Your Guide
to Access & Recreation

Pennsylvania's
PRESERVED LANDS

JEFFREY F. WILLIAMS

Schiffer
Publishing Ltd.
1880 Lower Valley Road • Atglen, PA 19310

Designed by Molly Shields
Type set in Superclarendon/Cambria

ISBN: 978-0-7643-5752-7
Printed in China

Published by Schiffer Publishing, Ltd.
4880 Lower Valley Road
Atglen, PA 19310
Phone: (610) 593-1777; Fax: (610) 593-2002
E-mail: Info@schifferbooks.com
Web: www.schifferbooks.com

For our complete selection of fine books on this and related subjects, please visit our website at www.schifferbooks.com. You may also write for a free catalog.

Schiffer Publishing's titles are available at special discounts for bulk purchases for sales promotions or premiums. Special editions, including personalized covers, corporate imprints, and excerpts, can be created in large quantities for special needs. For more information, contact the publisher.

We are always looking for people to write books on new and related subjects. If you have an idea for a book, please contact us at proposals@schifferbooks.com.

To my parents, Walt and Joan Williams, who encouraged their three sons to explore the world we live in.
To my wife, Alice, whose tremendous support, advice, encouragement, and patience was greatly appreciated.

DISCLAIMER

Outdoor activities have inherent risks, and many factors, such as location, weather, missing trail signs, wildlife, and others, can cause injury. Please respect the potential dangers, use common sense, do not take risks, and be prepared when you participate in outdoor activities. All persons using the information in this book do so at their own risk. The author and publisher disclaim any and all liability for conditions and inaccuracies of information where activities take place, occurrences, and information contained herein. Enjoy the natural world safely.

I encourage readers to forward corrections and comments to me at jfwilliams3691@gmail.com

Contents

ACKNOWLEDGMENTS

I want to thank my good friends: Dave Scheuermann, who took me flying countless times for aerial landscape and architectural photography; Pam Cooper, who proofread this book; and Rudy Blomstrom, who is an excellent studio photographer and helped me during the early years of my career.

I met many people who provided me with information and suggested I explore their favorite places. They were always willing to contribute as much time as I needed: Kathleen Sandt, Delaware Water Gap NRA; John Kolodziejski, Shenango River Lake; Brent Chonister, Raystown Lake; Jared Sayers, Linesville Fish Hatchery; Rick Wiltraut, Jacobsburg SP; Dale Luthringer, Cook Forest SP; Doug D'Amore, Sproul SF; Steve Repash, Bethlehem Authority; Bud Cook, Nature Conservancy; James Adovasio, Meadowcroft Rockshelter; Nathaniel Shank, Appalachian Trail Museum; Darryle Speicher, Tannersville Cranberry Bog; and Luke DeGroote and Mary Shindel, Powdermill Avian Research Center.

I would also like to thank the many nature enthusiasts I met who were knowledgeable about an area and provided excellent suggestions.

I certainly want to thank my publishers, Nancy and Peter Schiffer, and editors Ian Robertson and Kim Grandizio.

Cotter Swamp, Poconos

INTRODUCTION AND INFORMATION

It is not surprising that Pennsylvania's five million acres of preserved land host well over fifty million visitors annually. They come to experience Pennsylvania's spectacular natural world: its forested mountains, waterfalls, glacial bogs, old-growth forests, vistas, lakes and rivers, canyons, wildflowers, unique plants, and abundant wildlife. They also visit for the tremendous recreational opportunities and to relax and unwind in a beautiful, serene setting where the only sounds are nature's voice.

Whether you are an experienced outdoor enthusiast or just like to sightsee and want to explore new places, or you simply want to learn more about Pennsylvania's impressive natural environment, unique features, and wildlife, then *Pennsylvania's Preserved Lands* was written for you. The book combines informative text and photographs to present a clear picture of the best and most-important natural and recreational locations in Pennsylvania. Seventy locations, covering more than 120 specific areas, were selected with equal representation from each of the state's six regions. The locations are owned and managed by eight categories of landholders: the federal government, the Army Corps of Engineers, the Bureau of State Forests, the Bureau of State Parks, the Pennsylvania Game Commission, the Pennsylvania Fish and Boat Commission, conservation organizations, and large private landowners.

The book has information that is difficult to find or does not exist in brochures or on the internet. The information might include the best time of year to visit, how to reach a remote area, the best nature or scenic trails, warnings about difficult trails or other hazards, history of the area, interesting information about a particular species of wildlife, and the location's past and current environmental issues. Much of the information and all of the photographs are from my visits to more than 200 locations. To truly get to know the featured locations, I traveled approximately 35,000 miles throughout Pennsylvania during a period of ten years. I also gained valuable information from conversations with park and forest rangers, land managers with conservation organizations, and private landowners, as well as naturalists and experts in fields such as ornithology, herpetology, and biology. An extremely valuable source of information was the people I met who were out enjoying nature. They told me about places I would never have known existed.

Pennsylvania's Preserved Lands will make it easier for you to choose where to go and what to see and do when you get there. Keep in mind that

Following: Indian Creek Reservoir, Fayette County

there are many equally wonderful places not included in this book, due to limited space. I hope the book encourages you to visit the natural world more often and to explore places off the beaten path.

Information: Avoid crowds when possible by visiting places on weekdays, off-season, and early in the morning. Visiting a special place and having it all to yourself is far more rewarding and memorable.

Take the time to preplan your visit to a location you are not familiar with. Print pertinent information, maps, and directions, and know where you are going to spend the night.

A surprisingly large percentage of central and western Pennsylvania does not have cell phone service. Without it, you cannot make last-minute reservations at a campground, look up the nearest places to eat or camp, or use your GPS. Always bring a map or, preferably, a Pennsylvania atlas.

Entering an address into your GPS does not always take you where you wanted to go, so double-check the route against your map.

In remote areas, the nearest restaurant or gas station could be more than twenty miles away, so plan accordingly.

Never take unnecessary risks or overestimate your abilities. Nothing is worth getting injured, or worse.

Indian Ladders, Second Falls, Delaware Water Gap NRA

DEFINITIONS AND ABBREVIATIONS

bog: A bog generally begins as a small lake or pond—often glacially created—and is characterized by spongy peat deposits, acidic water, and a thick cover of sphagnum moss. Bogs receive all, or almost all, of their water from precipitation, rather than from runoff, streams, or groundwater. Lacking bacteria for decomposition, the yearly deposit of dead moss becomes acidic peat. This process creates acidic tea-colored water. Over time, the moss buildup forms spongy mats around the perimeter and will eventually fill the lake. Carnivorous plants, orchids, and insects have adapted to the low-nutrient, acidic, waterlogged conditions.

fen: Fens are similar to bogs, in that they are peat-forming wetlands. The difference is that they receive their source of water from streams, springs, or groundwater. This water has higher levels of nutrients and is less acidic. Fens can support a more diversified plant and animal community. It is important to note that fens and bogs can be destroyed by humans in a few days, but the natural process took thousands of years to become what we see today.

marsh: A marsh is a wetland that is frequently or continually inundated with water and is characterized by emergent soft-stemmed vegetation adapted to saturated soil conditions. Marshes are divided into two categories: tidal and nontidal. In Pennsylvania, nontidal marshes include wet meadows and vernal pools.

natural: The word "natural," as it is used in "natural environment" or "natural area," is often misunderstood. Its definition cannot mean "as it was 500 years ago or before European settlement," because the environment has always evolved and always will evolve on its own. Human activities have only increased the rate and magnitude of change. So my definition of "natural" is simply "land that is not significantly developed." More than 60 percent of the land in Pennsylvania falls within this definition.

natural area: The DCNR's Bureau of Forestry describes a designated "natural area" as an area with scenic, historic, geologic, or ecological significance that will remain in an undisturbed state, with development and maintenance being limited to that required for health and safety. Natural areas are maintained in a natural condition by allowing physical and biological processes to operate, usually without direct human intervention. Natural areas are usually small but may be up to several thousand acres. Within the state forest system there are currently sixty designated natural areas with a total of 78,600 acres.

old-growth forest: A number of different definitions have been used by agencies and organizations, but generally, this is a forest with trees that predate the earliest logging in the area. It usually has trees of mixed ages and has suffered few if any intrusions by humans.

old-growth tree: This is equally difficult to define. An "old-growth tree" generally refers to a naturally grown, substantially old tree within an old-growth forest. An "old tree" can be any individual tree of substantial age located anywhere. The use of the word "old" is determined by the age of the specific species. A white birch seldom lives longer than ninety years, while hemlocks can live well over 400 years. The size of a tree is not necessarily an indicator of its age.

swamp: A swamp is any wetland that is dominated by woody plants. There are two types of swamps—forested swamps and shrub swamps—but many swamps have areas both with shrubs and trees.

vernal pools: Vernal pools are seasonal wetlands in depressed land, with bedrock or a hard clay layer beneath the pool to retain the water. They hold shallow water for variable periods, usually from winter to early summer. They are usually dry from late summer through fall. Unusual seasonal climate conditions can alter this general rule. Certain species of amphibians are dependent on vernal pools.

wet meadow: Wet meadows are a type of marsh that commonly occur in poorly drained areas, such as low-lying farmland and land between shallow marshes and upland areas. For most of the year, wet meadows are without standing water, though the high water table allows the soil to remain saturated. Grasses, sedges, and wetland wildflowers proliferate in the fertile soil.

wetland: Wetlands are simply areas of land that are temporarily or permanently wet, and they are characterized by the vegetation. There are several types of wetlands in Pennsylvania.

wild area: This is an area within the state forest system that retains an undeveloped, wild character and is designated as a wild area to assure that this primitive character is perpetuated. Development and disturbance of permanent nature will be prohibited. The size should be no less than 3,000 acres and is seldom more than 15,000 acres. There are currently nineteen wild areas with a total of 152,916 acres.

Abbreviations

ACE: Army Corps of Engineers

CC: Cross-Country

CCC: Civilian Conservation Corps

DCNR: Department of Conservation and Natural Resources

EEC: Environmental Education Center

GC: Game Commission

NA: Natural Area

NC: Nature Conservancy

NF: National Forest

NFWS: National Fish and Wildlife Service

NHS: National Historic Site

NPO: Nonprofit Organization

NPCO: Nonprofit Conservation Organization

NR: Nature Reserve

NRA: National Recreation Area

NWR: National Wildlife Refuge

PFBC: Pennsylvania Fish and Boat Commission

RA: Recreation Area

SGL: State Game Land

SF: State Forest

SP: State Park

WA: Wild Area

WMA: Wildlife Management Area

WPC: Western Pennsylvania Conservancy

WR: Wildlife Refuge/Reserve

INTERESTING FACTS

Pennsylvania's black bears are the largest in North America. Eleven of the twenty largest black bears in North America recorded by the Boone and Crockett Club came from Pennsylvania, including the largest bear ever harvested by a hunter. Almost as amazing, the eleven bears came from ten different counties. One reason Pennsylvania has so many large bears is that the dense cover in the northeast swamps and the rugged mountains in many parts of the state allow bears to hide and grow old. The second factor is the abundant sources of high-calorie food. In 2016, bears were harvested in fifty-seven of the state's sixty-seven counties.

Biologists have recorded 3,319 different wild plants in Pennsylvania, of which 2,076 are native. Two hundred species of trees have been recorded, and of those, 135 are native.

Pennsylvania is home to the box huckleberry, a dwarf evergreen shrub that is the oldest and largest living organism in the world. The shrub exists in 100 scattered colonies in seven states. The two Pennsylvania colonies are in Perry County. The oldest-known colony in the world is on private land in Losh Run, Pennsylvania, and is approximately 13,000 years old. Botanists determined that the shrub spreads by its rhizomes 6 inches per year. This 12-inch-high shrub measured 6,500 feet long. Unfortunately, part of the colony was destroyed when a highway was built. The other Pennsylvania colony is protected in the Hoverter & Scholl Box Huckleberry NA, in Tuscarora SF. It is approximately 1,300 years old.

Pennsylvania has two of the country's most notable birding locations: Presque Isle SP and Hawk Mountain Reserve. A total of 414 species of birds have been identified in Pennsylvania.

Hickory Creek Wilderness, in the Allegheny NF, is the only federally designated wilderness area east of the Mississippi.

Archbald Pothole SP, in Lackawanna County, has the largest pothole in the world. It is believed to have been formed approximately 15,000 years ago by massive amounts of meltwater on the surface of the glacier, which probably fell 1,000 feet or more down a crevasse to bedrock. The swirling water, along with rocks and sand, scoured the bedrock for many years, creating a 38-foot-deep elliptical hole measuring 42 by 24 feet. A larger hole was discovered 1,000 feet north, but it remains filled due to the excessive cost to excavate the material.

The most numerous old-growth tree species in Pennsylvania is the eastern hemlock. These giant trees grew from a seed so small that 200,000 seeds will weigh only one pound. Their cones are less than 1 inch long.

Pennsylvania has more miles of streams and rivers than any state except Alaska.

Sixty different species of native orchids have been found, documented, and photographed in Pennsylvania. Orchids are the world's largest plant family, representing 10 percent of all plant species. Some of Pennsylvania's species are unique. One grows for seven years before it blooms, while others bloom and then remain dormant for one to ten years before blooming again, and many bloom for only one to three days. Most species bloom from May to September, and they will almost always die if transplanted.

Beneath one of your footprints on the forest floor are approximately 12,000 different microorganisms and billions of bacteria. They recycle everything that lives and dies on land.

The Delaware Water Gap NRA is the largest federal recreation area in the eastern US, and the Delaware River is the longest undammed river east of the Rockies.

The Delaware River hosts the largest wintering population of bald eagles in the eastern US.

During the second half of the 1800s, Pennsylvania led the nation in iron and coal mining, timber products, iron/steel production, and oil/gas extraction.

For those who think that our land, plants, and wildlife are securely protected, consider that Pennsylvania's most common and valuable tree, the American chestnut, is now essentially extinct. The most numerous species of wildlife, the passenger pigeon, is extinct, and the beautiful mountain ash tree will be virtually extinct by 2024.

Hummingbirds can fly backward, on their side, and even briefly on their back. They can't walk or hop. An adult ruby-throated hummingbird weighs 3 grams; a nickel weighs 4.5 grams. Their hearts beat more than 1,000 times per minute when feeding, they breathe an average of 250 breaths per minute, and when they feed, they lick ten to fifteen times per second. They can dive 60 mph and can turn with a g-force that would cause a trained fighter pilot to black out.

For those who do not believe the climate is changing, consider the following. The US Department of Agriculture has shifted the location of the numerical growing zones to the north. The increasing rate of death of our hemlocks and other trees is partly due to recent decades of mild winters, which have allowed the hemlock woolly adelgid and other insects to survive and spread rapidly. Kudzu—the dreaded vine of the south—has gradually moved north and has been identified in 140 locations in Pennsylvania.

Between the 1880s and 1930s, the ice industry in the Poconos shipped as many as 100 railroad cars of ice every day to eastern cities, and as far south as Florida and the Caribbean. Ice houses were completely filled, with some buildings measuring 300 × 100 × 50 feet high. The largest company used 1,500 men and 100 horses during the ice season, The men lived in dorms and received meals, and for the hard, cold, dangerous work, they were paid thirty to thirty-five cents per hour.

Where is the most remote place in Pennsylvania? The word "remote" has several interpretations, but two places stand out above all others: the southern section of Sproul SF and Quehanna WA, with the surrounding preserved lands.

Pennsylvania's Natural World

Abstract

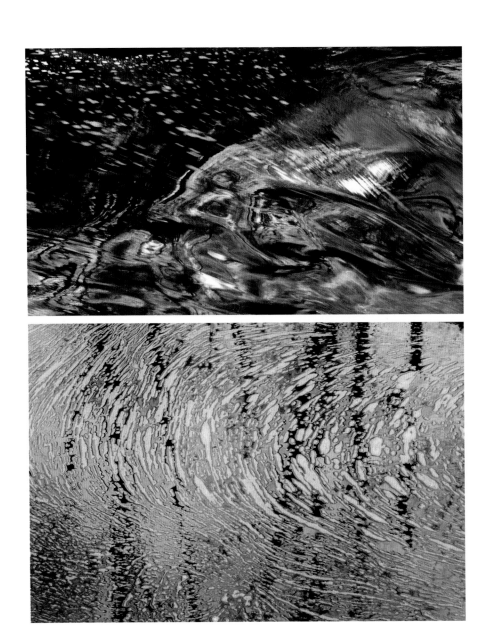

Green moss, tannic-colored water, and blue-sky reflection, Adams Falls, Ricketts Glen SP

Reflection of trees on water with foam, Tobyhanna Creek, Tobyhanna SP

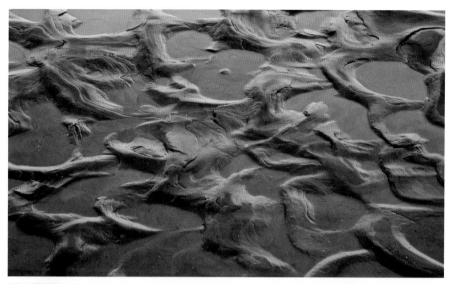

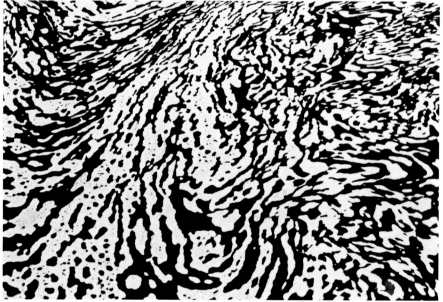

Wave-carved bedrock along Lake Erie's
shoreline, Erie Bluffs SP

Swirling foam on dark water with red leaf,
Stillwater Dam, Monroe County

Small Wonders

Bizarre-looking brown saddleback caterpillar will become a moth.

Japanese beetle surrounded by jewels of the morning, Erie Bluffs SP

Wind-blown lady bugs seek shelter in a knot on driftwood, Presque Isle SP

A red eft during terrestrial phase of the red spotted newt, Allegheny NF

Flora

A wild blue flag flower, Mud Run NA, Hickory Run SP

Even thistle plants have redeeming qualities; John Heinz NWR

Early-morning frost forms on the plant's leaf hairs. SGL 14, Elk County

Indian pipe—a member of the blueberry family—does not use chlorophyll. Instead, it is parasitic on fungus, which taps into tree roots for its energy.

Natural Beauty

This perspective is deceiving. The rock is nearly the size of a small Volkswagen. Shohola Falls, SGL 180.

Ice- and snow-covered branches with a visible moon north of Hyner Run SP

Reflection of sky in pools of water on an
ice-covered lake, Tobyhanna SP

Sunrise on a cliff high above the Delaware
River, Delaware Water Gap NRA

Interesting Nature

A Baltimore oriole wondering why the other bird does not respond; Presque Isle SP

The kids were proud to show me the crayfish they caught; Lyman Run SP

When the colony became too large they created a second queen. Thousands followed the departing queen to this branch, then they moved deeper into the woods to start a new colony.

Pileated woodpeckers use their heads as hammers thousands of times every day.

Recreation

An expert paraskier on Presque Isle Bay's rough ice, Presque Isle SP

Ready to launch at one of the best hang-gliding locations in the northeastern US, Hyner View SP

Looking for elk while horseback riding near Benezette, Elk SF

Hunting for morels requires a keen eye. Modest, personal-use harvesting is allowed on DCNR's parks and forest land.

Preserved-Land Ownership

Federal Agencies

Six federal agencies own and manage land in the US. The four that offer public access and recreational opportunities in Pennsylvania are the US Forest Service (513,418 acres), the National Park Service (50,014 acres), the US Fish and Wildlife Service (9,962 acres), and the Army Corps of Engineers (ACE ownership is described separately). The largest federal land agency—the Bureau of Land Management—does not own land in Pennsylvania, and the Department of Defense, with 43,502 acres in Pennsylvania, obviously does not allow public access for recreation.

National Forest Service. The NFS was created in 1905 to preserve forest land, protect water, and manage a sustainable timber harvest. In 1960, their responsibilities were expanded to include recreation, livestock grazing, and wildlife and fish habitat. Four years later, wilderness management was added. These multiple uses are to be managed in a "harmonious and coordinated" manner "in the combination that will best meet the needs of the American people." This balancing act is often difficult and controversial. Pennsylvania's only NF, Allegheny National Forest (ANF), has had its share of controversial issues; by simply visiting you would not know it. Established in 1923, the ANF has set aside approximately 140,000 acres of their 513,000 acres for preservation and recreation. Much of that land is a wilderness paradise. The rest of the land is leased for timber operations and oil and gas extraction but is still accessible to the public. When the federal government purchased the land, 93 percent of the acreage did not include rights below the surface. Consequently, the ANF has approximately 100,000 abandoned wells and approximately 12,000 active oil and gas wells—more than any NF in the country. The following four designated areas within the ANF are managed by the National Forest Service:

Allegheny National Recreation Area. This NRA, with 20,152 acres, was created when the Kinzue Dam was completed in 1965. The NRA includes the land surrounding the reservoir south of the Pennsylvania border with New York. Another designated RA is along the Allegheny River south of Warren.

National Scenic Areas. Within the ANF are two National Scenic Areas: Tionesta, with 2,018 acres, and Hearts Content, with 120 acres. They are preserved for their old-growth forest. The Tionesta Research Area is also an old-growth forest, with 2,113 acres.

National Wilderness Areas. The two NWAs are Hickory Creek, with 8,663 acres, and Allegheny Wilderness Islands, with 368 acres. These are the only National Wilderness Areas in the eastern US.

National Wild and Scenic Rivers. The two National Wild and Scenic Rivers that form part of the ANF's borders are the 86.6-mile section of the Allegheny

River downstream from the Kinzue Dam and the 52-mile section of the Clarion River downstream from Ridgeway.

National Park Service. The NPS, created in 1916, has the responsibility of managing 417 units in the US with 80 million acres, of which most is in Alaska. The types of units include national parks, monuments, preserves, historic sites, recreation areas, trail systems, battlefields, forts, and many more. Parks are established by Congress, and monuments are proclaimed by the president. The National Park Service manages two Recreation Areas in Pennsylvania.

National Recreation Areas. The ACE's plan to build the Tocks Island Dam on the Upper Delaware River was abandoned in 1975. Management of the 70,000 acres, which was allocated by Congress, was transferred to the National Park Service, and the area became Delaware Water Gap National Recreation Area. The 40-mile-long park has a total of 28,164 acres in Pennsylvania. It is visited by 3.5 million people annually for its outstanding natural features, including more than twenty spectacular waterfalls in its numerous steep ravines. The state's third NRA is Conemaugh River Lake, a reservoir in an area with historic canals, a railroad line with bridges, and a tunnel that ran between Philadelphia and Pittsburgh.

National Wild and Scenic River. In addition to the Allegheny and Clarion Rivers, two sections of the Delaware River have been designated wild and scenic. The Upper Delaware section flows from Hancock to Port Jervis, and the lower section flows from I-80 at Delaware Water Gap to I-95 at Washington's Crossing.

National Scenic Trails. Of the three in Pennsylvania, the most famous is the Appalachian Trail, which is 2,180 miles long, with 229 miles within the state's borders. It was completed in 1937 and is the most popular hiking trail in the world. Pine Grove Furnace SP is the halfway point. The North Country Trail, from New York to North Dakota, will be 4,000 miles long when completed. The trail enters Pennsylvania at the ANF, passes through three state parks and SGLs, and exits at the Ohio border. The Potomac Heritage Trail runs between Ohiopyle SP and the Potomac's tidal water below Washington, DC.

National Natural Landmarks. Twenty-seven National Natural Landmarks have been designated in Pennsylvania by the National Park Service.

US Fish and Wildlife Service. The first wildlife refuge was established in 1903, but it was not until 1966 that the nation's refuges were consolidated and administered by the US Fish and Wildlife Service. Their main mission is to conserve plants and animals. Other uses are permitted as long as they are compatible with the species' needs. Today, there are more than 500 refuges in the US. The following three Pennsylvania refuges are managed by the US FWS.

Erie National Wildlife Refuge. The refuge is two separate tracts of land in Crawford County, with a total of 8,777 acres.

John Heinz National Wildlife Refuge. This 1,000-acre refuge contains the only freshwater tidal marsh in Pennsylvania. Even though it is in Philadelphia, next to the international airport, it is teeming with wildlife.

Cherry Valley National Wildlife Refuge. This more than 2,000-acre refuge is a patchwork of preserved land along the north side and ridgeline of the Kittatinny Ridge in Monroe and Northampton Counties. It protects five federally threatened or endangered species and a major migratory bird flyway.

Delaware Water Gap NRA, Monroe County

Army Corps of Engineers

The Army Corp of Engineers (ACE) serves the armed forces and the nation by providing vital engineering services across a wide range of operations from peace to war in support of national interests. Their main activities in Pennsylvania are operating and maintaining twenty-four flood-control dams and operating locks on western Pennsylvania rivers. The landholdings surrounding the reservoirs are usually substantial because in heavy-rain events, controllers will raise the level of the reservoir and flood their own land. ACE projects have a variety of developed facilities and recreation, which may include camping, swimming, boating, fishing, and hiking. The properties are also maintained to enhance and diversify the habitat for many wildlife species. Some of the projects became state parks, with ACE controlling the dam operation, and several projects lease land to the Game Commission. Ten ACE projects are featured in this book. Most people are not aware that some of the state's recreational areas were created by ACE. Their website lists the locations and facilities, but it can be a bit confusing because the projects are in two separate districts, with headquarters in Pittsburgh and Baltimore. I advise calling the office of the location you want to visit to learn more about camping and other facilities. Also verify the height of the reservoir's water. If it is high, facilities could be closed, and if it is unusually low, boat launches could be closed.

Kinzua Dam, Allegheny Reservoir, Warren County

DCNR and Bureau of Forestry

Department of Conservation and Natural Resources. Pennsylvania's state-owned forests are managed by the Bureau of Forestry, which is under the auspices of the Department of Conservation and Natural Resources. The DCNR oversees four other bureaus, including state parks. Pennsylvania has lost at least 156 species of native plants and vertebrates since the early 1700s. Another 351 species have become endangered or threatened, and more than half of its wetland acreage has been lost since 1780. To prevent future losses, the DCNR has developed, coordinated, and promoted a multitude of services and programs. The following are just a few of the many programs conducted by the DCNR.

Education: Go Teach Workshops and Get Outdoors Program

Biodiversity: Pennsylvania Natural Heritage Program, which provides expertise, conducts surveys, and collects data on locations of plants and wildlife. The Wild Resource Conservation Program provides funding to protect nongame wildlife and wild plants.

Native Plants and Wildlife: The DCNR determines whether subjects are classified as rare, threatened, or endangered and how to conserve them, as well as addressing invasive species issues; the Wild Plant Sanctuary Program acknowledges exceptional properties, and the Eastern Hemlock Conservation Plan is working to save hemlock trees.

Recreation: Pennsylvania has 10,000 miles of trails and more than 50,000 miles of streams and rivers. As part of a program to encourage youth and the general public to get outdoors, many parks conduct courses in outdoor recreation skills and will kindly loan fishing gear.

Bureau of Forestry. The Bureau of Forestry is divided into twenty State Forest Districts that manage a total of 2.2 million acres in forty-eight counties. The bureau promotes clean water and air, recreation, and education; protects wildlife, trees, plants, and habitat; and gains economic benefits through leasing land for timber, mineral, gas, and oil resources. They also manage forest fires, prescribed burns, and destructive insects and disease, as well as conducting extensive research. Since state forests are usually large blocks of forest, they provide a unique opportunity for solitude and low-impact recreation. In total, 30 percent of Pennsylvania's forest is publicly owned. The rest is owned by private individuals, NPOs, and corporations. A surprising 78 percent of the timber harvested in Pennsylvania comes from private land.

Seventeen million acres (approximately 60%) of Pennsylvania's land is forest, and Pennsylvania has the finest hardwood forests in the nation. Timber and wood products are the seventh-largest industry in the state, employing 60,000 people. The largest type of forest in Pennsylvania—

encompassing 54 percent—is mixed oak, which are mostly in the southern portion of the state. They include red oak, chestnut oak, shagbark hickory, red maple, and tulip poplar. The second-largest is northern hardwoods, at 32 percent, comprising sugar maple, black cherry, aspen, birch, hemlock, and ash. The five largest forest districts are Sproul, 280,000 acres; Susquehannock, 265,000 acres; Rothrock, 215,500 acres; Tiadaghton, 215,500 acres; and Elk, 200,000 acres. The smallest district is William Penn SF in Chester County, with 812 acres.

When the earliest settlers arrived in "Penn's Woods," the state was more than 90 percent forest, which equates to 28 million acres. Forests were a hindrance to expansion, and timber was cut with little regard for the environment or future generations. Giant white pines were used for British ship masts. Iron furnaces required at least 20,000 acres of timber to produce charcoal. Giant hemlocks were cut for their bark, used by the tanning industry. The railroads required 80,000,000 crossties every year for their expanding lines, plus wood to fuel steam transportation. The growing population needed wood for bridges, homes, barns, stores, wagons, ships, tools, and furniture. Subsequent fires scorched the earth, mountainsides eroded and silted streams, and floods destroyed property, especially mills and bridges. Mining, oil, and gas industries added to the land's degradation. In the late 1800s, Pennsylvania led the nation in timber, oil, and iron production. By 1900, the forest was down to 10 million acres of mostly second- and third-growth trees, and wildlife was decimated. Yet, aggressive logging continued for another twenty years. Today, Pennsylvania has 17 million acres, but sadly, only a tiny fraction of one percent of the virgin forest remains.

In 1893, the Commission of Forestry was created and Joseph Rothrock was named its first commissioner. During his tenure the state purchased 500,000 acres and opened a series of state forest parks. The first was Franklin County's Mont Alto Park in 1902. It was a 30,000-acre iron furnace community and popular summer resort that attracted more than 60,000 visitors annually. Visitors arrived by train from Washington, Philadelphia, and other cities. This was also the site of the state's forestry school—the Academy of Forestry—with the first official graduation in 1906. The following year two more recreational areas were purchased: Caledonia and Promised Land.

Managing today's forests and the thousands of miles of forest roads is a daunting task, but the Bureau of Forestry's greatest concern is the widespread attack on the forests' trees by invasive insects and disease. The DCNR lists seventeen insects and diseases of significant concern. The emerald ash borer, discovered in Michigan in 2002, has already destroyed millions of ash trees across Pennsylvania. It is likely that 99 percent of the ash trees will be killed within the next decade. The hemlock woolly adelgid entered Pennsylvania in 1967 and has killed many of the stately old hemlock trees, with no end in sight. In 1990—the height of the gypsy moth outbreak—4.3 million acres of oak forests were defoliated, and in 2007, another 680,000 acres were hit.

Big Pine Hill Vista, Lackawanna SF,
Lackawanna County

Beech bark disease is another major concern. In the 1940s, the state's chestnut trees were wiped out due to chestnut blight. That makes the possible loss of beech and oak trees even more devastating, since they are the largest remaining sources of hard mast for wildlife. Currently, the only way to save many of the species is the extremely expensive process of injecting pesticides into the soil near the roots.

State Forest Natural Areas. The Bureau of Forestry has designated sixty-one sections of forest as natural areas. The objective is to "protect areas of scenic, historic, geologic, and ecological significance, which will remain in an undisturbed state with development and maintenance being limited to that required for health and safety. Physical and biological processes will be allowed to operate."

State Forest Wild Areas. Sixteen sections of SF have been designated as wild areas. The objective is to "set aside certain areas of land where development or disturbance of permanent nature will be prohibited, thereby preserving the wild character of the area. The areas selected must already have a wild character. The general public will be permitted to see, use, and enjoy activities such as hiking, hunting, fishing, and the pursuit of peace and solitude. The size of the area should be no less than 3,000 acres and seldom more than 15,000 acres." Hammersley WA, one of the newest WAs, consists of about 30,000 acres in Susquehannock SF and is the largest roadless area in Pennsylvania.

DCNR, Bureau of State Parks

The Bureau of State Parks is responsible for 120 state parks, including three environmental-education centers with a total of 300,000 acres. Eight of the parks are operated in cooperation with other public and private organizations. The parks range in size from 3 to 21,122 acres. Within the state parks you will find outstanding natural features, abundant wildlife, and opportunities for practically every conceivable form of outdoor recreation. Most parks have a campground, swimming areas, boating, hiking, fishing, winter activities, and environmental education. Several parks also offer some less common activities, including rock climbing, ice climbing, iceboating, geocaching, disc golf, cave exploring, astronomy, and fossil and mushroom hunting. Other parks have spectacular natural features, such as waterfalls, geologic formations, vistas, bogs, dark skies, old-growth forests, and deep canyons. You might be surprised to learn that a number of parks have historic buildings, museums with historic artifacts on display, and nature exhibits, and show interesting documentaries. Some of the best places in Pennsylvania to view wildlife, birds, and wildflowers are the state parks.

In Pennsylvania, land acquisition and preservation began as early as 1812, with the creation of Fairmount Park in Philadelphia. The first state park in the US was Yosemite, which was established in 1865. The US Congress designated Yellowstone as the first national park in 1872. In Pennsylvania during the late 1800s, groups of concerned citizens organized to preserve historic sites, forests, and wildlife. In 1893, the governor signed Act 130 for the purchase of ground at Valley Forge. Several years later, George Washington's headquarters and additional land were purchased for a public park, becoming Pennsylvania's first state park. In 1976, the park was transferred to the federal government and is now a national historical park.

Surveys conducted in 1921 and 1922 concluded that the state owned 1.1 million acres of forest—ranking second behind New York—but the only state park was Valley Forge. Recreational use of the forest was estimated at 600,000 visitors, mainly due to increased use of the automobile. The survey also stated that more than half of the visitors were campers. Interestingly, another category, totaling 120,000 people, was recorded as visitors of the state's 116 fire towers, which were open to the public. The Department of Forestry turned its attention toward creating park areas for recreation. A 7-mile peninsula at Lake Erie was already a local park when the commonwealth purchased it. The Pennsylvania state park at Erie became the second state park in Pennsylvania.

The greatest boost to the park system occurred during the Great Depression. President Franklin D. Roosevelt created the Civilian Conservation Corps (CCC), which hired three million unemployed, unmarried young men to live in camps across the nation and work on forestry and park projects. The CCC built many of our state parks' dams, beaches, stonework, cabins, pavilions, trails, water and sewer systems, and roads. They planted seedlings in what had become deserts. After World War II and through the 1950s, society's disposable income and mobility increased, and the five-day workweek became standard. In 1955, Dr Maurice Goddard, the new secretary of the Department of Forest and Waters, advocated that parks be built closer to cities and within 25 miles of every citizen. He also urged the governor to fund the park system expansion with oil and gas royalties from state-owned land.

In recent years, the Bureau of State Parks has spent tens of millions of dollars modernizing facilities and improving other services. In 2010, the Nature Inn at Bald Eagle SP was built. The popularity of the park system's first inn led to the planning of more inns.

Boulder field, Hickory Run SP, Carbon County

Pennsylvania Game Commission

The Game Commission is responsible for wildlife protection, habitat management, establishing laws and regulations, enforcing laws, officer training, hunter safety, public education, managing natural resources and funding, and much more. The wildlife includes sixty-four mammal species and 414 species of birds. Since 1901, the GC has purchased land for wildlife and recreational use not only for hunters, but all citizens, which now totals more than 1.5 million acres. The GC receives no funding from the state but does need legislative approval to enact game laws and establish license fees. Their approximately $105,000,000 budget is funded by hunting-license fees, timber leases and royalties for oil and gas extraction on game lands, and federal reimbursement from excise taxes on the sale of guns and ammunition. Eight commissioners are appointed by the governor. The commission employs more than 700 wildlife conservation officers (WCOs), deputy WCOs, biologists, wildlife experts, and the Food and Cover Corps. WCOs are trained at the GC's Ross Leffler School of Conservation in Harrisburg. Approximately 935,000 hunting licenses were sold in 2015.

The GC is recognized nationally for their efforts and success with wildlife and habitat management. In 1905, the GC established one of the county's first state-owned game refuges in Clinton County. The refuges were located on state forest land and were similar to today's propagation areas. Much of the GC's land was purchased through the efforts and contributions of numerous conservation organizations, and many properties have been donated by private citizens. Other efforts to help wildlife include building nesting platforms and boxes, gating caves to protect bats, conducting surveys and scientific research, creating a diversified habitat with successional growth and prescribed burns, planting food plots, creating shallow water impoundments and wetlands, and establishing propagation areas that are closed all year to human encroachment. For more than sixty years, the GC has been publishing an excellent magazine about the state's wildlife, *Pennsylvania Game News*.

Perhaps one of their greatest success stories that many people do not realize is species reintroduction. By 1900, many species were drastically reduced in numbers or were completely extirpated from Pennsylvania. In 1906, the GC bought fifty deer from a Michigan propagator, and another 193 deer in 1916, to restock the almost nonexistent Pennsylvania deer herd. In 1913, the GC worked with federal agencies that wanted to thin the elk herd in Yellowstone NP. Fifty elk arrived by train and were released in Clinton and Clearfield Counties, and another twenty-two elk were released in Monroe and Centre Counties. Other wildlife that have been

David M. Roderick WR, SGL 314, Erie County

reintroduced include beaver, Canada geese, fishers, river otters, bald eagles, osprey, and peregrine falcon.

In the early decades of its existence, the GC tried many methods to increase the population of game animals. Stocking farm-raised game and exotic game and paying bounties on predators proved expensive and ineffective and eventually ended. They learned early on that high-quality habitat was the only method that guaranteed positive results. When game laws were initially approved by the legislature, the public was not receptive. They wanted more game, but not more laws. The GC had no employees, so law enforcement was delegated to local constables who rarely enforced the law. To rectify the situation, the legislature said that the commissioners could hire game protectors who would receive half of the game violators' fines, but the commissioners knew that would be a problem. With no other choice, in 1903, nine game protectors were appointed from nine districts in the state. That same year the first field officer was shot at but was not hit. Assaults were common though. The following year, three officers were shot. In 1906, fourteen officers were shot at, seven were hit, and three died. The last officer to be killed in Pennsylvania was shot by a young poacher from Carbon County in 1915. It was not until 1913 that the legislature approved a source of revenue. Hunters of big game over age twenty-one had to buy a $1 license.

Hunting safety laws were nonexistent in the early days. The GC did promote wearing red and hunter safety. They also convinced the assembly to pass a law banning semiautomatic guns for hunting. In 1931, a staggering 439 people were accidently shot while hunting. In 1935, fifty-five hunters were killed and 252 were injured in hunting accidents. That same year, the GC was authorized to revoke hunting licenses from people who handled guns carelessly. Over the years, many safety regulations have been enacted, and the commission has worked hard at educating hunters, especially youth. More than 2,200 volunteers teach hunter and off-road vehicle safety courses, and 35,000 students receive their Basic Hunter-Trapper Education Certification before they can purchase a license. In 2016, with more than 935,000 hunters during a four-month season, there were twenty-five hunter-related shooting incidents and no fatalities.

The commission's Howard Nursery, next to Bald Eagle SP, produces about five million seedlings annually to improve habitat on public and private land. They also have visitor centers at Middle Creek WMA and Pymatuning WMA, and viewing blinds at Winslow Hill Elk Center and many other open areas across the state.

Pennsylvania Fish and Boat Commission

The Fish and Boat Commission was established in 1866 to address the issue of the newly built Columbia Dam blocking the shad run on the Susquehanna River. The commission is an independent agency similar to the Game Commission, whose responsibility is to protect, conserve, and enhance the state's aquatic resources, protect wildlife, and provide fishing and boating opportunities. The types of wildlife they protect and manage are fishes, reptiles, amphibians, and aquatic invertebrates. The PFBC monitors their population, health, and water quality, as well as conducts research, improves habitat, establishes regulations and policies, enforces laws, and educates the public. They manage and maintain fifteen state hatcheries, sixty-two public lakes, and nearly 250 boat access areas. The PFBC also works with other state agencies, conservation organizations, and thousands of volunteers on 700 habitat improvement projects, such as stream bank restoration, dam removal, and underwater structures for fish habitat. The PFBC publishes an excellent magazine, *Pennsylvania Angler & Boater*.

The PFBC consists of ten commissioners appointed by the governor and approved by legislators. The executive director oversees operations and a staff of approximately 425 employees. New candidates for the position of waterway control officer must attend the Stackhouse School of Fishery Conservation and Water Safety for fifty-two weeks of full-time training and seven months of on-the-job training. Pennsylvania has approximately 880,000 licensed anglers. To address the nation's declining hunting and fishing participation trend, the PFBC has initiated several projects, including multiyear licenses, early-season fishing for youths, and Keystone Select locations, where 14- to 20-inch trout are stocked at a rate of up to 250 per mile. The PFBC has never received general-fund tax revenue to support its programs. Reduced license sales means reduced funding, which is a major issue. The estimated capital improvement costs to repair eighteen dams deemed by the DEP to be unsafe is $58 million, and to upgrade hatcheries and improve access areas is $95 million. The PFBC has drawn down five dams as a precaution.

Eight hatcheries produce a total of four million adult trout annually, which are stocked throughout the state to supplement natural reproducing populations. Six hatcheries produce 100 million juvenile fish of popular species, such as walleye, catfish, striped bass, smallmouth and largemouth bass, muskellunge, crappie, pike, pickerel, and perch. Three hatcheries raise steelhead trout for Lake Erie's tributary streams. PFBC biologists and staff also monitor and work to restore populations of shad, paddlefish, American sturgeon, American eel, panfish, and baitfish. Pennsylvania's native reptile and amphibian species include twenty-two salamanders (two endangered), sixteen frogs and toads (four endangered), thirteen turtles (one endangered), four lizards and skinks (none are endangered), and twenty-one snakes, of which three are poisonous (three endangered).

A detailed chronology of historic events can be found on the PFBC's website, www.fishandboat.com. In 1867—one year after the commission was created—the first fishway was built at the Columbia Dam on the Susquehanna River. Also the first fish stocking was performed by a private citizen, who paid $313 for 450 bass from the Potomac River to be released into the Delaware River at Easton. The first brown trout eggs were shipped from Germany in 1886, and the first recorded stocking of rainbow trout occurred in the Susquehanna River in 1888. In 1921, Warden Shoemaker became the first PFBC officer killed in the line of duty. The following year the first resident fishing license was established at a cost of $1 for citizens over twenty-one years old. The license produced $207,425. I was surprised to learn that in 1931, a license was required to operate motorboats; the cost was $1 per cylinder and $2 for electric motors.

Stocking trout, Northampton County

Nonprofit Conservation Organizations

Pennsylvanians are fortunate to have some of the best state parks, state forests, fish, and game agencies in the country, but these four agencies by themselves cannot accomplish what still needs to be done. Nonprofit conservation organizations (NPCOs) deserve credit for much of the past success and are vital to the future health of the state's natural habitat and wildlife. Within Pennsylvania there are several hundred NPCOs, ranging from organizations that are involved in conservation around the world to small local groups of citizens. Their varied focus is on land preservation, landownership, conservation easements, habitat protection and management, wildlife rehabilitation, research, political issues, and environmental education. The list of NPCO accomplishments is endless. The following NPCOs are large land and wildlife protectors and land preservationists in Pennsylvania.

Western Pennsylvania Conservancy. Founded in 1932, WPC is the state's first conservancy and has conserved more than 254,000 acres in western Pennsylvania. That is half of all the land protected by land trust organizations in Pennsylvania. Of the twenty-two western Pennsylvania locations that are featured in this book, eleven have received land or are owned by WPC. The WPC owns nine preserved properties and has protected seventy-nine others. One of their properties is Fallingwater, the famous home designed by Frank Lloyd Wright. They partner with more than 12,000 volunteers to plant and maintain more than 130 gardens and green projects. WPC also partners with the PGC, PFBC, and DCNR in the PA Natural Heritage Program to provide scientific information, expertise, and assistance to support the conservation of biodiversity and monitor and keep records of species of concern. The conservancy has experts in many of the plant and animal professional disciplines. They also conduct energy impact research.

Audubon Pennsylvania. Audubon Pennsylvania, founded in 1896 as the country's second state chapter, is one of the largest NPCOs in Pennsylvania. They have twenty-two local chapters, ten state offices, and 24,000 members in Pennsylvania. Their five-state regional headquarters is in Harrisburg. They own and manage the John James Audubon Center at Mill Grove—Audubon's home in 1803, and where he began his painting. The museum and historic site combine nature and art and display all of his major works. The Pennsylvania chapter also owns Hawkwatch, at Waggoner's Gap on the Kittatinny Ridge, one of the best raptor migration sites in Pennsylvania. The national organization's website features twelve live bird cams throughout North America. Their bird experts and regional partners throughout the state and country have established "important bird areas" (IBAs) to identify and conserve areas that are vital to birds and biodiversity.

Nature Conservancy, PA Chapter. The Nature Conservancy is the largest conservation organization in the world. They have chapters in every state and numerous countries and work with 600 scientists in seventy-two counties. The Pennsylvania Chapter, headquartered in Harrisburg, owns fourteen preserves in Pennsylvania and has conserved tens of thousands of acres. In 2011, the NE Pennsylvania Chapter and the Bethlehem Authority signed the largest conservation easement in the state. The easement conserves 22,000 acres of woodland and some of the most valued wetland and heath barren habitat in North America. The NE Pennsylvania Chapter's Hauser Nature Center can provide information about Long Pond Preserve and guided nature walks.

Natural Land Trust. The trust was founded in 1951 to save the tidal wetlands that are now John Heinz NWR. They are headquartered in Media, Pennsylvania, and to date they have preserved more than 125,000 acres in Pennsylvania and southern New Jersey. They own forty-four nature preserves totaling more than 23,000 acres in thirteen counties in both states. Eighteen preserves are open to the public, with parking and trails. The Natural Land Trust works with landowners and holds conservation easements on 22,000 acres. They also provide a range of consulting services to 150 municipalities in Pennsylvania.

Wildlands Conservancy. The Wildlands Conservancy's headquarters and EEC are in Emmaus, Lehigh County; the organization was founded in 1975 by Robert Rodale, promoter of organic foods and healthful living, and Leonard Pool, founder of Air Products. The organization works to protect high-value natural land in northeastern Pennsylvania. They own nine nature preserves totaling 2,600 acres and hold seventy conservation easements. Since 2003, they have preserved more than 50,000 acres in the Lehigh River watershed. Thousands of students visit their environmental education center year-round to participate in outdoor nature study on their 72-acre wildlife sanctuary. The Bike and Boat Adventures program connects students of all ages to the natural world that is close to home in an urban area.

Lancaster County Conservancy. Founded in 1970, this conservancy protects ecologically valuable land in Lancaster County and surrounding counties. They own thirty-eight publicly accessible nature preserves and have protected 7,974 acres, including the recent transfer of PPL's 2,500 acres on both sides of the Susquehanna River at Holtwood. Many of their preserves along the Susquehanna River are rock overlooks or steep ravines with a profusion of wildflowers. The conservancy also works with twelve school districts to advance environmental education.

Keystone Trails Association. This association has forty-nine hiking clubs as members and works with all landowners to secure access and maintain trails across the state. Their mission is to provide, protect, preserve, and promote recreational hiking opportunities in Pennsylvania. Their volunteers contribute 3,000–4,000 hours of trail labor annually.

I hope this book provides inspiration for people to get outdoors more often. The best way to protect the natural environment is to know and appreciate the natural environment. While photographing natural areas, I met many people who volunteered because they wanted to make our world a better place to live. Tens of thousands of volunteers throughout Pennsylvania remove invasive plants, maintain trails, remove manmade debris from streams, improve stream habitat, install bird-nesting boxes and fish structures, conduct research, band birds, assist at wildlife rehab facilities, plant trees, create flower gardens, assist at museums and outdoor shops, help with fundraising events, conduct nature lectures and walks, and much more. Consider what has been accomplished and how important it is to continue our financial and volunteer support for conservation organizations and agencies. Please help.

Hawk Mountain Sanctuary, Berks County

Private Landowners

Electric companies, water authorities, and logging companies are not what most people think of when it comes to land preservation, wildlife conservation, and recreation, but the truth is surprisingly positive. You might be surprised at what is available near you if you are willing to investigate. The following are four of the largest private landowners that allow public access to most or all of their land.

Collins Pennsylvania Forest and its subsidiary, Kane Hardwoods, is the largest private landowner in Pennsylvania, with 119,000 acres. They practice sustainable timber harvesting with FSC certification. Their land is open to the public, with no fee for hunting (permit required through GC), fishing, hiking, biking, and other nonmotorized activities.

Exelon Corporation owns power-generation facilities across the country. Along the Susquehanna River in Pennsylvania, they own thousands of preserved acres at their three power plants. Much of this land, including beautiful Muddy Run Recreation Area (camping, boating, hiking trails, eagles, and osprey), is open to the public. The land includes river islands, deep ravines, and awesome river rock formations. Another corporation, Talon Corp., releases water from their Susquehanna River Holtwood Dam during early spring and late fall for kayakers to enjoy the new whitewater hydraulics at the Playpark.

Boy Scouts of America camps are scattered across Pennsylvania. Many are more than 500 acres, and most are open to the public for specific activities (fishing, hiking, and birding). Permits with a nominal fee are sometimes required. Call your local BSA council for more information. Most of the land at the camps has been left to nature for many decades. The three camps in the Poconos that I am very familiar with are gorgeous. They have excellent lake fishing and fly fishing for native trout. Their land also includes sand springs, wetlands, deep forests, and waterfalls and is teeming with wildlife and native plants. Off-season and on weekdays you will have nature to yourself.

Bethlehem Authority owns 22,000 acres in two areas of the Pocono region and, as mentioned earlier, signed a conservation easement with the Nature Conservancy to preserve both properties. A portion of their property in Long Pond has more species of concern than any other location in Pennsylvania. Other than their two reservoirs and a few fire lanes and dirt patrol roads, their land is natural and wild. It has no developed areas or facilities, no maps, few trails, and few places to park. It is open to the public for hiking, biking, and birding. Bring your map and compass.

Long Pine Run Reservoir, Chambersburg
Water Department

Western Pennsylvania

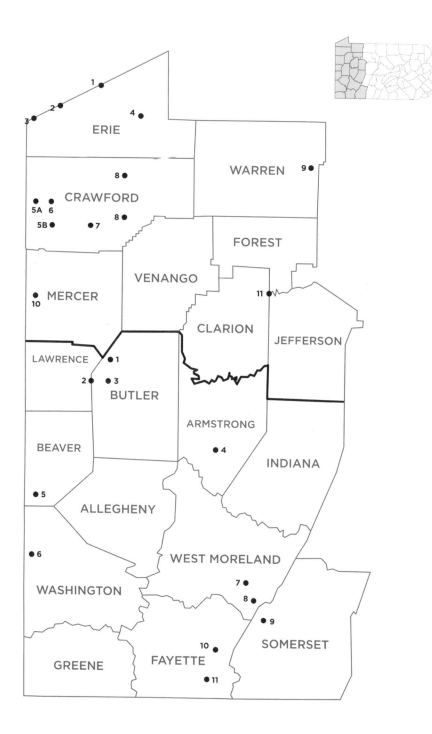

ERIE

1

2

3

4

CRAWFORD

8

5A 6

5B 8

7

WARREN

9

FOREST

VENANGO

MERCER

10

CLARION

JEFFERSON

11

LAWRENCE

1

2 3

BUTLER

ARMSTRONG

INDIANA

4

BEAVER

ALLEGHENY

5

WEST MORELAND

6

7

8

WASHINGTON

9

SOMERSET

10

GREENE

FAYETTE

11

Northwest Region

NW1 Presque Isle State Park, Erie County

Presque Isle SP is a narrow, 7-mile-long, sandy, hook-shaped peninsula jutting out into Lake Erie. Its unique environments and outstanding recreational opportunities attract four million visitors annually—more than any state park in Pennsylvania. Wind, waves, and currents continuously transform the shape of the land and create a diverse habitat for wildlife. In 1967, Presque Isle was designated a National Natural Landmark.

Geologic History. Approximately 20,000 years ago, the Wisconsinan glacier reached its farthest advance into what is now Lake Erie. Like a plow, the glacier pushed a wall of clay, sand, and rock across Lake Erie. When the climate warmed and the glacier began to retreat, a lake of glacial meltwater built up behind this ridge and eventually cut through, creating two peninsulas: Presque Isle in Pennsylvania and Long Point in Canada. As the lake level rose between 12,000 and 3,500 years ago, waves and currents transported loose sediment from the moraine and the lake's shoreline and deposited it on Presque Isle's eastern tip, creating sandbars and wide beaches. This transformation still continues to remove sand from the shoreline, creating the steep bluffs we see to the west. Over thousands of years, the entire peninsula has slowly migrated about 3 miles from its original location. Windblown sand is also transported to the bay side of the peninsula.

Since 1819, storms have broken through the peninsula's narrow neck four times, creating an island. In 1832, a storm cut an opening that grew nearly a mile long and remained open for thirty years. Both nature and human actions have filled in the openings, but to eliminate future problems, a rock-and-concrete seawall was built along the vulnerable neck. Every year before the lake freezes, winter storms wreak havoc on the beaches. I have seen sections of beach with drop-offs 4 feet high. To help reduce beach erosion, the Army Corps of Engineers built perpendicular jetties along the beaches and fifty-eight rock breakwaters offshore. Despite this effort, human intervention is needed every spring to replenish the sand and grade the beach.

Natural Environment. For me, witnessing the results of nature's relentless power is one of the reasons Presque Isle is so special. During the winter, the lake's surface freezes and expands. With the additional force from the prevailing west winds, the ice pushes against the beach. The pressure builds until large, 1- to 2-foot-thick slabs of ice heave up, forming ice dunes. Never attempt to climb the ice dunes. They look benign, but falling between slabs into frigid water could be deadly. Standing alone on the snow-covered beach, with a 180-degree view of the ice dunes and hundreds of ice

Sunset on the beach

formations on the expansive frozen lake, makes you think you are on the arctic coast. "Ice out" occurs in March and provides a beautiful contrast between the bright white ice and the open blue water.

East of Beach 10, there are no jetties or breakwaters; nature is allowed to take its course. From the Beach 10 parking lot, walk east along the shore or take the Gull Point Trail and you will see places where waves from storms have overrun low-lying land. Trees and shrubs are damaged or are ripped out, and sand has washed over the vegetation. This destruction occurs every year and is an impressive sight.

The park's seven ecological zones harbor more of the state's endangered, threatened, and rare species than any other location of comparable size in Pennsylvania. It is astounding that you can visit all seven zones within a one-hour walk. The extraordinarily diverse environment provides habitat for huge numbers of species. The list includes Lake Erie's eighty species of fish and six species of crustaceans, eighty-nine dragonflies and damselflies, thirty-five moths and butterflies, eighty-four different spiders, forty-eight mammals, thirteen amphibians, and at least 633 species of plants and trees.

Wildlife. Presque Isle is a birder's paradise. Its impressive list of 320 birds—of which thirty-nine are listed as endangered or threatened—ranks it number one in the state and one of the top birding locations in the country. The lagoon and ponds support migratory and nesting waterfowl, osprey, eagles, and numerous wetland birds. The most fragile environment and the best birding area is 319-acre Gull Point, at the tip of the peninsula. Many of the plants found here are endangered or threatened, and the area is an important stopover for migrating birds to rest and refuel. Sixty-eight acres at the eastern end of Gull Point were designated a natural rea. It is closed during nesting season between April 1 and November 30, to protect the many shorebirds that nest there. The 1.5-mile Gull Point Trail begins at the eastern end of the Beach 10 parking lot and takes you through the most recently created ecological zones. The trail ends at the point's observation tower, which is not considered to be in the natural area. The park's other observation platform, overlooking a wetland and pond, is on the bay side, near parking lot 3. On just one floating log I counted twenty-seven turtles sunning themselves.

I always enjoy visiting this park before sunrise on a beautiful day in the off-season. Whether I am on a trail or the beach, or kayaking on a pond, I feel like an explorer entering an untamed land. One morning in March, I stood on the bridge near the Perry Monument. As the sun rose, so did the squawking from countless gulls and waterfowl. After a night packed together in the limited open water they began to take flight a few at a time against the bright orange sky. Shortly after sunrise I heard a turkey nearby, gobbling with conviction, and within a few minutes, four toms were gobbling for the next hour. As I drove away a coal-black mink loped across the road in front of me. Later that morning, the ranger told me a coyote was raising her pups in a pipe under the road for the second year in a row. The park gate officially opens at sunrise, but usually a ranger will arrive earlier.

Sightseeing. Presque Isle has several historic attractions. Misery Bay and Perry Monument honor Adm. Perry and the sailors under his command who defeated the British fleet in 1813, and those who died during the two winters of 1812–1814. The Erie Harbor North Pier Light is a steel structure brought from France and erected in 1858. The 72-foot-tall, red-brick Presque Isle Light was constructed in 1872 and is open on weekends during the summer months. The lifesaving station—now the Coast Guard Station—has been serving mariners since 1876. Horseshoe Pond is a neighborhood for twenty-four families living on their floating homes. The homes were built on 2,000-square-foot platforms permanently anchored in their designated position. From May to October, kayaks, jet skis, boats, and fishing rods are close at hand, ready to go. Owners, visitors, groceries, garbage, furniture, and construction materials are transported by boat or, in the winter, by sled.

Recreation. The most popular of the park's sixteen trails, the 13.5-mile National Recreation Trail is paved and level and provides access throughout the park for bicycling, hiking, inline skating, and cross-country skiing. Bike rentals are available at the waterworks pump house. Winter sports include ice fishing, cross-country skiing, ice skating, iceboat sailing, and parasail

Ice formations on Lake Erie's 12-inch-thick frozen surface

Erie Harbor North Pier Light on a windy day. Alice and I were the only people there.

Gulls resting at sunset on one of the rock breakwaters.

View of the beach near the peninsula's tip. The last breakwater can be seen in the distance.

Large ice dunes form along Lake Erie's shoreline. Wind chill was minus ten degrees.

Patience prevails for this great blue heron.

skiing. Eleven large, sandy beaches have lifeguards, and four beaches have a concession and changing building. At the end of the day you can watch the sunset over Lake Erie. Boating is a very popular activity in Lake Erie and Presque Isle Bay. The park's multiservice marina, open from April 1 to November 30, has over 400 slips for permanent and temporary mooring. Water sports include waterskiing, windsurfing, sailing, jet skis, and scuba diving (registration required). The park rents canoes and kayaks to explore the interior wetlands, and motorboats and pontoon boats to cruise the bay. The concession for the Scenic Boat Tour is at the Perry Monument.

Fishing. Lake Erie and Presque Isle Bay provide some of the best fishing in the state. The bay is known for its excellent perch and very good smallmouth and crappie fishing. In March 2016, the state-record perch, weighing 2 pounds, 14 ounces, was caught in the bay. Walleye, northern pike, muskie, and steelhead are also present. In winter, ice fishermen set up temporary shelters in Misery Bay, Horseshoe Pond, and the western end of the bay. Lake Erie is a renowned fishery for three species of salmon, steelhead, lake trout, walleye, smallmouth bass, and brown trout. Five

A day at the beach

species of fish caught in the lake are state records. When boating on the lake, pay close attention to the weather because it can change quickly.

Environmental Education. The modern, 65,000-square-foot Tom Ridge Environmental Center, with its 75-foot glass observation tower, was opened in 2006. In addition to educational displays, the building houses classrooms, research labs, conference rooms, a gift shop, a café, a four-story large-format theater, and offices. The park offers a wide range of EE programs and tours for all age groups throughout the year.

NW2 Erie Bluffs State Park, Erie County

Erie Bluffs SP—one of Pennsylvania's newest state parks—is along Lake Erie's shoreline, approximately 18 miles southwest of Erie. The 587-acre day-use park has four outstanding natural features: the 80-foot-high sand bluff overlooking the lake, a mile-long undeveloped beach, a section of old-growth trees, and Elk Creek's world-class steelhead fishery. The land was purchased by the Western Pennsylvania Conservancy in 2004 and was turned over to the state's DCNR. The park has two parking lots off Route 5. The Elk Creek access area—the closest to the beach and fishing—has restrooms and a launch for small boats and kayaks. The second, smaller parking lot, called the "main lot," is a short distance west of Elk Creek and provides access to the park's fields, woods, bluffs, and trails.

Prime time for steelhead on Elk Creek
(November 1), 150 yards from Lake Erie.

Hiking. The park has ten very scenic hiking trails. The beach and bluffs can be accessed from both parking lots. From Elk Creek's lower parking lot, take the 0.2-mile Wildflower Way trail along the top of the western bank of Elk Creek. At the trail junction, take the 0.1-mile Fisherman's Footpath trail, which continues along the creek and then drops down to Lake Erie's beach and the sandbar at the creek's mouth. To reach the beach from the main lot, take the 1.1-mile Transition Trail toward the corner of the field and through the woods. At the trail junction, you can take the Lookout Trail (right) or the Bluffs Edge Trail (left). These trails meet again to form a loop. The Lookout Trail takes you through a section of old-growth trees, and the Bluffs Edge Trail provides views of the lake from the top of the bluff. Where the trails rejoin, take the Bluffs Edge Trail east to the Fisherman's Footpath trail to the beach. If you like to hike in solitude, another beautiful natural area with trails is Duck Run ravine, which is west of the main lot.

Natural Environment. Walking on the pristine beach without seeing another footprint is a unique experience. The scenery is the same as it was 1,000 years ago. You feel like you have traveled to an untamed, foreign land. The narrow beach is composed of rippled bedrock at the waterline, colorful smooth stones, small white shells, sand, a few boulders, and driftwood. The bluff's glacial till composition is clay and sand. The bluff's

The pristine, deserted, natural beach

Lake view from Bluffs Edge Trail

Sunset along the narrow beach

steep slope is held in place by vegetation, except where recent slides have occurred. Wind-driven waves and storm surge eat away at the bottom of the bluff until large sections of the bluff, including trees and boulders, slide down to the beach and lake. Almost immediately the waves and current wash the lighter material away. A USGS survey concluded that the average rate of bluff recession for Erie County ranges from 0.4 to 1.27 feet of land per year. The state park's bluffs lose an average of 0.7 feet per year.

Wildlife. Eagles feed and nest along Lake Erie's shoreline and are often seen flying along the bluffs. A colony of 3,000 bank swallows nest in holes in the bluff's upper layer of sandy clay. In 2004, the Western Pennsylvania Conservancy and Pennsylvania DCNR conducted a comprehensive wildlife survey and found eighty species of birds, nineteen mammals, an incredible 172 butterflies and moths, forty-six snails and mussels, fourteen reptiles and amphibians, and seven species of fish.

Fishing. Elk Creek is the county's largest and most popular Lake Erie tributary. The mouth of the stream is a small delta with shifting sandbars. Steelhead are the most sought-after fish. Between late September and mid-October, they begin to congregate inside the mouth of the creek and will travel upstream each time the water level rises after a hard rain. Fishermen wade into waist-deep water for the chance to battle these hard-fighting 5- to 8-pound fish, with rare heavyweights up to 15 pounds. Steelhead fishing continues upstream from the park through the winter months and ends in April. A few runs of Chinook and Coho salmon enter the stream between mid-September and October, and Brown trout are generally pursued in spring.

NW3 David M. Roderick Wildlife Reserve, SGL 314, Erie County

The Pennsylvania Game Commission's 3,455-acre SGL 314 was dedicated as Roderick Wildlife Reserve in 1991. It is a scenic gem—bordering Ohio and Lake Erie—that relatively few people, other than local residents, are aware of. Like most game lands, there are no facilities, and very little promotional marketing is done. Activities include hunting, bird watching, hiking, and sightseeing. In 1991, after US Steel decided not to build a steel plant on the property, they sold 3,131 acres to the Mellon Foundation and Western Pennsylvania Conservancy (WPC). David Roderick, the company's CEO at the time and an avid outdoorsman, was instrumental in preserving this land and sold it the day before he retired. The property was later sold to the Game Commission to protect and manage its wetlands, shrublands, and early successional forests, and the wildlife that live in this unique habitat. In recent years, the WPC has helped the PGC secure additional acreage.

The two miles of shoreline are the most dramatic feature of the property. It is the largest section of undeveloped shoreline on Lake Erie's southern shore. Dramatic bluffs as high as 80 feet rise steeply from the lake's natural beach. The Roderick Memorial overlook, near the state line, is an open grassy area on top of a section of bluff that juts out into the lake. The site provides one of Pennsylvania's most scenic and unique views, especially at sunset. Below the lookout, swirling currents create the circular pattern of stones on the point's beach.

Interior Environment. The vast majority of the property—called "the interior"—is relatively level, with progressive stages of forest, brushy fields,

As the ice begins to melt in March, currents at Roderick Point create this circular pattern.

wetlands, and shallow ponds. Much of the property was farmland abandoned in the 1940s and '50s. The combination of the water table near or at the surface and poor drainage made the ground too difficult to cultivate. Today, 50 percent of the property is either seasonal or permanent wetland. SGL 314 has two drainages: Raccoon Creek in the eastern section and Turkey Creek in the western section. Most of the property is northern hardwood forest cover, with red maple as the most common tree. About 8 percent of the forest is aspen groves, and a small portion is swamp hardwoods.

Since its acquisition, the Game Commission has placed a high value on the property's shrubland and early successional habitat. The GC's biologists consider it one of the most important areas in the state for the American woodcock. Populations of shrubland-dependent birds, such as the blue-winged warbler, field sparrow, grouse, and woodcock, have declined during the past fifty years due to significant loss of their specialized habitat. Many of Pennsylvania's abandoned fields and pastures have gradually reverted to pole stage forests, including large areas of this property. To rectify the situation, the GC, with the assistance of several government agencies and nonprofit organizations, began a major habitat restoration program. The plan specified whole-tree chipping on 700 acres in seventeen blocks and mechanical vegetation cutting on 90 acres of shrubland that is past its beneficial condition. Controlled burns also take

Walking the remote, deserted beach at sunset was both eerie and invigorating.

View from Roderick Point

Rudd Road is the main road through SGL 314.

Driftwood, colorful smooth stones, and boulders are products of the bluff.

place when needed. The GC's goal is to maintain 25 percent of the property in shrubland and early successional forest.

Shoreline Environment. Access to the beach is very limited. Climbing down the bluff is dangerous and exacerbates the natural erosion process. Besides, it is very difficult to climb back up. The only place where the beach is easily accessible is at the end of Rudd Road. This is a great place to walk along the beach. With reasonable effort you can also carry a kayak to the water. On the beach you enter a completely natural environment created by nature's dynamic forces. Recently fallen trees, driftwood, and millions of small shells and smooth stones of varied colors enhance the natural scene. From Rudd Road, the eastern property line is an approximately 0.5-mile walk. The most remote and scenic stretch of beach is to the west, past the cove. In the cove, the beach is very narrow, but passable when the wind is calm and the water level is normal. Beyond the cove, look for small holes along the upper face of the bluff made by nesting swallows.

To view the interesting two-toned spires along the bluff, park at the monument and walk approximately 300 yards east on Lake Road, then 30 yards through the woods to the top of the bluff. The spires are to your right. Do not get close to the edge of the drop-off. There are many deceptive overhangs that could collapse with your added weight, especially after a heavy rain.

Wildlife. SGL 314 was purchased for hunters and is maintained with funds provided by hunters, but it is open to the public. If you want to hike or bird watch in the interior during hunting season, wear orange clothing. A better option is to visit on Sundays, when hunting is closed. The game land's mixed habitat supports a variety of mammals, including deer, coyotes, rabbits, and squirrels. Birds include nesting eagles, migrating raptors, turkey, grouse, woodcock, waterfowl, and stocked pheasants.. Eagles are a common sight flying along the bluff in the early morning and evening hours. The Pennsylvania Audubon Society has identified SGL 314 as an "important bird area."

NW4 Lake Pleasant Conservation Area, Erie County

The beautiful 582-acre Lake Pleasant property, with its pristine 64-acre glacial lake, surrounding wetlands, and adjacent forest, was purchased by the Western Pennsylvania Conservancy in 1990. The lake is 14 miles southeast of Erie, in the upper portion of the French Creek watershed, which is one of the most biologically diverse in the northeastern US. A road runs along most of the lake's eastern shoreline, and several homes are along the western shoreline, but Lake Pleasant has the cleanest water and is the least developed kettle lake in the region.

History. Lake Pleasant, like all kettle lakes, was created between 20,000 and 12,000 years ago, during the Wisconsinan glacier's retreat. Pennsylvania has more than 2,500 lakes, but only fifty are glacial lakes, and only eight of those are in northwestern Pennsylvania. The water flowing into the lake and wetlands is almost entirely groundwater filtered as it travels through fine glacial sediments with a high amount of lime. Other factors contributing to the water's clarity are the lake's 44-foot depth, its relatively small watershed, and a ban on boat motors. The first thing I noticed after launching my kayak was that I could see the letters on my paddle 5 feet below the water's surface.

In 1991, George Moon was diving in the lake and found what looked like a bone protruding out of the lake sediment. He showed it to an anthropologist in Erie, who identified it as a shoulder bone from a woolly mammoth. Twenty dives later, Moon and five other divers recovered the nearly complete mammoth skeleton. They also found stone weights and fibers that might have been cords or nets. The skull and some bones showed evidence indicating that it was butchered and intentionally placed in the cold lake to preserve it for future use and to make it inaccessible to scavengers. The original scene occurred at least 10,000 years ago.

Nature. The preserved land north of the lake is forested wetland with a large beaver pond. Below the lake, the much-larger wetland area is composed of forests, scrub-shrub, and emergent wetlands and a few standing dead trees, called snags. Alder Run slowly meanders through the center of the wetlands. The wetlands and the lake's healthy population of fish attract a variety of migrating birds, including resident eagles and osprey.

Extensive wildlife surveys were conducted for the 2004 Lake Pleasant Watershed Assessment and Protection Plan. The list of species includes eight turtles, thirteen snakes, twelve salamanders, and eleven toads and frogs. An aquatic survey found twenty-one species of fish, of which three are listed as endangered in Pennsylvania. An abbreviated list of birds includes bald eagle, common moorhen, common loon, American coot, hooded merganser, pied-billed grebe, several species of hawks and sandpipers, bittern, woodcock, and many species of warblers.

North end of beautiful, crystal-clear Lake Pleasant

Of the 192 plants, twenty-three are species of concern (endangered, threatened, or rare).

If you bring a kayak or canoe, I recommend that you paddle down the outlet channel at the southern end of the lake. It is a scenic, 300-yard journey that dead-ends at a beaver dam. The dam has raised the level of the lake about 10 inches. From the channel, the dam appears to be just 2 feet high and only 20 feet long. What you can't see is the tremendous amount of work required to build the dam in the 5- to 6-foot-deep channel and extend it more than 100 feet each way into the thick wetland shrubs. Lodges were built at the dam on both sides of the channel. Another larger lodge is on the left side of the channel between the lake and dam. I was surprised to see the large branches the beavers hauled to build their lodge. They had to drag the branches for quite a distance, so they must have channels through the wetland to the wooded hillside.

Recreation. Activities include fishing, hunting, nature study, kayaking, bird watching, scuba diving, ice skating, and ice fishing. Hiking trails are planned for the future. Swimming is not allowed, with the exception of the few private-property residents. The lake attracts scuba divers for its clear water, schools of fish, healthy beds of weeds, and no boat motors. If you plan to scuba dive, contact the PFBC for a permit. Two dive clubs and the Erie County Search & Rescue Team use the lake for training and recreation.

One of several beaver lodges along the outlet channel

The outlet channel through the wetlands

Fishing is the most popular activity. The Pennsylvania Fish and Boat Commission stocks trout during the spring, fall, and early-winter seasons. Bass might be an underutilized fishery, especially since bass grow faster in this lake than in the average Pennsylvania lake. Their fast growth is due to the prime habitat and large numbers of bait fish. Other species of fish include northern pike, carp, grass pickerel, catfish, perch, and panfish. The PFBC manages the two small parking areas and kayak launch along Lake Pleasant Road. It is one of only two lakes in Pennsylvania where electric motors are prohibited. On the west side of Lake Pleasant, the WPC, with the support of the DCNR and other nonprofit organizations, built an access trail, boardwalk, and canoe/kayak launch. This is also the location of the WPC's Field Station, which they and other institutions use for environmental education and research. The field station property is a great place for bird watching and wildlife viewing.

NW5 Pymatuning State Park, SGL 214, Crawford County

The 21,122-acre Pymatuning SP encompasses three-quarters of Pymatuning Lake, which straddles the state's border with Ohio. It is the largest state park in Pennsylvania and ranks as the second most visited state park. Pymatuning Lake—the largest interior lake in Pennsylvania—is 17,088 acres and 17 miles long has seventy miles of shoreline, a maximum width of 1.6 miles, and a maximum depth of 35 feet. Within the park are two natural areas and two causeways that cross the lake, each more than 2 miles long. On the south side of the Linesville causeway is the GC's Pymatuning Waterfowl Area. The park and SGL 214 combined protect more than 30,000 acres of land, water, and wetlands, providing excellent habitat for wildlife.

History. When the most recent glacial ice sheet began to melt and retreat, the meltwater transported and filled the Shenango River valley with vast

The spillway bowl at Linesville Causeway

amounts of glacial material. This flat plain was called the Great Pymatuning Swamp. The severe flood of 1913 led to the initial efforts to build a dam. Construction began on the 2,400-foot earthen dam in 1931 and was completed three years later. The Civilian Conservation Corps, based in three camps, was part of the nearly 7,000-man construction workforce. In addition to the dam, the men cut 8,000 acres of timber and built the beautiful stone gatehouse and walls along the dam's roadway, the causeways, a concrete spillway bowl, and most of the park's roads and facilities.

Nature. Two natural areas are in the northern section of the lake. There are no trails in the natural areas, so the easiest way to visit is by boat. The 161-acre Clark Island NA has been separated from the mainland for more than eighty years. The island's shoreline is white sand, and the island has its own small pond. The 725-acre Blackjack Swamp NA, at the far north end of the lake, comprises several tributaries that flow through large wetlands, separated by sections of forest. Wildlife in the natural areas includes eagles, osprey, beaver, waterfowl, cormorant, and, at times, loons. One of my favorite places in the northern area is Wilson Boat Launch; it is quite scenic, quiet, and good for birding.

The Sugar Run Trail—a hidden gem—can be accessed from either side of the dam. It drops down below the dam, uses two bridges to cross the stream, and connects with an old railroad bed that follows the scenic Shenango River.

Brief snow squall at the bridge over the Shenango River, below the dam

A silent, deserted park preceding a winter storm. View is from the causeway.

This unmarked trail, with views of the cascading outflow, large hemlocks, maple trees, and the beautiful stream, is great for bird watching or simply unwinding in nature. The Tamarack Trail, near Jamestown Campground, takes you along Beaver Dam Pond and to the deciduous tamarack trees. Beaver Dam Trail goes through wetlands on a boardwalk to an observation deck.

The state park and game lands are well known for their large nesting and winter population of eagles. Pymatuning Lake is the only known place in Pennsylvania that has never lost its nesting population of bald eagles. One of the best places to see eagles is along the causeway, near the spillway

A male yellow warbler with a leg band at Wilson boat launch in May

Every year approximately 300,000 people feed the carp at the causeway.

bowl, at sunrise. During the winter, eagles congregate near the dam. For bird watching, the spring migration has slightly more species of birds than the fall migration. Also they are more active and their plumage is brighter.

Fishing. At Pymatuning SP, fishing is probably the most popular activity, followed by boating. The lake is famous for its outstanding warm-water fishery. The most-common species are largemouth and smallmouth bass, walleye, muskellunge, crappie, perch, and channel catfish. The excellent fishing is due to several factors: a well-managed stocking of millions of fingerlings and fry each year, extensive monitoring of the lake's fishery, a relatively shallow depth with large weed beds, and protected areas, and there are more than 1,000 manmade habitat structures built with the help of the Pymatuning Lake Association. Approximately fifty fishing tournaments are held each year. The breakwater piers at Espyville and Linesville Marinas are popular places to fish from shore.

Boating. The lake's size and miles of natural shoreline make it a favorite for boaters. Within the state park are more than forty mooring sites, eleven boat launches, and three marinas. The marinas rent pontoon boats, motorboats, and human-powered boats and sell boating supplies. The Linesville Marina and Boat Rental Concession was rebuilt in 2017. Boats are limited to 20-horsepower motors, reducing noise and making fishing, sailing, and kayaking more enjoyable. The wild, scenic islands; coves; and northern backwater areas are great places to visit with a kayak or canoe, especially at sunrise or sunset.

Recreation. Every year more than 300,000 people stop at the causeway's concession area and spillway bowl to feed the mass of gluttonous carp. It is quite a spectacle. The concession sells food both for fish and humans. The DCNR has made this activity a rare exception to their policy of not feeding wildlife. Notice that the lake on the south side is several feet higher than the main lake, and the unique spillway is a large, circular drain. Another place definitely worth visiting is the PFBC's Lineville Fish Hatchery, the largest in Pennsylvania and one of the largest in the world (see NW6). In addition to boating and fishing, the list of activities includes hunting, hiking, bird watching, swimming, camping, disc golf, sightseeing, and environmental-education programs. Winter sports include ice fishing, iceboating, snowmobiling on designated trails, cross-country skiing, ice skating, and sledding at the dam. The Jamestown concession—open most days during the winter—has refreshments and rents ice skates and cross-country skis.

The GC closed the Pymatuning Learning Center near the spillway, but the grounds are still maintained and worth visiting. The 0.25-mile paved nature trail takes you through meadows to an observation deck at the shoreline, a jungle of vines, several old-growth trees, and a fenced area to illustrate what vegetation looks like without deer. Markers identify the species of trees. The state park has two campgrounds with modern camp facilities, cabins, boat launch, and swimming beach. Jamestown CG—considerably larger than Linesville CG—has a store, amphitheater, playground, and cabins for year-round use. All four beaches have bathhouses.

Pymatuning Waterfowl Area and SGL 214. This 9,661-acre, 8-mile-long wildlife habitat is south of the Linesville causeway. An elevated railroad track runs at an angle through the middle of the wetland and separates the headwaters of two major streams: the Shenango River flows north and Crooked Creek flows south. The habitat both on the upper and lower sections consists of open-water impoundments, vast wetlands, fields, and forest. The water level in the northern section was raised when the causeway was built, to expand that section of lake to 2,500 acres. The lake is a wildlife propagation area, and access is forbidden. South of the railroad track, the GC, with help from Ducks Unlimited and other nonprofit organizations, built large impoundments with control structures to manage water levels.

To experience solitude, hike through the fields east of the waterfowl area. Park near any gate and follow the grass roads to the ponds and lake. One beautiful winter afternoon, I hiked several miles with 10 inches of snow on the ground and never saw a human track—just wildlife. The only trail in the waterfowl area and SGL is the 4-mile-long, grass-surfaced Erie Extension Canal Towpath Trail between Routes 285 and 322. It follows the old canal south through wetlands and around impoundments. This is a great way to see wildlife. Bring sunscreen, insect repellent, and water. There are no toilet facilities or shade, and the trail is not a loop.

A fresh imprint of a bald eagle that caught a rodent in the snow in February, SGL 214

An idyllic scene at sunset

NW6 Linesville State Fish Hatchery, Crawford County

The Fish and Boat Commission operates thirteen hatcheries in Pennsylvania. I had the pleasure of touring Linesville Fish Hatchery on Pymatuning Lake with manager Jared Sayer. Hatcheries have two main functions: the first is to replace the fish that anglers harvest, and the second is to constantly learn more about all aspects of fish and their habitat. In a natural situation, a lake's entire fishery and aquatic life would be balanced. The 97-acre hatchery is the largest in the state and contributes to the science and business of raising warm-water species of fish. I highly recommend visiting their grounds and visitor center, with its reptile and trophy-sized fish mounts, 10,000-gallon fish-viewing tank, and viewing area on the lower level. During most of the year—especially spring—you can watch the early stages of the hatchery process: egg fertilization and development, feeding methods, and tanks with tiny fry. The viewing tank holds many of the fish native to Pymatuning Lake, including a monster 62-pound flathead catfish. The state record is 53 pounds. The property's ponds and enclosed raceways are where various species of fry and large breeding fish are raised. The visitor center is open every day, except certain holidays.

Unlike most hatcheries that raise only trout, Linesville raises at least eleven different species from egg to fry or fingerling, and in some cases fish up to 10 inches long. The year-round process and timing is different for each species. The species they raise for inland lakes are yellow perch, walleye, muskellunge, channel catfish, largemouth bass, bluegill, golden shiner, white bass, black bass (crappie), and brown trout. For Lake Erie, they raise steelhead and brown trout. The hatchery will occasionally raise hybrid striped bass in cooperation with other hatcheries. Every year, the Linesville Hatchery makes 110 stocking trips to fifty-two bodies of water in twenty-nine counties. Fish biologists are continually analyzing and fine-tuning the answer to the question, "Is it better to release a large quantity of fry verses releasing a smaller quantity of fingerlings?" By electroshocking the water, then counting and measuring the fish and analyzing their scales, biologists can estimate the number of fish in each age class and compare results over many years.

Walleye: Soon after ice-out, for approximately two weeks, fourteen trap nets are set in shallow-water areas. As many as 6,000 adult walleye are collected and transported alive back to the hatch house, where their eggs and sperm are extracted and mixed. The adults are returned to the same area the next day. The fertilized eggs are suspended in 2-gallon egg jars with 50-degree oxygenated water. Eighteen days later, they are ready to hatch and are placed in indoor tanks. Their yolk sac provides sustenance for the first five days, and then they are fed and remain in the tanks for approximately thirty days. The 1.5–2-inch fry are placed in special bags with oxygen for transportation to lakes to be released. Some of the fry are moved to the ponds for sixty days, where they

The lower level of the Linesville Hatchery Visitor Center is the fish culture station, where fish eggs are fertilized and fry are raised.

The visitor center's fish tank is a great way to view Pymatuning's species of fish.

Some of the fish ponds at Linesville Hatchery

A young fox who lost its mother fends for itself at the ponds.

continue growing into fingerling size and are then stocked in lakes. These ponds are pretreated with lime and fertilizer to promote phytoplankton and zooplankton that walleye eat. The ponds are also designed to drain into catch basins at the deepest end to make removing the fish easier. The hatchery releases a phenomenal 70–90 million walleye every year.

Muskellung: After the walleye breed and the water is about 55 degrees, it is the muskie's turn. Trap nets are set in shallow water in Pymatuning Lake, and approximately 120 adults between 34 and 50 inches are collected. They are placed into tube-shaped sock nets for transportation by truck back to the hatchery house. The eggs are fertilized and placed in floating bags immersed in the egg jars. Fourteen days later, the hatched fry are placed in the tanks, where they lie on the bottom and do not eat until the yolk sacks are absorbed. Then they swim up and cling to special burlap hanging in the tank, similar to vegetation in the lake. Muskie are programmed to eat prey, so the first ten days they are fed brine shrimp. Gradually, fish food is mixed in with the brine, and within days they are feeding on fish food. They are kept in the indoor tanks until they are 4 inches in length. They are then moved to the outside enclosed raceways with automatic feeders. By October, they have grown to 10 inches and are ready to be released. Two weeks before release, they are fed minnows to get them back to their normal predator mindset. The hatchery releases approximately 50,000 muskie every year.

Largemouth Bass: The process for bass is different. When the water on the Game Commission's side of the lake reaches a temperature close to 70 degrees, the hatchery staff cruise shallow water for large, gold-colored schools of small bass fry. They net about 150,000 fry and place them in the hatchery ponds. When the bass are 2 to 3 inches, the pond water is lowered and they are caught and transported for release. When new or recently refilled lakes need to stock bass, the hatchery will keep some bass in the ponds until they are 5 to 8 inches and then transport them for release.

Brown Trout: Three- to four-year-old brown trout are kept in ponds for breeding. They spawn around November 4 and are raised indoors until March. Then they are moved to the raceways until June or July. Testing is done to make sure they are disease free. The goal is to release 100,000 into Lake Erie and send close to 200,000 to other hatcheries throughout the state, where they are raised until the following May and then released.

The business of raising a dozen species of fish requires complicated scheduling, diligent record keeping, and hard work. The pressure to produce good results never ends. It took decades to develop the current system and requires dedicated, experienced personnel to execute it. I came away with a new appreciation of where my money goes when I buy my fishing license.

NW7 Conneaut Marsh, SGL 213, Crawford County

The 5,500-acre Conneaut Marsh is one of the largest wetlands in Pennsylvania. The Western Pennsylvania Conservancy purchased the original 684 acres in 1978 and transferred ownership to the Game Commission. The size of the marsh and its location near two other large protected waterfowl areas make it one of the state's premier habitats for migrating and nesting birds. The 12-mile-long marsh begins at the outflow of Conneaut Lake, the largest natural lake in Pennsylvania. Slow-moving water in the channel called

Secluded Brown Hill Road is only 2 feet higher than the wetland forest and marsh.

Conneaut Outlet snakes through a mixed habitat of emergent marsh, wooded wetlands, and open water. The land adjacent to the wetlands is mostly deciduous forest and a few cultivated fields. Twelve thousand years ago, glacial meltwater filled the valley with silt to a depth of more than 100 feet. Stories have been written about heavy construction equipment and railroad cars parked on dry land within the marsh that disappeared overnight, sinking deep into the muck. The marsh has three distinct sections—the upper, middle, and lower, each with its own characteristics.

Viewing the vast wetland can be frustrating due to very limited access, signage, information, and maps. I use Google Earth to print detailed aerial views of the areas I plan to visit. If you are going to kayak or canoe in the marsh, inform someone about your plans and always wear a life vest. In most areas, if you tip over it is virtually impossible to swim through the dense vegetation to the nearest shoreline. Also viewing wildlife from the high-traffic roads that cross the marsh is potentially deadly.

Nature. Conneaut Marsh was designated by the Audubon Society as one of Pennsylvania's important bird areas (IBAs). Several bird, mammal, and plant species are listed as rare or of special conservation concern. At least four pairs of eagles nest each year near the marsh's perimeter, and an average of eight eagles feed in the marsh throughout the winter. Beavers inhabit most of the marsh, and in some areas their dams can restrict boating. The state-protected reptile—the massassagua rattlesnake—resides here but is rarely observed. In spring, the wetlands come alive with the chorus of thousands of frogs. To protect wildlife, the GC created a propagation area, which is off-limits to human encroachment. The following is a short list of unique migrant birds: common loon, sandhill crane, tundra swan, yellow rail, and rusty blackbird, a federally listed "Bird of Greatest Concern." Boaters might encounter muskrat, mink, and beaver.

A 3.6-acre stand of old-growth trees is near the parking area on the east side of the Route 19 bridge. The stand is on the edge of the wetland, with some trees in the hummocks about 100 yards from dry land. Dale Luthringer, a naturalist with the DCNR, measured about fifty large trees of an impressive sixteen different species, including six species of oak.

Recreation. The best way to view wildlife is from the water, but the launch areas for kayaks and canoes are primitive, and some require a long carry from the parking area. Also keep in mind that there are no public facilities. Conneaut Marsh is a favorite place for waterfowl hunters, so caution is in order during hunting season. Whether you hike into the marsh on manmade peninsulas or float in, you will experience solitude and a feeling of adventure. To avoid heat, insects, and other people, visit in the off-season.

View from the Geneva Road Bridge, looking north

A group of geese take off while another group ponders what to do.

Fishing. The most-common species of fish are crappie and bowfin, but bass, carp, and pike are occasionally caught. Bowfin are found only in a few locations in Pennsylvania, and the marsh is probably the best place to fish for them. Bowfin look prehistoric, with a flattened head and a long dorsal fin that runs almost to their rounded tail. Their ability to survive in water with a low oxygen level is one reason why they flourish in this marsh. Bowfin can grow to 32 inches and weigh up to 10 pounds. They have lots of sharp teeth and a reputation for being fearsome fighters. Bowfin are protected in Pennsylvania, so release them to fight another day.

The natural channel through the marsh, looking south from Brown Hill Road

A bald eagle is leaving its perch for a better hunting location.

Upper Section. This approximately 2.6-mile-long section extends from the lake's outflow to Brown Hill Road, which crosses the wetland. There is not much open water in this section; therefore, kayaking is limited to the channel. Swamp forest is the dominant habitat, with emergent vegetation located in the north and south ends. To reach the GC access from Route 285, take Route 322 east for three blocks, turn right onto the GC's dirt road, and continue to the end. A gorgeous area is along Brown Hill Road, with parking adjacent to the channel. Be aware that parking areas are not plowed in the winter. A good place to spot eagles is from the GC's waterfowl farm road.

Middle Section. This 2.5-mile-long section extends from Brown Hill Road to Geneva Road. It is the widest section with the most open water, and the best place to kayak and view waterfowl. Vegetation includes cattails, smartweed, and spatterduck. Large numbers of migrating waterfowl use this section to rest and refuel. Shorebirds are occasionally seen feeding on the mudflats. The marsh is prime habitat for a long list of nesting species, including American and least bitterns, American coot, common moorhen, Virginia rail, sora, marsh wren, black tern, and bald eagles. The Geneva Road bridge is a good place to spot eagles perched on nearby snags. The best place to launch a canoe or kayak is to park at the Y intersection, north of the Geneva Road bridge.

Lower Section. The 7-mile-long section south of Geneva Road begins to narrow in width. Wetland shrubs are more prevalent here. Large areas of dense cattails, bulrushes, reeds, and hummocks are favorite habitat for northern shoveler, pintail, gadwall, American wigeon, and both green- and blue-winged teals. In more-open water you may find common goldeneye, canvasback, ruddy ducks, northern shoveler, and both species of scaup. Swamp forest borders the marsh and is a good place to see blue herons, bald eagles, bitterns, and rare redheaded woodpeckers. The GC's access road along Route 285 is approximately 1.6 miles west of the I-79 exit. Turn right onto the GC's dirt road, drive about 200 yards, and park in the small lot. Walk straight ahead on the GC road approximately 0.4 miles to the end. Two other access locations are at the north end of the Route 19 bridge and the Mercer Pike bridge.

NW8 Erie National Wildlife Refuge, Crawford County

Erie National Wildlife Refuge is owned and managed by the US Fish and Wildlife Service. The refuge is composed of two separate properties: the 5,206-acre Sugar Lake Division and, 10 miles to the north, the 3,609-acre Seneca Division. The land was bought in 1959, with funds generated from the sale of federal duck stamps purchased by waterfowl hunters. Each division has its own distinct characteristics. Erie NWR is known for its excellent habitat, which attracts and supports impressive numbers of species of birds and mammals. The refuge headquarters is in the Sugar Lake Division, 0.75 miles east of Guys Mills on Route 198. Turn right onto a gravel road called Wood Duck Lane and drive past the ponds to the office. Be aware that many of the refuge road names do not match the names on a GPS and that your GPS will not lead you to the refuge office.

Pool 9, Sugar Lake Division

From the observation deck at Pool K, Sugar Lake Division

Beavers raise the water level and the dead trees provide nesting habitat.

The covered observation deck at Pool 9

A wood duck with a leg band is napping at the first viewing area off Boland Road.

Sugar Lake Division. This large property is a mosaic of habitats, including wetlands, numerous natural ponds, manmade impoundments, twisting channels, and small tributary streams. Wet and dry meadows, cultivated fields, and forests are on the higher rolling terrain. Route 198 cuts across the refuge at a slightly higher elevation, separating the north-flowing watershed of Woodcock Creek from the south-flowing watershed of Lake Creek.

Seneca Division. The Seneca property is mostly wetlands, with Muddy Creek and Dead Creek forming the two main channels. Each channel winds back and forth in seemingly endless loops. Other than the channels, there are few areas of open water. From the air, you can see the old isolated channels. Meadows, cultivated fields, and patches of forest complete the habitat.

Wildlife. In total, 237 species of birds have been identified on the refuge, with 113 species nesting on the two properties. The refuge was designated an important bird area by the National Audubon Society. Thousands of migrating ducks and geese use the wetlands to rest and refuel. Red-tailed hawks, American kestrels, several species of owls, and bald eagles nest here. Shorebirds feed on the mudflats, and great blue herons nest in rookeries. A staggering thirty-nine species of warblers have been recorded. Tundra swans and sandhill cranes are occasional visitors. A partial list of imperiled or rare species includes peregrine falcon, American bittern, short-eared owl, upland sandpiper, sedge and marsh wrens, Swainson's thrush, northern goshawk, northern harrier, and black-crowned night heron.

The refuge provides habitat for forty-seven species of mammals and thirty-seven species of amphibians and reptiles.

Predatory birds and mammals rely on the refuge's healthy population of diminutive but important shrews, moles, voles, bog lemmings, and mice. The wetlands are home to beaver, muskrat, and river otter. Turtles include box, snapping, midland painted, spotted, and eastern spiny softshell. Five nonvenomous species of snakes live here. Mussels contribute an important role in the health of the streams by filtering the water. The refuge protects the rare northern riffleshell and pearly clubshell mussels, which are found in only 5 percent of their historical range. The refuge has the healthiest population of riffleshell in the world.

French Creek, on the northern border of Seneca Division, is the most biologically diverse stream in Pennsylvania. The stream is home to twenty-seven species of mussels, of which four are federally endangered and ten others are endangered in Pennsylvania. The creek has a phenomenal eighty species of fish, and eight are listed as endangered or threatened in Pennsylvania. The mud puppy and eastern hellbender are huge, ugly salamanders. The hellbender can grow up to 29 inches long and weigh more than 5 pounds. During the past decade, the Western Pennsylvania Conservancy and many other organizations have contributed professional, volunteer, and financial resources to protect and monitor the stream and its aquatic life.

Flora. The Fish and Wildlife Service maintains the habitat with water-level control structures, prescribed burns, grassland and shrubland maintenance, invasive-species removal, and new plantings. A cooperative farming program permits farmers to cultivate grain crops on refuge land, which provides supplemental food for wildlife. Along just three trails—Tusuga, Beaver Run, and Deer Run—more than 100 species of wildflowers bloom from April to September. The most-common trees in the upland forest are red, striped, and mountain maple; white ash; American basswood; white pine; and black cherry. The riparian forests are composed of water-tolerant trees such as sycamore, black willow, river birch, hemlock, box elder, pin oak, and silver maple. Scattered throughout the refuge are large, solitary, old-growth trees that somehow avoided the axe.

Recreation. Before visiting, print the online information or stop at the refuge office on weekdays for brochures describing the trails and wildlife. The fishing brochure has the only map showing the trails, locations for parking, and observation blinds. The two refuges are vast, so my advice is to pick some trails or destinations, park your car, and explore. There are three viewing areas along Boland Road and one off Allen Road. The popular Tsuga nature trail is behind the NWR office. The 3-mile-long Deer Run trail takes you through a variety of habitats to an observation deck and the Pool 9 dike. Parking lots are at both ends of the trail. Another excellent trail is the 1-mile Muddy Creek Holly boardwalk trail from Johnstown Road. It is an out-and-back trail through less visited Seneca wetlands. Without question, the best way to observe the scenery and wildlife is from a kayak or canoe. Motors are prohibited. Certain areas are closed between January 15 and August 15 to protect breeding birds. Kayaking along the Muddy Creek channel would be an awesome trip. The refuge is open to hunting and trapping, but special permits are required.

Beaver Meadows Recreation Area, looking west. The floating boardwalk is to the right.

NW9 Allegheny National Forest, Wild Areas, Natural Areas, and National Recreation Area; Warren, Forest, McKean, and Elk Counties

The vast 513,257-acre Allegheny National Forest (ANF) is the only national forest in Pennsylvania. It is also the largest protected land in the state and offers more recreational opportunities than any other place in Pennsylvania. It hosts four million visitors but rarely seems crowded. Its wilderness provides solitude and serenity. The National Forest Service ranger stations are in Marienville and Bradford. A map of the ANF can be ordered on their website or purchased at their offices.

The ANF encompasses the Allegheny Reservoir, two national wilderness areas, two national scenic rivers, two national recreation areas, and two national scenic areas with old-growth forests. These protected areas equate to 140,000 acres where logging and drilling are prohibited. Like all national forests, the ANF is managed primarily for the extraction of natural resources, but the Forest Service must also maintain a healthy, sustainable forest; protect the watershed, natural features, and wildlife; and develop recreational opportunities. Balancing this list of tasks is difficult, and at times contentious.

Forest History. The one constant that describes the ANF is that it is always changing. The trees were mostly eastern hemlock and beech, with white

View from Rim Rock Overlook

pine and oaks in the lower valleys. Fallen trees decomposed and enriched the forest soil. Natural predation by mountain lions, wolves, and bears kept the deer population low, allowing a diversified understory to grow. The forest ecosystem was balanced.

In the early 1800s, the forest began its rapid evolution when the first settlers moved into the area. Over the next hundred years, the forest was clear-cut, followed by slash-feed fires, soil erosion, and stream degradation. The 23,000-acre Owls Nest fire was so hot that it sterilized the soil in places, which remained bare for decades. Only three pockets of old-growth forest were spared. Soon after the world's first oil well was drilled just 40 miles west, oil wells began to sprout up by the thousands. During the 1860s, Pennsylvania led the world both in lumber and oil production. In 1911, the Weeks Act allowed the federal government to purchase land in the east. Twelve years later, the Allegheny National Forest was established. Unfortunately, only 7 percent of the land that was purchased included mineral rights.

Today, the forest is not diversified or balanced. Less than 1 percent of the original forest was black cherry, but it dominates the forest today and accounts for 80 percent of the value of the wood produced, and supplies a third of the world's cherry veneer. The Forest Service still allows clear-cutting, but in many areas other methods are used. One method removes only trees that are dead or diseased. Another method selectively harvests most of the tallest trees. This opens up the forest canopy and allows new growth but leaves a variety of mature trees to start the regeneration process. Wetlands constitute 4 percent of the ANF.

Environmental Issues. The ANF has a phenomenal 100,000 wells that are inactive and abandoned. Many are not sealed. The recently developed fracking process for oil and gas extraction has added 6,000 new wells, doubling the number of active wells to 12,000. Each fracking well requires 3 acres of cleared forest versus the previous 1 acre. In addition, drilling each well requires an incredible average of 3.6 million gallons of fresh water pumped from nearby lakes and rivers and hauled by truck to the well site. The ANF has more wells than any of the country's 155 national forests. In the areas that most people visit, logging and oil and gas production are prohibited.

Diseases and insects are killing many species of trees throughout the ANF. In 2014, an outbreak of the cherry scallop-shell moth––a native species—defoliated 17,000 acres of black cherry trees. The outbreak rarely kills the tree, but it does reduce growth, causing tight tree rings, which reduces the value of the finished cherry wood. The hemlock woolly adelgid—an invasive insect—has gradually killed some of the ANF's eastern hemlock trees, including some old-growth hemlocks. The scale insect is responsible for a fatal fungus called beech bark disease, which eventually destroys the tree. The fungus is evident on the bark of several old-growth beech trees in Hearts Content Scenic Area. The gypsy moth, ash borer, and leaf roller are other insects that threaten the health of the ANF's trees. Several days of severely cold temperatures would help keep some of these insects in check. Instead, our winters seem to be getting milder. The high population of deer is another issue. To combat the problem, the Forest Service has erected more than 100 miles of 8-foot-high fence.

Allegheny Reservoir. The 12,080-acre Allegheny Reservoir, with 7,783 acres in Pennsylvania, is the most dominant feature in the ANF and one of the premier boating destinations in the state. In 1965, the Army Corps of Engineers completed the Kinzue Dam, creating the 27-mile-long reservoir—the deepest in Pennsylvania—with 91 miles of shoreline. Ten of the ANF's campgrounds are along the lake's undeveloped, forested shoreline, and five of those are primitive camp sites, with access only by boat or forest trail. Numerous coves, clean water, and scenery make this a great place for kayaking. The best places to view the dam are the Big Bend Visitor Center and the nearby overlook parking area along Route 59. Kinzua Wolf Run Marina has boat rentals, supplies, and a nice restaurant and bar with a view of the lake.

The reservoir is famous for its outstanding fishery. Anglers focus mainly on walleye, northern pike, smallmouth bass, muskellunge, yellow perch, channel catfish, and brown trout. The reservoir produced Pennsylvania's

Looking up at the shear face of Rim Rock. Cool air pours out of the rock separation.

This newly fallen tree will eventually look like the other fallen moss-covered trees.

state-record northern pike (33 lbs., 8 oz.) and walleye (17 lbs., 9 oz.). It is believed that more muskie over 40 pounds have been caught here than any place in the eastern US. Perhaps the most scenic place to fish is the narrow valley below the dam. The Allegheny River's large boulders, islands, and deep pools create tremendous habitat for huge brown trout weighing up to 10 pounds. Large muskie, pike, and walleye are also caught below the dam. Eagles, osprey, and blue herons are often seen feeding in this stretch of river.

National Scenic Areas. Tionesta and Hearts Content National Scenic Areas' old-growth forests were also designated national natural landmarks. Hearts Content is only 121 acres but is far more accessible. This is the place to introduce your children and grandchildren to the forest that once existed in Pennsylvania. The easy-to-follow 1-mile trail heads into a majestic stand of 300–400-year-old hemlock, white pine, oak, and beech trees. Notice the hemlocks with bent trunks formed by competing for sunlight with neighboring trees. On a recent visit, I saw several giants that fell during a windstorm earlier that year. The splintered trunks, shattered limbs, and the smaller crushed trees made me wonder how violent and frightening it would have been to be out in the storm and close to where it fell. The fallen trees are host to moss, ferns, and young saplings, and many have deteriorated to the point where they are almost indiscernible.

The 2,018-acre Tionesta Scenic Area was the largest stand of old-growth trees in Pennsylvania. Sadly, the infamous 1985 tornado cut a path of destruction across 954 acres. This remote area is a haven for wildlife, including black bear, fisher, bobcat, and forest birds such as barred owl, pileated woodpecker, Swanson's thrush, and yellow-bellied flycatcher. The best access is the North Country National Scenic Trail. Along the trail you will enter stands of ancient hemlock and beech, and open areas with dense saplings. Bushwhacking through the blowdown area is nearly impossible.

National Wilderness Areas. The 8,663-acre Hickory Creek Wilderness Area and the 368-acre Allegheny River Wilderness Area are the only federal wilderness areas east of the Mississippi. The Hickory Creek WA is a third-generation forest with two streams, wetlands, and wet meadows. Hemlock and birch trees are primarily found in the valleys, and an oak-hickory forest is on the higher plateau. This wild place is home to all of the region's deep-woods mammals. The only major trail is the 11.1-mile Hickory Creek loop trail. Hickory Creek's wetlands were inadvertently created by logging. In flat areas large trees transpired the groundwater. After they were cut, the water table rose to the surface. Now only wetland vegetation grows.

The Allegheny River Wilderness Area, the country's smallest national wilderness area, comprises seven islands scattered along a 31-mile section of the Allegheny River. The islands, ranging from 10 to 96 acres, are anchored with large sycamore trees, raritan vegetation, and wildflowers. The 1985 tornado flattened the trees on Baker Island, and a 1975 windstorm knocked down trees on Thompson's Island. Cull's Island—the largest—has an old-growth river bottom forest, and Kings Island has several 3- to 4-foot-diameter trees. Boaters floating down the Allegheny enjoy primitive camping, fishing, and exploring on the islands.

The trail through the old-growth forest in
Hearts Content National Scenic Area

National Wild and Scenic Rivers. The Allegheny and Clarion Rivers, bordering the ANF, are two of Pennsylvania's four national wild and scenic rivers. The Allegheny's features include steep, forested mountains rising 500 feet above the river, deep pools, more than thirty islands (of which most are privately owned), excellent primitive camping, and fishing and bird watching. The designated 51.7-mile section of the Clarion River is one of the top paddling trips in the northeast. This section of river starts near Ridgeway and flows west along the ANF's southern border past Cook Forest SP, ending at the backwaters of Piney Reservoir. The serpentine river flows through forested valleys with miles of beautiful scenery. Gentle to moderate rapids precede long deep pools with large boulders and wildflowers lining the shoreline. Be aware that when the river level is high, some rapids pose a real danger to canoeists and kayakers. Otters, eagles, osprey, and many species of waterfowl can be seen as you float down the river. The fishing and primitive camping are also superb. The two sections with the best scenery and fewest people on the river are Ridgeway to Hallton and Cook Forest SP to the reservoir.

Overlooks. Three overlooks well worth visiting are Rim Rock, Jake's Rocks, and Tidioute. Rim Rock overlooks the reservoir from 700 feet above. When you visit, check out the boulders from the trail below the lookout. Take the stairs down through the rocks, turn left, and hike along the bottom of the massive 80-foot-high vertical rocks. A significant amount of cool air emanates from the bottom of two crevasses. To visit Jake's Rock, take the road up the mountain, and at the sign that reads, "Overlook left and picnic area right," turn right. Park at the end of the lot and take the 400-yard paved trail to the lookout. The view is the west arm of the reservoir. Two nearby overlooks with views of the dam are along the road to the left of the intersection. The Tidioute Overlook is off Route 62 and provides views of the Allegheny River and the town below from two overlooks. From the parking lot, take the left trail to the town overlook and the right trail to the river overlook.

Recreation. Outdoor activities include 200 miles of hiking trails, plus the North Country National Scenic Trail, rock climbing, hunting, boating, waterskiing, swimming in four developed areas, fishing, biking, ATV riding on 106 miles of trails, equestrian trails, bird watching, sightseeing, cross-country skiing on 54 miles of trails, ice fishing, and snowmobiling on 360 miles of trails and forest roads. Within the ANF are seventeen campgrounds in prime locations. The developed campgrounds have modern facilities, a beach, and boat launch. Some sites are along the shoreline, so you can beach your boat at your site.

The Forest Service has established fourteen boat launch sites; five of these are no-motor areas. The ANF's mountain streams provide the unique opportunity to fish for native brook trout. You might also consider hiking

View from Route 59, looking south into
Kinzua Bay

Hector Falls

to small but scenic Hector, Bent Run, and Logan waterfalls. The best place for cross-country skiing is the Laurel Mill Cross Country Ski and Hiking Area, where most trails are groomed. This is also a great area to hike, especially in early spring, when wildflowers are in bloom. Tracy Ridge and Minister Creek Trails offer natural areas with boulder cities and vistas.

One of my favorite places, Beaver Meadows has a small primitive campground, but the outstanding scenery, lake, and trails make it well worth a visit. Take the Beaver Meadows Trail around the lake to the expansive wetlands. Stop on the floating walkway to soak in the dramatic, wild scenery; it looks and feels like you are in northern Canada. Another great wildlife area to visit for birding and fishing is Buzzard Swamp Habitat Management Area. In the 1960s, the Pennsylvania Game Commission built dikes along Muddy Fork to create fifteen shallow ponds for waterfowl. The fishing entices anglers who hike in with their raft or kayak.

NW10 Shenango River Lake Recreation Area, Mercer County

Shenango River Lake is a 15,071-acre Army Corps of Engineer project in the relatively flat Shenango River valley, near the Ohio border. At "summer level," the narrow, 11-mile-long reservoir covers 3,560 acres. Its virtually undeveloped forested shoreline, clean water, countless islands, deep coves, shallow deltas, and peninsulas make this beautiful lake the gem it is. The dam, completed in 1965, provides flood control and maintains adequate water flow for aquatic life and water usage in the rivers below. As with most flood-control reservoirs, the water level in the reservoir is usually drawn down to "winter level" between January and mid-March and rises back to normal "summer level" in late spring. The level is also drawn down during periods of low rainfall. During a major flood event, the dam has the capability

A quiet cove in the vast reservoir

A beaver pond along Route 846, north of the reservoir

In late 2016, Shenango's water, like all reservoirs in the state, was below normal.

to raise the lake level 23 feet higher than normal. At maximum height, the lake would triple in size to 11,090 acres, flooding most of the property.

Nature. The Pennsylvania Game Commission leases 3,150 acres to develop habitat improvements for wildlife. Shallow impoundments were built, and food plots are grown each year to attract waterfowl. Entering the Propagation Area is prohibited. The developed habitat supports many species of waterfowl, eagles, osprey, river otters, beaver, deer, and turkey. Eagles are often spotted along the lake's shoreline and the dam's outlet, where they look for dead fish. From the parking lot above the dam, a paved trail leads to an observation deck overlooking the dam. You can walk to the dam's outlet by continuing downhill on the trail, or by driving to the lower parking lot and walking from there. The 0.5-mile Seth Myers Trail and 0.3-mile Coonie Trail are self-guided, interpretive nature trails that meander through the scenic habitat. Along Route 846, 0.3 miles north of the lake, is a beautiful wetland with snags where beavers control the water level. Nearby, an eagle's nest sits on top of an electric utility tower, and ospreys have a nest on top of a wood utility pole. Bird watchers should also visit the Golden Run Wildlife Area.

Recreation. The lake is a boaters' paradise, with areas that allow boats with unlimited horsepower and waterskiing, restricted zones for electric motors only, and a large area at the northwest end of the lake limited to 10-horsepower motors. Canoeists and kayakers can take advantage of the restricted zones and the many coves and points that reduce wind and waves. The property has six access areas with boat ramps (no fee) and a few parking areas where canoes and kayaks can be launched. RC's Marina is a privately run, full-service facility with docks, boat rentals, and a boat launch (fee charged).

The most popular activity is fishing. The Pennsylvania Fish and Boat Commission annually stocks muskellunge fingerlings, hybrid striped-bass fingerlings, and walleye fingerlings and fry. The lake is well known for its good crappie fishing. The lake's naturally reproducing game fish are white crappie, northern pike, channel catfish, medium-size largemouth bass, a small population of smallmouth bass, increasing numbers of yellow perch, and panfish. Fishing in the dam's outflow or river can be very productive for trout, which are stocked year-round, crappie, pike, smallmouth bass, and muskie.

The Shenango Recreation Area has a huge modern campground with 330 shaded and open sites, with several close to the water. Next to the campground is a wide boat launch with parking. The Chestnut Run Swim Beach is on an island with a narrow connection to the mainland. It has a wide, sandy beach with an expansive grass area and basic facilities. Mahaney Recreation Area offers a disc golf course, and the Bayview Off-Road Vehicle Area has trails for ATV riders (see website for rules). Hunting and trapping are permitted on the property, except in developed recreational, wildlife, and posted areas. The Erie Extension Canal towpath is on the property and is part of the Shenango Trail.

NW11 Cook Forest State Park and Clarion River Lands, Clarion County

The magnificent old-growth forests in Cook Forest SP make it one of the most revered parks in Pennsylvania. The 8,500-acre park and 3,136-acre Clarion River Lands attract both outdoor enthusiasts and people who want to experience the natural environment similar to how it looked hundreds of years ago. The park has eleven areas of old-growth trees totaling 2,300 acres. Forest Cathedral Natural Area and Seneca Natural Area are the finest

A February winter scene on the beautiful
Clarion River, a half mile west of the park

stands of white pine and hemlock trees in the northeast US. Forest Cathedral was designated a national natural landmark for its 225–450-year-old trees. The park's third prominent area of virgin forest is Swamp Natural Area. Three other treasures include the Clarion River, designated as a national wild and scenic river; the park's historic buildings, registered as national historic sites; and Seneca Point, with its overlook, fire tower, and River Trail.

History. In 1828, the region's first settler, John Cook, brought his wife and ten children to live in the cabin he built on 765 acres. John and succeeding generations of Cooks built several mills, logged the forests, rafted logs down the Clarion and Allegheny Rivers, and built flatboats and a store. John's sons built the original Cook Forest Inn and the Cook Homestead. In 1910, Israel McCreight visited Forest Cathedral with owner A. W. Cook and made the statement, "Cook, no greater crime could be committed than to destroy this; it shall not be destroyed; it must be saved for humanity's sake." McCreight formed the Pennsylvania Conservation Association and with other members raised $200,000 and petitioned the state legislature to appropriate the additional $450,000 to purchase the 6,055-acre property. After sixteen years of lobbying, Cook Forest finally became the first state park in Pennsylvania that was purchased to preserve a natural landmark.

Old-Growth Areas. During your first visit to Cook Forest, you will likely agree that photographs and words cannot convey the feeling you have when you walk through an ancient forest. The very accessible 448-acre Forest Cathedral NA contains more white pines over 150 feet than any other place in the northeast US. It is also home to the second-tallest white pine in the East: 350-year-old Longfellow Pine, at 183 feet. Most of the majestic old-growth trees began life as seedlings after the drought and fire of 1644, the same year William Penn was born. The trees that survived the fire helped reseed the mountainside. One such tree was an ancient cucumber magnolia that fell in 2006. It was core-drilled 21 feet above the base and was determined to be at least 436 years old; it is believed to be the oldest cucumber magnolia ever found by an impressive sixty-one years.

Hemlocks are the most dominant old tree species in all three NAs, and white pine account for 30 percent in Forest Cathedral, 15 percent in Seneca, and virtually none in Swamp NA. I am always amazed to see pairs of giant trees separated by only a few feet and groups of trees within 15 feet from each other. Most of the forest floor is barren, but where blowdowns occur, ferns and saplings quickly fill in. One huge hemlock fell recently, which is always an impressive yet sad sight.

Old-Growth Information. The definition of a primary old-growth forest is a forest with trees that predate the history of logging for that area. In the southeastern portion of Pennsylvania that would be 250 years ago. In Cook Forest it would predate the 1820s. The far less common secondary old-growth forest occurs in places such as the Philadelphia area, where second-generation forests are 250 years old. The age of a tree cannot be determined by its size. Trees that grow on exposed rocky ridges with poor soil or in acidic bogs grow very slowly. A 14-inch diameter tree could be 250 years old. An old-growth forest should also have multiaged trees.

One of the differences between today's old-growth forests in Pennsylvania and the same forest a hundred years ago is the diminished understory. Deer, whose densities were not nearly as high back then, overbrowse new growth in our forests. In fact, there were so few deer a hundred years ago, the Game Commission had to import deer from other states to rebuild the population. The second difference is that eastern hemlocks are being killed by nonnative insects: the hemlock woolly adelgid (HWA) and the elongated hemlock scale (not in Pennsylvania yet). Several years ago, forest managers began treating old hemlocks for HWA with a chemical that is injected into the soil and absorbed by the roots, but the cost has limited the number of areas treated and it works for only about seven years. The chemical used to treat elongated hemlock scale is twice as expensive and lasts only two years. Pockets of old-growth forests are still being discovered on NF and SF land. These forests are typically on ridges, where the trees are small for their age. Also there are some old-growth forests that are privately owned. Records for the largest and tallest trees in Pennsylvania, called Champion Trees, are kept by the nonprofit association Pennsylvania Forestry Association.

The junction of Longfellow and Ancient Forest
Trails in Cathedral Forest

Trails. Numerous trails can be combined to adjust the length of your hike in Forest Cathedral and along Tom's Run. The 1.3-mile Forest Cathedral Trail begins at the Log Cabin Environmental Center and takes you past the Memorial Fountain, uphill to an area that suffered wind damage in the 1950s, and then into the heart of the forest. A popular return trail is the 0.3-mile Ancient Forest Trail. Another great combination is the Birch Trail and Toms Run Trail, which follow the valley's stream, Tom's Run. Pause at the swinging bridge and beautiful arched bridge to view the babbling stream, 100-year-old rhododendron, old-growth trees, boulder-lined pools of water, and a small tributary waterfall. The more difficult but very scenic 1.1-mile Indian Trail starts near the fishing pond, ascends steeply past rock outcrops and house-size boulders, and connects with Longfellow Trail.

The Seneca and Mohawk Trails can be combined for an awesome but steep hike through the Seneca Natural Area. The park naturalist informed me that this area has the largest concentration of old-growth trees in Pennsylvania, and the "Seneca Hemlock," 30 feet from the Seneca Trail, is the tallest hemlock in the northeastern US. Make your assent on the Mohawk Trail. Most likely you will not see another person on this trail. During the hike, you will begin to feel that you were transported back in time to a primeval wildness. At the end of Mohawk Trail, use the North Country Trail to connect to the Seneca Trail for your descent back to Route 36. Old-growth trees in the Seneca NA include pitch pine, white pine, hemlock, beech, red oak, chestnut oak, and white oak.

The 246-acre Swamp Natural Area is traversed by only one trail, the North Country Trail. The tract has a large, forested wetland and many

One of the bridges in the old-growth forest along Tom's Run

Winds brought two hollow, old-growth trees down in Forest Cathedral.

Paddling down the 8-mile sections above and below the park is a first-class experience.

The overlook at Seneca Point

species of old-growth trees, including red, black, and white oaks; beech; sugar maple; hemlock; and black cherry. In other parts of the park are old-growth species such as black gum, yellow and black birch, white ash, red maple, and cucumber magnolia.

Clarion River Lands. Perhaps the second most popular activity in the park is floating down the Clarion River. Private concessionaries near the park rent canoes, kayaks, and tubes and provide transportation upriver either for 4- or 10-mile float trips back to the park. The scenery is gorgeous in the forested valley, with boulders and wildflowers along the banks. On a weekday trip in August, I was the only person on the water for the first 6 miles, but I was not alone. I shared the river with cedar waxwings, orioles, blue herons, squawking kingfishers, mergansers, several species of ducks, and, most memorable of all, three river otters sunning themselves on a boulder. We stared at each other in disbelief for a few seconds before they dove into the river and somehow disappeared. Eagles are also spotted along the river. For a more wilderness-oriented experience, paddle from Ridgeway to Halltown, or from the Route 36 bridge to Mill Creek takeout. Be aware of the occasional large rock lurking just below the surface, and if the river is high, the X, Y, and Z rapids below Arroyo can flip a canoe or kayak.

Recreation. The modern campground has 210 sites. The Indian Cabins and River Cabins were built by the CCC in the 1930s and are available for rent. The Clarion provides fishing for trout and warm-water fish, and Tom's Run is stocked with trout. The stocked fishing pond behind the office is open to children under twelve and people with disabilities. Almost all of the park's twenty-six hiking trails have signage and are blazed and maintained. Approximately 12,000 acres of the state park and river lands are open to hunting. The Log Cabin EEC has a display of logging tools and artifacts and provides a wide range of environmental programs. The historic Sawmill Center for the Arts offers craft demonstrations and presents plays during the summer and fall. Specific trails and forest roads are designated for bike and horseback riding. Winter activities include ice skating on a lighted pond, snowmobiling, sledding near the river cabins, cross-country skiing, and hiking. River otters are still active during the winter and seem to enjoy sliding in the snow.

The two views at Seneca Point should not be missed. From the parking lot, the trail winds through a forest garden of mountain laurel and rhododendron, and trees with exposed roots cling to large rock slabs. Seneca Lookout is a large sandstone outcrop at the plateau's precipice above the river. The 1929 fire tower's 108 steps can be climbed for expansive views of the Clarion River valley and beyond. Seneca Point River Trail is one of the park's most beautiful and strenuous trails. It descends down switchbacks through lush understory to the Clarion River and Indian Rock, then follows the scenic river for 0.6 miles before heading back up the mountain.

Nature. The list of flora identified in the park includes 159 wildflowers, fourteen species of ferns, fifty different fungi and mushrooms, and forty-five trees and shrubs. The park's thirty-nine mammals include bobcat, fisher, river otter, porcupine, black bear, coyote, and deer. Native brook trout are one of the park's nineteen species of fish. The park also has thirteen species of amphibians and ten different reptiles, including the timber rattlesnake. Of the park's eighty-two species of birds, the hardest to spot are birds that seek the high canopy in conifer forests.

Two otters on a rock and one in the background along the Clarion River

This tranquil scene is at the children's fishing pond behind the office.

Southwest Region

SW1 Wolf Creek Narrows Natural Area, Butler County

Beautiful Wolf Creek flows through a narrow horseshoe-shaped gorge that is renowned for its 1.5-mile trail through a profusion of spring wildflowers and remnant old-growth trees. The Western Pennsylvania Conservancy (WPC) bought the original 112-acre Wolf Creek property in 1979. After purchasing five additional tracts of land, the WPC now owns a total of 241 acres. A separate preserved property called Miller Woods is on the opposite side of the road and is owned by Slippery Rock University. Geologists believe that the gorge was created from what was originally a long cave that lost its roof due to erosion from glacial meltwater. Limited logging by previous generations of owners has left now-mature stands of sugar maple and black cherry on the upper slopes and a mixed hemlock and hardwood forest along the stream.

My favorite time to visit the property is from late April to the first week in May, when the spring wildflowers bloom. Hiking the trail is the best way to see the natural scenery. Park in the gravel lot on the south side of Miller Road, walk across the bridge, and then turn left and enter the open floodplain area. Look for the kiosk and read the information and map before heading

White trillium cover the forest floor on the preserve's higher ground in April.

Wolf Creek gradually cuts into the layered rock on the stream's outside bend.

Wildflowers and wetland plants grow between the creek and vernal pools in late April.

A water snake suns itself on leaves packed in branches 2 feet above the ground.

off. In season, this section of forest floor is covered with bluebells, spring beauties, and a few trillium and trout lily. The vernal pools between the flowers and hillside are all that remain of the old creek channel. Skunk cabbage grows in the wet ground, and the pools, before they dry out in late summer, support several species of amphibians. On the other side of the stream, Wolf Creek continues to slowly cut into the bottom of the limestone cliff as it makes its way around the sweeping curve. Groundwater seeps out of fissures in the steep rock walls, and in the winter the water forms glassy walls of ice. The streambed is composed of solid layers of rock with bright-green, mosslike aquatic vegetation that clings to the rock.

A few old-growth hemlocks stand tall along the streamside trail. The open forest—lacking understory—is typical of mature forests in Pennsylvania. Continue on the trail as it ascends the hill, and in early May you will see huge areas of the forest floor carpeted with white trillium. I believe it is the largest bed of trillium in the state. Please appreciate and protect their beauty by staying on the trail. Also, cutting the flower could kill the plant, or it will take seven years before it blooms again. This mature upland deciduous forest creates an environment that is a pleasure to visit any time of year. The trail makes a loop and takes you back to your starting point. Peak time for blooming varies year to year with seasonal weather. My last visit was on May 1, and it was perfect for the trillium, but a little late for the peak of the bluebells.

The forest floor is covered with blooming trillium in all directions.

SW2 McConnells Mill State Park, Butler County

The 2,546-acre McConnells Mill SP was established to preserve the exceptionally scenic Slippery Rock Creek Gorge, and for the public to see and experience the outstanding natural environment. You can't help being impressed and exhilarated when you hike along the swift-flowing, crystal-clear stream lined with countless boulders that have tumbled down the steep sides of the gorge. When you visit the top of the gorge, house-size boulders have started their eventual decent into the gorge. Old-growth trees, wildflowers, water channels cut through rock, waterfalls, and vistas round out the park's list of natural features. The 930-acre Slippery Rock Gorge was designated a national natural landmark in 1974, and a state park natural area in 1998.

History. Between 20,000 and 140,000 years ago, glacial ice blocked rivers and created Lake Pouty, Lake Watts, a larger version of today's Lake Arthur, and Lake Edmund. When the continental glacier started to melt 20,000 years ago, a massive amount of water poured off the glacier. Lake Pouty spilled over the ridge near the park's Cleland Rock and began the swift process of erosion in the valley. Lake Watts also drained its water, followed by Lake Edmund. The massive amount of glacier meltwater and lake overflows funneled through the valley and eventually cut a gorge more than 400 feet deep. This recent glacial and geologic activity ended approximately 10,000 years ago and is why the gorge looks so wild and rugged.

Hells Hollow Falls

The first gristmill on Slippery Rock Creek was built in 1852. After a fire it was rebuilt and then was sold to Thomas McConnell in 1875. McConnell modernized the methods used for the mill's power and grinding, making it one of the first rolling mills in the country. The mill processed grain until it closed in 1928. (Tours are conducted daily during the summer months.) The nearby covered bridge, built in 1874, is a national historic landmark. The Western Pennsylvania Conservancy bought the land along the gorge in 1942 and transferred ownership to the state in 1957, when it became a state park.

Slippery Rocks. The gorge got its name for a good reason. An oily film coats the rocks in the stream and along the bank within 30 feet of the stream. I can't emphasize enough just how slippery the rocks are. I saw a photographer slip off a large boulder and fall head first. He was dirty and bruised but very fortunate to be able to walk out. As a further warning to others, I slipped on the rocks twice on one hike. The second fall was in a small tributary just off the trail. Fortunately, my camera was not damaged and I had only an ankle sprain, but hobbling 2 miles back to the car was not fun. I have been extremely cautious on every visit since then.

Trails. To really experience the park, you need to hike its trails. The 0.5-mile, strenuous Alpha Pass Trail takes you from the Scenic Vista parking area straight down the side of the gorge to Slippery Rock Creek. Wooden steps and railings at the steepest section are very helpful, plus they help

Huge blocks of rock are slowly moving away from the plateau in the Rim Rock Climbing Area.

Practicing their skills; the ropes on the far right were set for a college climbing course.

Swift current and abrasive sand and pebbles
created numerous holes and unique formations.

to reduce erosion. After carefully reaching the bottom you have three choices: return by going back up the same trail, follow the trail downstream for a short distance and take the next trail that leads up to the Point parking area, or continue hiking downstream on Alpha Pass Trail to the historic mill area. It is all very scenic.

Hiking the 6.2-mile Slippery Rock Gorge Trail takes a fair amount of effort, but the scenery along the entire tail is absolutely gorgeous, entertaining, and varied. When I hiked the trail on a beautiful weekday in October, I saw no one else the entire day. From Eckert's Bridge, the trail follows the gorge downstream, ascending and descending the steep terrain around each of the tributary ravines. At mile 4.2, the trail turns north to follow Hell Run up the side valley, past Hell's Hollow Falls. Stands of old-growth red and white oak, yellow-poplar, and beech are near Hell Run. The trail follows along the bizarre, winding cut through solid rock made by Hell Run and ends at Hell's Hollow parking lot.

The Kildoo Trail's 2.1-mile loop is the most popular trail in the park. It begins at the covered bridge and heads downstream. The first 400 yards are paved for the interpretive nature trail that ends at Kildoo Run and the falls. You will notice that the air is cooler and more humid as the trail snakes its way through a dense forest of hemlock and deciduous trees and around exposed roots, ferns, and moss-covered boulders. The trail continues to Eckert Bridge and returns on the opposite side of Slippery Rock Creek.

A view of the boulder-filled stream while hiking on Kildoo Trail

Rock Features. The huge rock formations adjacent to Rim Road are one of the most dramatic examples of erosion in Pennsylvania. The flat-topped boulders are separated vertically from the plateau and each other. Trees are miraculously able to grow on solid rock thanks to their long, exposed roots snaking their way down to the forest floor. The site's northern end is the rock-climbing area, with three main boulders. Using extreme caution, you can step onto one and leap onto the second one. Try to find the stone steps that were built between the vertical faces of two boulders. It is the easiest way to reach the bottom of the boulders, other than repelling. Here you can view the boulders from a different perspective and watch climbers hone their skills. Another interesting rock marvel is the one-way road to and from the mill. The road traverses the steep-sided valley through narrow cuts in the rock and under overhanging rock. Imagine the amount of work it took to build this road with only hand tools, horses, and sticks of dynamite.

Recreation. Two sightseeing locations worth visiting for the view are Breakneck Bridge and Cleland Rock. Park along Breakneck Bridge Road. Walk to the middle of the bridge for a view high above Cheeseman Run ravine and the gorge. If you have a vehicle that can handle a very rough road, drive down to Eckert Bridge for a view above the creek. You can also park here and hike downstream on the Gorge Trail, or upstream on either side of the creek on the Kildoo Trail loop. Cleland Rock overlooks the gorge from a point approximately 500 feet above Slippery Rock Creek. McConnells Mill SP does not have a campground, and swimming is not allowed, but there are many other recreational opportunities. Kayaking down class II to IV rapids is a thrill for experienced paddlers. The run below the milldam to Harris Bridge is 4 miles and should be attempted when there is sufficient flow. Fishing for trout (stocked several times per year) and smallmouth bass is popular, mostly near the four bridge-access locations. The stream above and below Armstrong Bridge is a fly-fishing only catch-and-release area.

SW3 Moraine State Park, Butler County

The main focus of this large and very popular 16,725-acre state park is recreation centered on 3,225-acre Lake Arthur. One million annual visitors enjoy this beautiful park and its extensive recreational opportunities, facilities, and wildlife. The park's two developed areas—South Shore and North Shore—are on the western portion of the lake. Volunteers from the Moraine Preservation Fund contribute funding and personal time to establish and maintain conservation projects such as Nautical Nature tours, education programs, the Butterfly Trail, and the Owlet Gift Shop.

Sunrise view west from the parking area,
below the Route 528 bridge

A lone kayaker in one of the many coves in mid-October

History. In the mid-1800s, early settlers cut the forests and drained the wetlands to create pastures and farmland. Farming the glaciated soil proved to be difficult and was soon replaced by the mining industry. The land was opened to extract glacial deposits of sand, gravel, limestone, and clay, along with ancient deposits of shale and coal. Profitable coal was extracted from the surface and seven underground mines. In the late 1800s, hundreds of oil and gas wells were drilled, pumped dry, abandoned, and left unsealed. By 1940, the land was abandoned and in deplorable condition, and the streams were polluted from mine drainage.

Dr. Frank Preston, a local amateur geologist and naturalist, studied the area's glacial landforms for many decades and thought the land could be restored. In 1932, he and nine other concerned citizens formed the Western Pennsylvania Conservancy. Preston was the driving force behind the purchase of the original 3,000 acres between 1959 and 1964. With help from the state, 422 wells were capped, mines were sealed, strip mines were filled and contoured, soil was fertilized, and grasses, shrubs, and trees were planted. The dam was completed in 1968, and Moraine SP was dedicated two years later. Moraine SP is the finest example in the state of what can be done if we, as a society, care enough about our environment and our legacy.

Boating. Boating is probably the most popular activity, and the sizable lake can handle a large number of boaters. The length of the lake and reliable

Returning to the Barkley Road access area after a morning of duck hunting

What better way to enjoy a breezy day on the lake.

winds make it ideal for sailing, windsurfing, and iceboating. Boat motors are restricted to 20 horsepower. There are ten public boat launches, two marinas, and a boat rental marina. Crescent Bay Boat Rental, near the park office, has all types of boats for rent. Fuel, canoe storage, and supplies are also available. On the North Shore, Watts Bay Marina caters to sailboats and catamarans, with 138 onshore seasonal spaces and twenty day-use spaces. The huge Davis Hollow Marina, also on the North Shore, has 545 seasonal slips, plus offshore moorings, onshore spaces, short-term spaces, and supplies. Despite the size of Lake Arthur, there are countless calm water places to kayak. One example is Muddy Creek Cove, toward Duck Pond Dam at the far eastern end.

Fishing. Lake Arthur is considered the most productive lake in the state for 3- to 5-pound largemouth bass. During its heyday in the 1980s, more bass over 5 pounds were caught here than the rest of the state combined. Three key reasons for the number of large bass are the habitat, the Big Bass Program, and the high percentage of large bass that are released. The excellent muskellunge fishery is not well known by anglers. A PFBC trapnet survey in 2014 captured thirty-nine muskie between 28 and 49 inches, outperforming a similar survey at Pymatuning Lake. In 2014, the national nonprofit Recreational Boating and Fishing Foundation rated Moraine SP the fifteenth-best family fishing location in the country. Lake Arthur supports a reproducing fishery of largemouth bass, northern pike, black crappie, channel catfish, and bluegill. The PFBC stocks walleye, muskellunge, and striped bass. The park has three fishing piers. A map of the lake showing manmade structure locations and underwater features is available at the park marinas, office, and gift shop.

Nature. Moraine's wide range of habitat includes creeks, marshes, swamps, mudflats, meadows, thickets, abandoned fields, deciduous forests, and coniferous forests. A favorite place to see wildflowers and native plants is the self-guided Native Plant Butterfly Trail at McDanel's Launch. Stop at the office or gift shop for a checklist. The less developed portion of the lake is east of Route 528 and is composed of three long coves: Muddy Creek and Swamp Run—each 3 miles long—and Shannon Run, which is 1.5 miles long. Other than the four boat launches, it is a large, protected natural habitat for wildlife. A propagation area is in Swamp Run.

The park's habitat supports many species of nesting and migrating birds. In 1993, the Game Commission began a hatching program for osprey, and three years later a pair successfully produced the first fledglings. Today more than six pairs of osprey raise their young in or near the park. Two pairs of bald eagles have each produced an average of two young for the past several years. The park is on the primary migration flyway for tens of thousands of tundra swans. The wetlands in the eastern coves attract blue and green heron, Virginia rail, sora, American coot, mergansers, and many species of waterfowl. If the lake is drawn down in the summer, the South Shore mudflats are a great place to see as many as twenty-one species of shorebirds. The park's extensive list of birds includes twenty-seven species of warblers, of which twenty-one have nested in the park. A waterfowl observation deck is at the end of a short trail along Park Road.

Trails. The park has 28 miles of trails designated for hiking only. A beautiful, paved 7-mile bike path begins at the bike rental location and follows the north shoreline. A 6-mile trail for experienced mountain bikers is near Davis Hollow Marina. There are also 20 miles of trails for horseback riding and 26 miles of trails for snowmobiling. The North Country Trail crosses the north side of the park and heads west to McConnells Mill SP and north to Jennings EEC.

Recreation. Both the North Shore and South Shore have a sandy beach with a clothes-changing and concession building. Eleven modern cabins are available for rent, and there are two organized-group camping areas. This is a day-use park, so there is no campground. Bear Run is the nearest private campground and has some of the best tent sites in Pennsylvania; reservations are a must during the summer months. Hunting is allowed on 13,600 acres.

The paved bike trail is fairly level and follows the north shore for several miles.

Most duck hunters depart from the Barkley Road launch and head for the remote shallow areas. Other activities are disc golf, a boat tour on the thirty-seven-passenger *Nautical Nature*, environmental programs, and a visit to Owlet Gift Shop. Winter activities include sledding, ice skating, cross-country skiing, snowmobiling, ice fishing, and iceboating. Two events that are seasonal highlights are the "Regatta at Lake Arthur"—a dynamic two-day event in early August—and "Winterfest," with a dozen activities in early February.

SW4 Crooked Creek Lake Recreation Area, Armstrong County

Crooked Creek Lake is a 2,664-acre Army Corps of Engineers project and is aptly named for its many 180-degree bends. The 143-foot-high dam, completed in 1940, created the long, narrow, 350-acre lake. The lake winds through a steep-sided forest valley surrounded by mostly farmland on the rolling Allegheny Plateau. At summer elevation, the lake is 42 feet deep at the dam, but if extreme flood control is needed, the lake level can rise as much as 75 feet, creating a huge 1,940-acre lake—more than five times its normal size. For a great view of the lake, Crooked Creek, and the surrounding countryside, drive across the dam and park in the lot near the control tower. Notice the record high watermark on the control tower from Hurricane Agnes in 1972.

I had the entire lake to myself.

One boat launch provides access to the lake.   Overlook view from the dam area

A successful evening for this hunter

Boating and Fishing. The two main activities are boating and fishing. There is one boat launch in the center of this unlimited-horsepower lake, but if the lake's water level is high the launch will be closed (ACE's lake report and launch status recording number is 724-763-2764). Due to the lake's steep banks and thick woods, only a small percentage of the shoreline is accessible to walk-in anglers. Fishing from a boat is far more productive. Large motors are unnecessary on this lake unless you are waterskiing. In fact, the lake is a great place to canoe or kayak. From the boat launch, if you head left through the narrow gap toward the dam, the lake is fairly deep. To the right it gets shallower and, in places, is loaded with submerged logs and debris. With a little luck, you will see eagles perched along the shoreline, waiting for their next meal to surface.

Anglers enjoy this lake for its excellent largemouth bass and crappie fishing and, during most of the year, minimal boat traffic. Other fish that are caught less frequently are smallmouth bass, tiger muskellunge over 40 inches long, channel catfish up to 38 inches, carp, and sunfish. Every year a few anglers catch several largemouth bass over 3 pounds, with the largest over 6 pounds. On an evening kayak trip in early October, the only sounds I heard were chirping birds and splashing from bass feeding on the surface.

Recreation. Crooked Creek Lake has a sandy swimming beach with restrooms at the end of a long, narrow peninsula. The campground, playground, and visitor center are in an open grassy area along the lake near the peninsula. The Army Corps also provides several picnic areas and six pavilions. Within the park are six trails, plus a section of the 141-mile Baker Trail, which parallels the lake and the creek below the dam. Shrub Swamp Trail—below the dam—is an easy walk along the creek's lowland habitat. You can find a variety of birds, aquatic life, and wildflowers. Crooked Creek Horse Park was established on leased land for trail riding. Other activities include hunting, bird watching, ice fishing, ice skating, sledding, and cross-country skiing. Before visiting, print the map and trail information from ACE's Pittsburgh District website.

SW5 Raccoon Creek State Park and Wildflower Reserve, Beaver County

Raccoon Creek SP is a gorgeous 7,572-acre park with two lakes, excellent facilities, and lots of recreational activities. What makes this park stand out is that it is arguably the best place in Pennsylvania to see spring wildflowers. Flowers are found throughout the park, but the Wildflower Reserve should be your first stop.

History. During the 1930s, the National Park Service established the park as a recreational demonstration area. Depression-era CCC and WPA crews built the park's facilities and infrastructure. In 1945, the Park Service transferred the property to the state, creating Raccoon Creek State Park. Over the years, park administrators added the lake, campground, cabins, and trails.

In the early 1800s, well-known Frankford Mineral Springs attracted people seeking its "medicinal qualities and delightful retreat from the cares and drudgeries of Pittsburgh." Water from seven springs that flowed over the grotto contained fifteen different minerals. In 1827, Edward McGinnis bought 12 acres surrounding the springs and built a health resort that catered to wealthy patrons from Pittsburgh and throughout the country. The resort's main building had guest rooms, a parlor for social gatherings, and a ballroom, kitchen, and dining hall. The resort also had a three-story guest building, dance hall, stables, and a walkway that led

A sunny spring day on the lake

Along the Mineral Springs Loop Trail in late
April are red, yellow, and white trillium.

to the springs. By the early 1900s, its popularity began to fade, and in 1927
a fire destroyed the main building. The other facilities were used for several
more decades until all but one cottage were eventually lost. A few remnants
of the resort remain.

Wildflower Reserve. The reserve is a 314-acre tract of mostly forested
land and is home to an incredible 715 species of plants. To protect this
unique environment, the WPC purchased the property in 1962 and
transferred it to the DCNR. Ten interconnecting trails totaling 5 miles take
you along Raccoon Creek, past old trees, and through habitats such as
oak-hickory forest, pine plantation, meadows, and floodplain forest. The
peak time for spring wildflowers to bloom is late April and early May, but
some bloom much earlier and others bloom through September. It is
important for most flowering plants in mature forests to grow and bloom
before the forest canopy closes in and blocks sunlight. The plants' next
task is pollination, then storing enough energy in their roots to make it
through the winter and start the cycle again in spring. Some plants begin
to wither as early as July.

The staff at the Wildflower Reserve Interpretive Center will provide
you with a trail map and brochures and inform you about the plants that
are flowering and the trails to take for the most productive hike. You can
also call in advance to sign up for their guided walks and evening programs.
One of the most popular trail combinations begins on the Old Wagon Road
Trail and then turns left onto Jennings Trail. Continue on Jennings as it

Water with a high iron content pours out of fissures in the rock, leaving the orange stain.

Trout lily at Wildflower Reserve in late April

Dwarf larkspur

makes the turn around the ridge, turn left at the cutoff trail, and turn right onto the Audubon Trail to head back to the center. You will appreciate that many species of plants are identified with small placards. When you visit, it is important to stay on the trails and take photos—and nothing else.

Trails. The park has nearly 100 miles of hiking and multiuse trails. The Wetland Trail and Camp Trail provide the best opportunities to view wildlife. The trails take you past 12-acre Upper Lake, which is a great place to hike for seclusion, bird watching, and fishing. Along sections of the 6.2-mile Forest Trail you will find beautiful spring flowers on display. The Mineral Springs Loop is very popular, especially when spring wildflowers are blooming. Impressive masses of white-, red-, and yellow-colored trillium thrive along the trail and hillside. The trail follows the spring-fed tributary to a beautiful area of exposed rock ledges, a grotto with a small waterfall, a rock face that is stained orange where water spouts out between the layers of rock, and impressive 150-year-old stone steps and walls.

Recreation. The 101-acre Raccoon Lake has a large sandy beach, two boat launches for electric- and human-powered boats, mooring spaces, kayak and canoe rentals, and a fishing pier. The clean lake holds a healthy

White trillium

population of largemouth and smallmouth bass, perch, walleye, muskellunge, and panfish. Brook trout and rainbow trout are stocked in the streams and lake. A small fishing pond for children is behind the park office. The park has a modern campground with 172 sites, ten modern cabins, picnic areas, and organized-group tent and cabin camping. Raccoon Creek SP is open year-round for primitive camping and winter activities on the lake and designated trails. Other activities include horseback riding, mountain biking, bird watching, and hunting.

SW6 Meadowcroft Rockshelter, Washington County

Meadowcroft Rockshelter is recognized as one of the most important, if not the most important, archeological site in North America. The excavation, led by Dr. James Adovasio beginning in 1973, established Meadowcroft as the first identified archeological site with 16,000 years of continuous human habitation. Twenty-seven years of meticulous work has yielded an astonishing two million items—more than any site in the world—including seeds, sticks, bones, charcoal hearths, stone tools, and pottery. The oldest artifact is a cut piece of bark that may have been used as a basket; it has been radiocarbon dated at 19,000 years old. The site was designated a national historic landmark.

For forty years prior to the Meadowcroft discoveries, most archeologists believed that the "Clovis" people were the first to enter the New World approximately 13,500 years ago.

Clovis is a term that describes a group of people, a period of time, and a projectile point. In 1929, in Clovis, New Mexico, several uniquely designed, chipped-stone projectile points were found in context with mastodon bones that dated to 11,000 years before present (BP). Since then, at sites across the country and as far south as Venezuela, similar projectile points have been discovered. They were made by using high-quality material and were finely flaked with a flute chipped out of the center on both sides of the base.

Until Meadowcroft, no sites had definitive, human-made artifacts in a context dating earlier than 13,500 years BP. As you can imagine, the results from Meadowcroft were immediately disputed by many archeologists, who stubbornly insisted that the Clovis people were the first to enter the New World. It took another thirty years and more discoveries to convince all but a few skeptics.

The Meadowcroft excavation also turned another widely held believe on its head. Most experts believed that the environment in Pennsylvania 16,000 years ago was tundra, with permafrost below. Meadowcroft is just 47 miles from Moraine SP—marking the farthest advance of the most recent Wisconsinan glacier—yet the archeological site has enough evidence to show that a mix of boreal trees and deciduous trees, along with white-tailed deer, were present 16,000 years ago. As the climate warmed, Pennsylvania became a mosaic of environments with local conditions varying greatly, mainly on the basis of elevation.

Rockshelter. Meadowcroft is on a farm that was owned by Albert Miller. In 1950, Mr. Miller discovered chert flakes and a burnt bone at a groundhog hole. After digging in the loose soil he found a chert knife. Fearing looters might ruin the site, he buried the evidence and kept the discovery to himself until he could find a professional willing to excavate the site. Twenty-three years later, James Adovasio, an anthropology professor at the University of Pittsburgh, was searching for a site in western Pennsylvania to excavate with his students, and he met Miller. They both had found what they were looking for, and fieldwork began in June 1973. From the beginning, Adovasio insisted on using the most advanced technology and thorough methodology. Meadowcroft was the first archeological site to use computers in the field, which were connected to the university's mainframe. The site was surveyed and photographed. Geologic studies of the surrounding area and the rockshelter were conducted. Razor blades were used to scrape minute layers of soil to a depth of 10 feet, and electron microscopes were used to study particles of sand and pollen. Fifty-three radiocarbon dating tests were performed, of which thirteen proved to be from pre-Clovis strata. An essential component was excellent financial support from the National Geographic Foundation, the National Science Foundation, the Miller Family via the Meadowcroft Foundation, and others.

The rockshelter is 50 feet above Cross Creek and faces west. At one time, when the creek bed was higher, it carved into the sandstone rock and created the shelter. The shelter was also substantially larger than it is today. Over time the edge of the ceiling moved back and the floor grew in elevation from the sediments that washed in from the sides and the fine particles and large rocks that fell from the ceiling. The ceiling boulders that fell protected the layers of soil from being disturbed. Today the shelter is 49 feet wide, 20 feet deep, and 43 feet high. In 2008, a $4,000,000 enclosure was completed. A

A view from the back wall of the rockshelter.
Rocks from the ceiling sealed the strata below.

Main observation deck

roof, two sides, and an observation deck were built to protect the site and provide better access and viewing for visitors. The main deck faces the excavated area, and a second viewing area is along the back wall and overlooks the site. A long set of stairs, lighting, monitors, and a rollup security door were also added. One-third of the site was intentionally left unexcavated for future generations of archeologists with advanced technology.

Meadowcroft served primarily as a seasonal campsite during the fall, and visitors probably did not stay long. They gathered nuts and berries, such as the readily available hackberry. Deer, elk, and small mammal bones were found, but only a few fragments of megafauna bone remained. When food sources were depleted they moved elsewhere for a few years. The stone tools found in the lowest strata were made from chert found in New York, Ohio, and West Virginia, indicating they most likely traded with other groups.

A portion of the site was left unexcavated for future generations of archeologists.

The shelter sits on the hillside, well above the stream.

Care was taken to mark each layer and record the position of every item found.

Paleo History. Ice ages have occurred in cycles of approximately 120,000 years for 1.7 million years. The warm interglacial periods are short lived, lasting only 10,000 to 20,000 years. When the Wisconsinan glacier reached its maximum extent 20,000 years ago, the ocean was approximately 400 feet lower than today. Land was gradually exposed between Asia and North America and grew up to 1,000 miles wide. Long before the glacier's maximum extent, waves of humans were able to cross the land bridge. The climate began warming and the edge of the glacier vacillated for several thousand years. It began retreating 15,000 years ago, was out of Pennsylvania 9,000 years ago, and retreated to its current position about 6,000 years ago. We will never know when, where, or why the first groups and subsequent groups arrived, but we do know what they encountered. The climate was colder than today, and wildlife consisted of a mix of supersized mammals, called megafauna, and many of the mammals we are familiar with today. Megafauna species included three types of mammoth, mastodon, the huge lion, cheetah, two types of tigers (including the sabertooth), large bison, camelids, horse, giant sloth, dire wolf, and beaver weighing 350 pounds. The dominant predator was the short-faced bear. It was as high at the shoulder as today's moose, and when it reared up, it was 15 feet high. An 11,000-year-old nearly complete mastodon was excavated in Pennsylvania's Pocono region. Woolly mammoths survived on Wrangle Island off Siberia until 2,500 years ago.

Early humans probably scavenged far more often than hunting for large, dangerous beasts. They also took advantage of opportunistic situations, such as large mammals mired in mud. Their survival depended mainly on plants, nuts, berries, and small mammals, rather than big game. Most likely, the majority of animals they killed were driven into nets made with woven vegetation. Their beautifully made, thin projectile points are certainly an item to admire, but their most important everyday items were bone needles, hole punches, flaking tools, woven cordage, baskets, nets, and stone tools such as scrapers, awls, and knives, as well as stones for hammering, grinding, and hafting.

Visit their website for information about touring the site and lectures conducted by Dr. Adovasio.

SW7 Powdermill Avian Research Center and Nature Reserve, Westmoreland County

Powdermill Nature Reserve and Powdermill Avian Research Center (PARC) are fine examples of what can be accomplished by dedicated people who care about our natural world. The reserve was established in 1956 as a biological research field station for the Carnegie Museum of Natural History. In 1983, environmental education was added when the Nimick Nature Center was built. PARC has conducted bird banding and avian research at the field station since 1961, making it the longest continually operating program in the country. As of 2017, they have captured and recorded more than 700,000 birds, more than any other bird-banding facility in the world.

Powdermill Nature Reserve. The 2,200-acre reserve is in the Laurel Highlands. The original 1,160 acres were donated to the Carnegie Museum of Natural History for the long-term study of nature, ecological relationships, acid mine drainage pollution, and changes in the environment and populations of wildlife. It also serves as a refuge for increasingly rare plants due to the loss of habitat across Pennsylvania. The reserve hosts students, interns, and researchers from around the world who conduct studies in ornithology, botany, herpetology, and invertebrate zoology. The reserve's facilities can accommodate up to forty-five guests in cabins and dorms. The Nature Center has wildlife displays, environmental-education exhibits and programs, office space, and wildflower gardens. The building uses its own wastewater management system of pumps, gravity, sunlight, and plants to purify and recycle water.

The property's habitats include wooded floodplain, deciduous forest, and young stands of hawthorn, locust, aspen, black birch, and black cherry trees. The habitat also includes a sugar maple orchard, hedgerows, marsh ponds, and alder- and willow-lined streams. The 0.75-mile Black Birch Trail begins behind the Nature Center and enters a young forest, then follows the stream before heading back. Across the road is the 1.25-mile Sugar Camp Trail, named for the seasonal sugar maple camps that farmers used to set up to boil sap and extract the syrup.

Powdermill Avian Research Center. The research center is certainly one of the most interesting places I have visited in Pennsylvania. Robert Leberman established the highly regarded bird-banding operation and guided it for forty-three years. Every year the center bands ten to twelve thousand birds and records another two to three thousand previously banded birds. An average of 122 species are banded each year, and almost 200 species have been banded since the program began. Surprisingly, of the annual two to three thousand recaptured birds, an average of only three birds were banded somewhere other than at PARC.

Banding a Swainson's thrush

Some people might ask, "Why band birds?" The first answer is that we should protect all species of birds simply because we love to see and hear them. They enrich our lives. We owe them our protection. By banding birds, we are able to monitor their health and population trends. The second reason is that birds are the best indicator species for monitoring the health of the world we live in. Birds travel long distances, live in all types of environments, and are sensitive to harmful environmental and habitat changes that will eventually affect us. Early miners took parakeets into the mines to warn them about the presence of deadly gases. During the 1960s, ornithologists noticed eagles and other bird populations were declining dramatically. Researchers discovered that the eggshells were too thin and would easily break due to DDT that was sprayed to kill mosquitoes. This new knowledge led to the next discovery—that DDT is an agent of cancer in humans.

Bird Banding. Each morning before sunrise, mist nets are unrolled and anchored to a line of poles that run down pathways bordered by hedges and vegetation, or along the edge of ponds or forest habitats. Field personnel check their six or seven color-coded nets every thirty minutes. The birds are carefully untangled from the net and placed in individual sacks, with their capture location noted. Two-way radios are used if instant communication is needed between personnel. The sacks are brought to the station, where the lab team functions like an assembly line. The first person removes the bird from the sack and attaches the appropriate size band, unless the bird already has a band. The next person verbally identifies the band, species, sex, wing length, fat deposits, weight, and health

Excellent habitat, developed over decades, is the key to attracting birds.

Mist nets are strung between hedges of the same height.

and examines its feathers to determine age and whether it is molting, on the nest (a bare patch), or migrating. A third person enters the verbal information into PARC's database. The bird is then released out a side window. Sometimes a fourth person will photograph a bird of special interest before it is released. Newly fledged birds are carried back to the location where they were caught and then released to reunite with their parents. The fine-tuned process takes about one minute and has proven to be safe. The health of the birds is the staff's main priority. A good example illustrating that the birds are handled with care is the black-capped chickadee that was caught in 2016 for the forty-second time over a period of eight years.

I also learned that the birds that PARC handles cannot outgrow their bands, because after they leave the nest their legs never grow thicker. Bands are supplied by the US Geological Survey, and bird longevity records are kept by the National Banding Lab in Maryland. The peak months for numbers of birds are May, September, and October. Banding at PARC takes place six hours a day for six days each week and is canceled for bad weather, high winds, or when the temperature is over 78 degrees. From early November to the end of February, they band only two days each week. The six species that are banded most often are cedar waxwing, ruby-crowned kinglet, gold finch, magnolia warbler, Swainson's thrush, and catbird. A partial list of warblers that were captured during my two-hour visit on August 31 is common yellow throat, Canada, hooded, Connecticut, morning, and black-throated blue warblers. Other birds were ruby-throated hummingbird, blue-headed vireo, red-eyed vireo, and Swainson's thrush.

Research. Every year, millions of birds die by flying into reflective glass in homes and commercial buildings. PARC's Flight Tunnel Project began in 2010 to determine how birds react to various glass and window treatments. The 40-foot-long flight tunnel—one of only two in the world— can be rotated on a central axis to face away from the sun for consistency.

Each bird's age, sex, wing length, fat content, weight, and general health are recorded.

Two different pieces of glass (clear glass and test glass) are placed at one end of the black tunnel, with a special net in front to safely protect the bird. Selected birds from the banding program are recorded and then placed through a hole at the other end of the tunnel. A video camera records which piece of glass the bird chooses to avoid on its flight to escape. The bird is then immediately released unharmed.

PARC's well-designed website, http://powdermillarc.org, is a tremendous source of valuable and fascinating information. The site's "Banding Summaries" go back to 2010, and the "Pictorial Highlights" has detailed photos of selected birds, with a wealth of interesting information about the species and that individual bird. Information about visiting or taking PARC's five-day beginner or advanced Bird Bander Training Workshop is posted on their website.

Hummingbird. The hummingbird is certainly one of the world's most remarkable birds. There are about 340 species in the Western Hemisphere, and of those, twenty-seven have been recorded in the US; only one, the ruby-throated hummingbird, is found in the eastern US. When I visited PARC and held a ruby-throated hummingbird in my hand, I could feel its heartbeat, and placing it next to my ear, I heard its heart beating at its typical rate of 200 beats per minute. While feeding, their heart rate is an astounding 1,000 beats per minute. They breathe 250 times per minute. A hummer's wings are different from all other bird species. Its hand bones are longer than its arm bones, allowing the wing to rotate 180 degrees in both directions. This enables them to fly backward and sideways, hover, fly with one wing, and fly upside down for a short time. Their normal wing beat is a phenomenal seventy beats per second, and during a dive they beat 200 times per second. They are also speedy flyers: normal fight is 25 mph, and dives reach 60 mph. Perhaps the most incredible feat for this tiny bird is their annual 4,000-mile round-trip migration to Mexico or Central America, which for some hummers requires a nonstop, eighteen-

This young rufous-throated hummingbird is starting to get his trademark plumage.

Black-throated blue warbler

Connecticut warbler

to twenty-hour, 500-mile flight over the Gulf of Mexico. Another quirky characteristic is that they do not walk; they can only perch. Hummers also have the largest brain-to-body-size ratio in the animal kingdom. They visit hundreds of flowers every day and can remember every location and how long it takes for each flower to refill with nectar. They can even recognize human faces; who fills the feeder and who does not.

SW8 Laurel Mountains, Forbes State Forest, Southwestern Pennsylvania

The Laurel Mountains, or Highlands as they are frequently called, is a 70-mile-long area of preserved forest providing nearly every type of outdoor recreation. The Highlands are basically two parallel mountains: Laurel Ridge, which has most of the preserved land, and Chestnut Ridge, which is west of Ohiopyle SP. Negro Mountain, east of Ohiopyle SP, is also considered part of the Highlands. The mountains are broken up by countless deep stream cuts, including the Youghiogheny River. This rugged land supports abundant wildlife and diversified habitat in a patchwork of state game lands, state parks, state forest, and nonprofit organizations' preserves.

The following is a dizzying list of preserved land that totals approximately 151,000 acres. Forbes SF is more than 60,000 acres. The seven state parks and their acreages are Kooser's 250 acres, Linn Run's 612 acres, Laurel Mt.'s 493 acres, Laurel Summit's 6 acres, Laurel Hill's 4,062 acres, Laurel Ridge's 14,964 acres, and Ohiopyle's 20,500 acres. Game Commission lands include four state game lands (SGLs) totaling 42,500 acres. Bear Run Nature Reserve is 5,000 acres and Powdermill Nature Reserve is 2,200 acres. There are two designated SF natural areas, one SF wild area, and two SP natural areas. The following are locations that are not featured individually in this book.

Linn Run SP: Linn Run SP is a small day-use park with cabins for rent. The two natural features are Adams Falls and Flat Rock Slide; both are across the bridge. To hike to Adams Falls, turn right onto the gravel road, then right at the sign for Adams Falls Trail. The 15-foot waterfall is on a small tributary of Linn Run. The map shows that Adams Falls Trail is a loop trail, but it dead-ends just past the falls. I recommend you return the way you came in. To reach Flat Rock, turn left and walk through the picnic area, then follow the wide forest lane downstream for 0.5 mile. It is a very scenic place with a wide streambed of flat rock. When I visited, kids were having a blast sliding down the 40 feet of gently sloped rock. Be aware that it is slippery, and the park brochure states that swimming is not allowed.

Spruce Flats Bog: Within Forbes SF is the 28-acre Spruce Flats Bog, a natural depression on top of Laurel Ridge. It is easy to access on the short trail from the Laurel Summit picnic area. For thousands of years the bog was filling in and eventually became a forested swamp. When logging removed the trees, their transpiration of water stopped and the wetland quickly reverted back to a bog that is too wet for trees to grow. The bog supports unique wetland plants and wildlife.

The popular rockslide at Linn Run SP

Picturesque Adams Falls, Linn Run SP

Lookouts: Two nearby SF overlooks are Beam Rocks and Wolf Rocks. Beam Rocks offers a better view, and its shorter quarter-mile trail is gravel and level. The trail initially takes you through a young forest with ferns covering the forest floor. It then winds through a section of thick mountain laurel. In addition to the great view, you might see rock climbers scaling the 90-foot-high rocks. The state's highest elevation of 3,213 feet is in Mount Davis NA. The high point is accessible by road or trails, and an observation tower next to the stone monument is open to the public. During your visit, look for numerous stone rings that resulted from centuries of soil freezing and expanding during the winter, then eroding during the rest of the year.

Natural & Wild Areas: Roaring Run NA preserves an entire watershed fed by springs near the top of Laurel Ridge. Roaring Run Trail follows the small stream, which is lined with dense rhododendron and is home to native brook trout. The scenery is gorgeous. A few old-growth chestnut oak and black birch trees are found near remote rock outcrops. The Quebec Run Wild Area is a rugged and remote area on the eastern slope of Chestnut Ridge. It was logged twice, with the most recent occurring during the 1930s. The Bureau of Forestry is creating 5-acre plots of open grassland to improve habitat for wildlife and provide opportunities for recreation.

Laurel Highlands Hiking Trail: The 70-mile-long LHT traverses Laurel Mountain Ridge and is one of three national scenic trails in Pennsylvania. The trail is recognized as one of the best and most popular trails in the state, and the

View from Beam Rocks, Laurel Summit Road, Forbes SF

average elevations are higher than any other long trail in Pennsylvania. The camp areas are reached by blue-blazed connector trails every 8 to 10 miles. Each camp has five Adirondack shelters with fireplaces, large areas for tents, well-water pumps, and pit toilets. The six trailheads have large parking areas with signage, and the trail has a mileage monument every mile. In spring, the forest wildflowers bloom, followed by mountain laurel and rhododendron. Many hikers visit for the fall foliage, and others enjoy the tranquility and silence that only a snow-covered forest can provide.

SW9 Laurel Hill State Park, Somerset County

Laurel Hill SP is a beautiful 4,062-acre multiuse park in the Laurel Highlands region. It is a wonderful combination of scenic natural environments, recreational development, and historic sites. My favorite place is the old-growth forest within the Hemlock Trail Natural Area along Laurel Hill Creek.

History. As is typical for most of Pennsylvania's mountain regions, its forests were clear-cut and then abandoned in poor condition. In 1935, the federal government's Emergency Relief Administration began buying land to rehabilitate. Laurel Hill was one of five areas in Pennsylvania that was developed into a recreational demonstration area. Two CCC camps of 200 men each arrived at Laurel Hill and built camp buildings, the dam, a beach house, roads, utilities, and the campground, and they also planted trees. The federal government transferred the land improvement project to the state in 1945. A total of 202 buildings—the largest collection of CCC buildings in Pennsylvania on 1,352 acres—were designated as a recreational demonstration area historic district. The information center at the campground entrance has a collection of CCC photos and wildlife displays. Across the road is a memorial to the young men of the CCC who created the treasures we have today.

An interesting historic site well worth visiting is the Jones, Scott, Singo Cemetery. The family cemetery has fifty-one burials that date back to the early 1800s. Rural families could not afford headstones, so they used flat field stones placed upright at the head and foot of the grave. The stones are unmarked and many are missing, but records of burials and locations are still kept. Historical information is posted at the cemetery. One other interesting fact is that family members have served in every US war: Revolutionary War, War of 1812, Civil War, Spanish-American War, World War I, World War II, Korean War, Vietnam War, and Persian Gulf War.

Recreation. The 63-acre Laurel Hill Lake has two boat launches and mooring sites and, during the summer months, rentals for self-propelled boats. Above

Laurel Hill Lake and beach from the dam,
early morning

Wonderful old-growth hemlocks along
Hemlock Trail near Buck Run Road

the large sandy beach is terraced landscaping, a food concession, and a changing building. Steep forested mountains border the eastern side of the lake. The lake supports trout, bass, crappie, and panfish. On most summer evenings you will see a few anglers fly fishing for trout on Laurel Hill Creek, below and above the bridge. Jones Mill Run is a smaller trout stream where I met two young boys who proudly showed me the 18-inch trout they had just caught. The Lake View building, with a large deck overlooking the lake, is one of the park's many facilities that are available to rent.

As you might expect, the park has a lot of camping and cabin options. The modern campground has 264 sites, 149 with electric. Also available are walled tents with bunk beds, refrigerator and electric, eight cottages, several large organized-group cabin camps and tent camps, the attractive five-bedroom Hufman Lodge, and the three-bedroom Copper Kettle Cabin. Most of the buildings are rustic, CCC built, and well maintained. The park has 2,200 acres that are open to hunting and ten trails totaling 14 miles of varying degrees of difficulty. The Copper Kettle Trail is paved and follows the lakeshore from the dam to the opposite end of the lake. The Pump House Trail leads to the scenic Jones Mill Run Dam, built by the CCC. Winter activities include a sledding hill with lights on weekends, snowmobiling on 10 miles of park trails connected to 120 miles of state forest trails, ice fishing, and 15 miles of trails for cross-country skiing and snowshoeing.

Scenic Laurel Hill Creek, upstream from the bridge

This ancient oak tree at the group cabins has eleven large lower branches and eight higher up.

Hemlock Trail Natural Area. The Hemlock Trail takes you along Laurel Hill Creek through a magnificent 6-acre grove of giant hemlocks. No one knows how these hemlocks were saved from the axe. At the Buck Run Road trailhead, I crossed Buck Run on a huge tree trunk split down the middle. Access to the stream is limited in this area due to thick rhododendrons that shade the water for native trout. The forest floor is covered with ferns or blankets of needles and not much else. These giant hemlocks began growing from tiny seeds that are so small that it would take 200,000 seeds to weigh one pound. The cones are only 0.75 inches long. Throughout the state, the massive trees were cut down for their bark, which was stripped off and processed for use by the tanning industry. Until the later years of the logging era the rest of the tree was left in the forest.

SW10 Bear Run Nature Reserve and Fallingwater, Fayette County

Bear Run Nature Reserve (BRNR) is a 5,115-acre forest with pristine streams on the western slope of Laurel Mountain. Within the reserve is the famous home named Fallingwater, designed by architectural genius Frank Lloyd Wright. The modern home, built above the 15-foot-high waterfall, is one of the finest examples of Wright's organic architecture. In 1963, the Kaufmann family donated their home, along with their entire collection of Wright-designed furniture and surrounding land, to the Western Pennsylvania Conservancy. It is well worth taking the guided tour of the home. You should purchase tour tickets online two weeks in advance of your visit. The highest ground at BRNR is at the top of Laurel Ridge, at an elevation of more than 2,600 feet, and the lowest point is 1,040 feet, where Laurel Run flows into the Youghiogheny River. From the main parking lot, a path leads to the unique visitor center pavilion. The information desk is in the center, and the perimeter has open areas to gardens and pathways that separate the café, museum store, gallery, and restrooms.

Nature. Nearly all of the watersheds of the reserve's four streams are within the property. Bear Run and Beaver Run are designated state scenic waterways. The Bear Run and upper Lick Run drainages are known to have species of federal and state concern and are designated biological diversity areas. The reserve is only one of three places in Pennsylvania where the endangered wildflower solitary pussytoes is found. The habitat supports more than 500 species of plants and a sizable list of trees, including beech, birch, striped and red maple, black gum, poplar, bigtooth aspen, cucumber magnolia, hemlock, white pine, and four types of oak. Larger mammals include deer, black bear, fisher, bobcat, and coyote. The best birding locations are in mountain laurel and rhododendron thickets, in the peninsula's meadows,

Fallingwater is Frank Lloyd Wright's most famous home design.

Bear Run flows under the cantilevered living area and patio above.

This gorgeous path from the visitor center
leads to the garden, stream, and home.

and where trails cross the mountain streams. Birds that you might see are Swainson's thrush, wood thrush, hermit thrush, northern waterthrush, yellow-breasted chat, veery, golden-crowned kinglet, northern parula, hooded and black-throated green warblers, turkey, and ruffed grouse.

Recreation. One of my favorite times of the year to hike the trails is mid-June, when the mountain laurel is blooming, and early July, for the rhododendron. Despite the fact that five million people have visited Fallingwater since it was opened to the public, the trails offer a surprisingly quiet retreat. Visit the nature center for maps and information about the eighteen color-coded trails, and register for one of the five campsites, including one for group camping. Hunting is permitted with a conservancy permit, and fishing is allowed with the exception of Bear Run downstream from Route 381.

Trails. The short trails between the visitor center and Fallingwater are beautiful, well maintained, and lined with tall rhododendron. All of the color-coded hiking trails begin at the reserve's nature center parking lot, at the barn on Route 381, 0.5 miles north of Fallingwater's entrance. For most hikes, you need to combine several trails to make a loop. The Peninsula Trail follows the river's 180-degree bend and passes two rock vistas with views of the river valley. The very scenic Laurel Run Trail, on the west side of Route 381, hugs the stream as it rushes down the steep ravine through stands of rhododendron.

Visitor center with restrooms, café, gift shop, and gallery at the perimeter of the octagon

The path to Lower Bear Run Trail, which parallels the steep ravine with old-growth trees

The short Arbutus Trail uses wooden bridges to cross the stream four times. The 0.9-mile Lower Bear Run Trail provides great views down into Bear Run's steep ravine, and a few old-growth hemlock, oak, and poplar trees are found along the trail. You will also see large trees that fell during recent storms.

SW11 Ohiopyle State Park and SGL 51, Fayette County

Ohiopyle SP is a 20,500-acre wonderland for millions of visitors who enjoy the park's outdoor recreation, spectacular scenery, rugged mountain terrain, preserved natural areas, waterfalls, and deep river gorge. It is the second-largest state park in Pennsylvania and is at the southern end of the Laurel Highlands. The park borders 5,500-acre Bear Run Nature Preserve and two state game lands that have a total of 28,000 acres. The Youghiogheny River Gorge is the centerpiece of the park, and the quaint town of Ohiopyle contributes to the park's charm and popularity. The "Yough" (pronounced "Yock"), as it is affectionately called, is one of the best and most popular whitewater-boating destinations in the eastern US.

History. The railroads opened the area to timber companies, and by the 1880s, railroads began to transport something new: tourists. One dollar covered the round trip from Pittsburgh to Ohiopyle. Hotels were built in town and on what is now the highly protected Ferncliff Peninsula. The peninsula also had a dance pavilion, a bowling alley, fountains, a boardwalk, and recreational areas for tennis and baseball. During the early 1900s, the forests were still being cut, and logs were sent to a three-story sawmill next to the falls. The mill also served as a power plant to supply electricity for the mill's operation and lights for the town. The tannery and acidic mine runoff polluted the river to a degree that fish could not survive. Society's changing cultural and landscape meant fewer visitors to the resort and the end of an era. In 1951, Edgar Kaufmann purchased the 100-acre peninsula to preserve the land and its rare plants. Western Pennsylvania Conservancy (WPC) received Kaufmann's land gift and worked with West Penn Power Company and Mrs. Keister, who donated land containing Cucumber Falls. In May 1963, the WPC transferred 2,800 acres to the state to form a new state park. Two years later, the conservancy had transferred nearly 10,000 acres, and the park was opened to the public. Over the years the WPC has continued its mission to add land to the park.

Water Features. Over millions of years the Youghiogheny River's 27-mile stretch within the park cut through Laurel Hill and the surrounding mountains with elevations up to 2,900 feet. The river now enters the town of Ohiopyle at 1,200 feet as it flows around Ferncliff Peninsula and over 20-foot Ohiopyle Falls. The ledges at the park's waterfalls and boulders in the river are of

The Youghiogheny River and 20-foot-high
Ohiopyle Falls are the heart of the park.

sandstone, which is harder than other layers of shale. Baughman Rock
Overlook on Sugarloaf Road provides an awesome view of the river gorge.

The most prominent of the park's waterfalls is Ohiopyle Falls. Three
observation decks near the parking lots provide a close view overlooking
the falls. Cucumber Falls is a sheet of water that drops 30 feet, with a huge,
cavernous area behind the falls. It is a great waterfall to photograph with
people standing behind the falls, whether you are at the top of the path or
in the ravine. Meadow Run has the best natural waterslide in the state. Over
thousands of years, the swift-flowing stream has cut a 100-foot-long, 2- to
6-foot-deep channel through the rock streambed. Most people relax on the
adjacent rocks and watch the less intimidated as they are washed down the
chute. It is definitely a spectator sport. Less than 1 mile above the waterslide
along the Meadow Run Trail is a small cascade. Two smaller waterfalls,
Jonathan and Sugar, can be reached by biking on the Great Allegheny Passage
trail downstream, then hiking a short distance up the respective creeks.

Ferncliff Peninsula NA. The NA was preserved for its long list of unusual, rare,
and endangered plants, many of which are at their most northern or southern
extent. In 1973, it was designated a national natural landmark, and in 1992,
as a state park NA. The well-maintained 1.7-mile Ferncliff Trail follows the
perimeter of the peninsula. A side trail leads to the falls, and another trail leads
to the river takeout area. As you hike the trail, look for old potholes and channels carved by the river. At the interpretive sign, look for ancient fossils. At least
nine species of plants are designated as rare or endangered. Within the 100

Cucumber Falls viewed from the stream. An observation area is at the falls' trailhead.

acres are eighty-seven species of trees and shrubs. A number of old-growth trees have circumferences over 9 feet and heights over 100 feet. A huge black oak near the parking lot has a 17-foot circumference. Along the Magnolia Trail are several umbrella magnolia trees, which are at their northern limit.

Nature. Throughout the park there are 127 species of trees and shrubs, including stands of rhododendron and mountain laurel. Checklists of trees, wildflowers, and birds are available at the park office. The list of birds includes an amazing thirty-four species of warblers, fourteen different sparrows, and ten species of flycatchers. The occasional sighting of an olive-sided flycatcher is extremely rare in Pennsylvania. In addition to trout, the

Shooting through Cucumber Rapids on the "Yough" downstream from Cucumber Run

Visit Meadow Run Waterslide in the early morning for the scenery. Later in the day, if there is enough water, watch brave people slide down the chute.

It is rare to see someone from an "older generation" running the chute.

river has native walleye, eel, and smallmouth bass. Fourteen types of reptiles have been found, including the timber rattlesnake and copperhead. The park has sixteen species of amphibians and twenty-four different mammals, including fisher, river otter, bobcat, black bear, and mink.

Whitewater Float Trips. The Youghiogheny River is recognized as one of the most floated rivers in the US. Its loyal fans come for the thrilling rapids and gorgeous scenery in the deep gorge. The Youghiogheny Dam releases a fairly consistent flow of water from spring to fall for float trips down the park's two sections of river. The park's upper, family-friendly section, with class I and II rapids, begins at Ramcat Put-In and flows 9 miles to Ohiopyle. The 7.5-mile lower section begins below Ohiopyle Falls and ends at the Bruner Run takeout. It has fourteen boulder-strewn class III and IV rapids.

Photographing a friend. The cavern behind the falls is just as impressive as the waterfall.

Six of those are in the first 1.7 miles, called "the loop." Many experienced kayakers hone their skills in the loop's rapids and then exit the river at the Loop Takeout and hoof it the half mile across the peninsula to run it again. A third whitewater section with class IV and V rapids is outside the park in West Virginia and Maryland. Commercial river tour companies provide guided float trips and transportation to all three sections of the river.

Recreation. Bike riders love to cruise through the scenic gorge on the park's 16 miles of rail to trail, called the Great Allegheny Passage. This trail connects with other trail systems for a continuous ride from Pittsburgh to Washington, DC. Heading downriver from the train station, you cross the river twice on former railroad bridges and continue along the river at a 3 percent grade past boulder-filled rapids to the Bruner Run takeout. The ride upriver from the station is a 1 percent grade. The park also has six off-road mountain biking trails with a total of 25 miles. Hikers have a choice of thirteen different hiking trails that traverse 44 miles of forest scenery. The most challenging trail is the 70-mile Laurel Highlands Trail, which begins with a 1,200-vertical-foot climb. My favorite trails are beautiful Meadows Run Trail, Great Gorge Trail, and Ferncliff Trail. The best place to watch and photograph boaters going through rapids is from the large boulders approximately 200 yards below Cucumber Run.

The PFBC has done an excellent job establishing a first-class fishery on the river's upper section. The dam's cold-water outflow and adequate water volume in the summer enable both trout and prey to flourish. Fly fishing in particular is gaining in popularity. The large quantity of stocked brown and rainbow fingerlings and special regulations have increased the likelihood of catching and releasing a trophy-size trout. Meadows Run has a 2.2-mile section that is designated delayed harvest and artificial lures only. The secluded campground is huge, with approximately 200 sites, twenty-seven walk-in sites, yurts, cottages, and organized-group tenting. Reservations should be made months in advance. Hunting is allowed on 18,000 acres. Eleven miles of the Sugarloaf Trail and Pressley Trail systems are open for equestrian riding. The three areas for rock climbing are Meadow Run, Bruner Run, and along the lower Youghiogheny River. Winter activities include cross-country skiing (34 miles), snowmobiling (16 miles), and a maintained sledding hill.

What better way to cool down on a hot summer day.

The rail trail crosses the river above and below the falls.

Rafters having a blast on a guided float trip down the lower section of the "Yough."

Central Pennsylvania

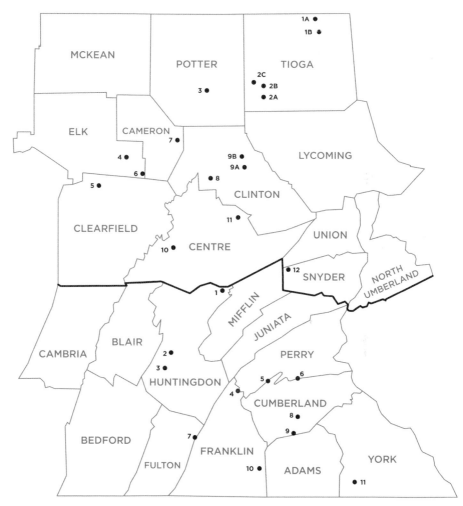

MCKEAN

POTTER

TIOGA

1A ●
1B ●

2C ●
● 2B
● 2A

3 ●

ELK

CAMERON

7 ●

LYCOMING

4 ●

9B ●
9A ●

6 ●

8 ●

5 ●

CLINTON

11 ●

CLEARFIELD

CENTRE

UNION

10 ●

● 12

SNYDER

NORTH
UMBERLAND

1 ●

MIFFLIN

CAMBRIA

BLAIR

JUNIATA

PERRY

2 ●

3 ●

HUNTINGDON

5 ●
● 6

4 ●

CUMBERLAND

8 ●

9 ●

BEDFORD

7 ●

FRANKLIN

YORK

FULTON

10 ●

ADAMS

11 ●

North-Central Region

NC1 Cowanesque and Tioga-Hammond Lakes, Tioga County

The large dams that created 498-acre Tioga Lake, 640-acre Hammond Lake, and 1,085-acre Cowanesque Lake were constructed by the Army Corps of Engineers to hold vast amounts of water during potential flood events. In 1972, the need for flood control was realized after tropical storm Agnes caused massive flooding, with damage that was twice the cost of the dams. The dams were completed in 1979 and 1980, at a total cost of $349 million. Subsequent work was done on the Cowanesque dam in the late 1980s to raise the lake level an additional 35 feet.

In addition to flood prevention, year-round control of released water helps maintain healthy aquatic life in the rivers. Recreational facilities are another benefit that ACE is required to provide. The Tioga-Hammond Lake Project also accomplished one other benefit, using a design unique to ACE. In the Tioga River watershed, acidic water carrying heavy metals seeps out of old coal mines and through tailings of strip mines, so the pH level in the river is so low it cannot support fish. When the two dams were built, a quarter-mile channel was carved through rock between the lakes, with Hammond Lake's normal water level 5 feet higher than Tioga Lake. The mixed water of the two lakes is a major improvement in downstream water quality, and aquatic life is thriving. One pleasant common characteristic

Kids enjoying Cowanesque Lake. It is a
relatively quiet retreat, considering its large size.

A favorite campsite over-
looking Cowanesque Lake

One of the displays at Hammond Lake Visitor Center

Osprey nest across the cove
at Hammond Lake's Pine Camp.

of all three parks and lakes is that they are less crowded than most of the other reservoirs in the state.

Cowanesque Lake. The 2,734-acre park is a great place to combine camping, boating, and fishing without the crowds. Tompkins Campground, on the north shore, has eighty-three wooded and open sites, with several sites along the lake. A couple of sites have a patio area with railings overlooking the lake. There are also sixteen primitive walk-in sites with more privacy and a group camping area. The campground has a grassy swim area with a concrete base in the lake, plus a camp store, bathhouse, boat launch, and overnight mooring. The Mid-State Trail follows the shoreline along the western half of the lake. Common sightings for bird watchers are migrating and breeding songbirds, waterfowl, osprey, and the occasional eagle.

The lake's 17-mile shoreline, wetlands near the inlet, and a maximum depth of 200 feet provide an excellent habitat that produces large fish. Species commonly caught are black crappie, channel catfish, tiger muskie, muskellunge up to 42 inches, walleye weighing 6 to 8 pounds, largemouth bass more than 5 pounds, hybrid striped bass, and football-shaped smallmouth bass. The west end of the lake is shallow, with islands, wetlands, trees, and a delta of silt that is perfect habitat for small fish and waterfowl,

View from the observation area through the
cut at Hammond Lake

and a favorite place for kayaking. There are two launches on the south
shore, and no limit on boat motor size. Waterskiing, Jet Skis, and sailing
are popular activities. Hunting is allowed in certain areas.

Tioga-Hammond Lakes. The office for all three lakes is at the west end
of Hammond Lake. Inside are wildlife displays, including the state record
crappie and a glass enclosure with a rattlesnake or two. Each year an
average of three rattlesnakes are found in public areas of the park. They
are transferred to the office for a few weeks and then released in their
more remote home habitat. On the other side of the office parking lot is
an arborarium with a paved trail through an extensive collection of trees,
with placards identifying species. I counted a total of nine different magnolia
trees, fifteen conifers—including two cypress and two redwood, seven
types of crabapple trees, and many maples, oaks, and other trees.

Ives Run Recreation Area has a full-service campground with 163 sites,
a camp store, swim beach, bathhouse, boat launch, and overnight mooring.
Primitive Pine Campground is on a peninsula approximately 0.8 mile east
of the Hickory Camp loop. The park has five trails of varying lengths and
degrees of difficulty. The 1-mile Archery Trail is unique, in that it has
targets and two tree stands to practice and improve your archery skills.
Boating and fishing are excellent and similar to Cowanesque Lake. I did
notice more eagles and osprey here. A pair of ospreys had a nest on a
platform near Pine Campground, and I saw three at another platform near
the dam. One of the best places to watch osprey is at the Tioga Dam outlet

and stream, where they hover and then dive for a meal. The outlet is also one of the best places to hook into a huge fish, but it is easy to get snagged in the rocks. I highly recommend you visit the overlook between Hammond and Tioga Lakes; the cut through solid rock is impressive. The 3,730-acre park shares its southern and eastern border with SGL 27. Lambs Creek boat launch serves Tioga Lake, which has far less boat traffic.

NC2 Pine Creek Gorge NA, Leonard Harrison State Park, and Colton Point State Park, Tioga and Lycoming Counties

The 12,163-acre Pine Creek Gorge NA is 18 miles of protected land on both sides of the deep gorge from Ansonia to Blackwell. It is the second-largest natural area in Pennsylvania, and Pine Creek was designated a Pennsylvania scenic and wild river. Colton Point SP, on the west rim of the gorge, and Leonard Harrison SP, on the east rim, are at the northern end of the gorge. The gorge, also known as the Grand Canyon of Pennsylvania, is 800 feet deep and 4,000 feet wide between the state parks. The gorge is protected south of the natural area by the Tioga SF, Tiadaghton SF, SGL 68, Wolf Run NA, and Algerine NA. The parks and protected lands attract hundreds of thousands of visitors every year, who come for the views, waterfalls, float trips, biking, hiking, fishing, and wildlife.

Leonard Harrison SP. Leonard Harrison SP has a large and impressive observation area with paths and terraces constructed with flagstone pavers, stone walls, and gardens of rhododendron and trees. The observation area also has a small museum with a video about the CCC, a food concession, a gift store, and benches. On a recent visit, I arrived early in the morning as the fog lifted and only a few people were there. Within the first half hour I watched a total of seven bald eagles fly low overhead. The Turkey Path is a popular trail from the observation area to Pine Creek and back. The scenery is gorgeous on this well-maintained trail, but it is steep, and some places are wet from seeps. Switchbacks and wooden stairs on the steepest sections

View of Pine Creek and side canyon from
Leonard Harrison SP lookout in late October

are helpful. The trail's upper half is shaded by hemlocks and leads to Little Four Mile Run, and the trail's lower section is mostly in a hardwood forest and parallels the stream. The stream is a continuous cascade down the ravine, with at least eight waterfalls 10 to 40 feet high. The stream is most dramatic during periods of high flow. The Overlook Trail takes you to Otter View vista. The small campground has showers, a dump station, and electric at some sites. The park also has picnic areas, a pavilion, and a play area.

Colton Point SP. In some respects, Colton Point SP is similar to Leonard Harrison SP, but the views of the canyon are from a different perspective, and the entrance road is a long, uphill drive. Along the edge of the plateau there are five vistas that overlook the canyon to the north or south. The 3-mile Turkey Path trail on this side of the canyon is longer and also somewhat difficult, but it is just as scenic along Four Mile Run. At the half-mile point is a 70-foot cascading waterfall, and farther down are more waterfalls. The park has a primitive campground, pavilions built by the CCC, and picnic areas.

Pine Creek Gorge. Pine Creek's 47-mile-long canyon is one of the most scenic and wild places in the state. The National Park Service designated the upper 12-mile section a national natural landmark and noted that it

Pine Creek Gorge Natural Area

is "one of the finest examples of a deep gorge in the eastern US." The 18-mile section from Ansonia to Blackwell was designated as an SF natural area. You can travel the entire length by floating down Pine Creek or biking and hiking on the Pine Creek Rail Trail, or a shorter section by hiking the 30-mile West Rim Trail. Add fishing, bird watching, and camping to the list of activities and it is understandable that the gorge is a major attraction for people in the mid-Atlantic region. Float trips are possible in spring and after heavy rains in summer and fall. An adequate river level of about 3 feet is needed, and wetsuits should be worn in spring. Equipment can be rented from outfitters in Ansonia.

Ansonia access points serve as the beginning of float and biking trips through the remote 18-mile section of the canyon. In the first 1.5 miles, Pine Creek cuts through the canyon past the spectacular cliffs at Owasee Rapid, the stream's most notorious rapid. The only road access in the canyon is at Tiadaghton, 9 miles below Ansonia. A designated primitive campground is here, and a camping permit is required. Camping above this access point is not allowed.

Rail/Trail. The Pine Creek Rail Trail is approximately 61 miles long, with the northern terminus near Route 6. If you start at the north end and your legs are up to it, take a break at Turkey Path and check out the falls before

Canyon view to the south from Colton Point SP

A snow-covered canyon presents a completely different scene; Colton Point SP.

Kayakers floating the stream after a substantial rainfall, Leonard Harrison SP

Ladies on a two-day, 94-mile, up-and-back bike ride on the canyon's rail trail

Stairs on Turkey Path Trail help preserve the steep mountainside in Leonard Harrison SP.

continuing south through the canyon. From Blackwell to Waterville, the trail and Route 414 parallel the stream for approximately 26 miles. This section has excellent fishing, numerous access points, and commercial campgrounds. The final 10 miles parallel Route 44 until you reach the southern terminus at Route 220, near Jersey Shore.

One of the waterfalls along Little Four Mile
Run, viewed from Turkey Path Trail

NC3 Cherry Springs State Park and Susquehannock
State Forest, Potter County

Cherry Springs SP is one of the finest examples of what Pennsylvania's
preserved lands have to offer. This park has become nationally recognized
as one of the best places in the eastern US for its dark night sky. In 2001,
the National Public Observatory picked it as the pilot for the "Stars in
Parks" program. In 2008, it was named an international dark sky by the
experts at the International Dark-Sky Association (IDA), which measures
night sky darkness. Many more accolades have been bestowed on Cherry

Springs SP since then. Amazingly, as recently as 1998, hardly anyone visited the 82-acre park to view the stars, but word quickly spread about its unique attribute. Since then, the DCNR has dedicated considerable funds for improvements to benefit the increasing numbers of amateur astronomers and the general public who simply want to experience a wondrous night sky. The park has thirty primitive campsites (no reservations) and picnic tables in a separate area from the astronomy fields. In the Astronomy Field is a huge, partially enclosed log pavilion built by the CCC in 1939.

Dark Sky. Several factors make this park ideal for superb night viewing. The fact that there is almost no light pollution is key. It is in the middle of the 262,000-acre Susquehannock SF, on a mountain plateau—not a peak—with an elevation of 2,300 feet. The view is 360 degrees. The DCNR, other state agencies, and nonprofit organizations have worked hard to reduce light pollution from all sources within a 20-mile radius. The Tri-County Electric Company installed light-shielding caps on residential outdoor lights for free. In 2007, the DCNR spent $395,000 to buy the mineral rights to prevent gas development in the state forest and park. The park's Dark Sky Fund/Association works to protect the dark sky, provides night sky information, organizes public stargazing programs, and promotes star parties between May and October.

The main Astronomy Field is across Route 44 from the parking lot and inside the fence. Fences were erected, rows of trees were planted, berms and parking areas were built, and lighting was eliminated or changed to red lenses and shielded. In 2005, three observation domes and a sky shed were built to help block wind and thermal current. Also, concrete pads and electric pedestals were installed. In 2006, the adjacent grass airfield was bought to develop a second viewing area. This field is next to the parking area and is used mainly for shorter visits and astronomy programs held throughout the summer. It has an amphitheater and a few concrete pads for telescopes. In a typical clear rural night sky, approximately 2,500 stars can be seen. At Cherry Springs SP the number of visible stars is 10,000.

Visiting. My first visit many years ago is a good example of what not to do. I arrived well after dark with my camera gear and flashlight and was politely informed by the ranger that I could not use my flashlight because it did not have a red lens. After getting directions to the field, I immediately realized that I was completely blind. I saw nothing: no road, path, or tree line. I had to shuffle along and feel whether I was on pavement, gravel, or grass. Along the path I heard voices but saw no one. I just stood in place for fifteen minutes until my pupils dilated enough to see faint silhouettes. To use my camera I had to borrow a red flashlight. While taking photos, I was stunned to see thousands of stars, the cloud-like Milky Way, and Jupiter. I was also generously invited by other visitors to look through their telescopes at nebulae and distant galaxies. Walking back to my car, I

Milky Way with one of the observer's red trailer lights on; camera exposure was eighty seconds

Some of the nearly 500 amateur astronomers setting up for the annual four-day Star Party

The park's observatory domes in the main field are used to block light and wind.

thought, "What a wonderful and memorable experience the natural world provided for me tonight!"

My most recent visit was on the weekend of an annual star party, with 550 amateur astronomers from all over the eastern US and Canada having camped and set up their equipment in the field. I was amazed at how sophisticated telescopes have become and how many people had them. The computer industry has changed the way we track the night sky.

There are a number of rules and suggestions for new visitors. Choose a clear night between five days before and three days after the new moon phase. You should always arrive before sunset and set up immediately. Assume you will be there for four hours or more. Keep in mind that prime observing does not occur until almost two hours after sunset. For families with children, it is probably best to set up in the viewing area next to the parking lot, since it is close to your car. If you want to stay overnight, you must park at the Observation Field and cannot leave until morning. There is a $15 fee and a form to fill out. You cannot stay overnight in the parking

Sunrise at Cherry Springs Vista, looking west along Route 144, Susquehannock SF, Potter County

Water Tank Hollow Vista, looking east along Route 144, Susquehannock SF lot. Suggestions of items to bring include two mini flashlights with red lens or red cellophane, blanket, chair, star chart, binoculars, and extra clothes. It gets much colder after dark than you might think. Taking photos will require a tripod and two-minute exposures. Quiet hours at both fields remain in effect until 11:00 a.m.

The Woodsmen's Show is held in the park in early August every year. Since 1952, the show has commemorated Potter County's lumber industry heritage. Thousands of people attend the weekend show, which features competitions and demonstrations in lumberjack skills, vendors with wood carvings and crafts for sale, kids' games, and food vendors.

NC4 Elk Country, Elk State Forest, and SGL 14, North-Central Counties

There are not many outdoor experiences that can equal watching a mature bull elk in his role as the dominant alpha male during the mating season. His high-pitched bugling sends a message to any challengers within a quarter mile that the cows are his. The young bulls are persistent but easily chased away. Large bulls of similar size are not intimidated and will try to steal his cows, so a battle ensues where the winner takes all. It is like watching a National Geographic special in person.

A brief nap before another night of fending off the competition, Elk County Visitor Center

Bugling bull elk at sunrise, Winslow Hill, SGL 311, mid-October

Between 1,000 and 1,100 wild elk—the largest number east of the Mississippi—roam the mountains of north-central Pennsylvania. The population is centered near the small town of Benezette, in Elk County. The best time of year to view elk is during the mating season, from mid-September to mid-October. Elk are crepuscular, meaning that they are most active during the first and last hours of the day. For most people, especially first-time visitors, the best place to view elk is the Elk Country Visitor Center. Fifty thousand people visit in September and October, so arrive at a viewing location at sunrise or two hours before sunset. My last visit, on a weekday evening, I arrived early and watched as 250 people arrived and stood ten deep, watching the drama unfold just 30 yards away. The center has wildlife exhibits, touch displays, a theater, a mounted 800-pound bull elk, monitors with live cams showing the fields, a gift shop, and trails that lead to observation areas. While you are there, pick up the set of large antlers on display and imagine carrying them on you head.

Viewing Locations. (1) The road to the visitor center is on the right side of Winslow Hill Road, 1.2 miles from Route 555 in Benezette. At the desk, ask about directions to specific viewing locations. (2) Winslow Hill Viewing Area is on the left side of Winslow Hill Road, 3.6 miles from Benezette. Park in the lot overlooking the valley or drive down Dewey Road through the game lands. You can walk on the dirt roads, but not into the fields or woods. (3) Woodring Farm is on the left side of Winslow Hill Road, 2.2 miles from

Elk-viewing area along
Route 555

This massive rack has an
impressive fifteen points.

The dominant bull must
constantly prove he's
worthy of the position.

Route 555. Take the 0.75-mile trail that leads into the game lands. (4) Dents Run Viewing Area is on Winslow Road, 3 miles from Benezette. It is a popular viewing area overlooking the surrounding fields. (5) Hicks Run Viewing Area is along Route 555, approximately 8.5 miles east of Benezette. There is a covered blind that overlooks fields. (6) The towns of Benezette and Medix and the nearby campground are good places to see elk. One morning before sunrise, I watched two excited spike bulls following a cow as they passed within 8 yards of my campsite. They do not seem to mind being close to civilization, because you will see them in town grazing on residents' lawns.

History. Prior to European colonization, elk inhabited all of Pennsylvania, but by the late 1870s, elk had been extirpated from Pennsylvania due to loss of habitat and unregulated hunting. In 1912, the Game Commission purchased fifty elk from the Yellowstone area at $30 each and shipped them by train to Pennsylvania. Another twenty-two were purchased from a Monroe County preserve. The elk were released in three north-central counties and Monroe County in the east. Two years later, the GC bought ninety-five more elk, which were released in six counties, including Monroe and Carbon. It was not long before crop damage became an issue, so the first hunting season for mature bull elk was opened in 1923. Twenty-three elk were taken the first year, but by 1931 the yearly harvest plummeted to one elk, and future seasons were closed. The number of elk remained low for fifty years. In 1974, only thirty-eight elk remained in Pennsylvania. The problems were a lack of suitable habitat, illegal killings, legal killing due to crop damage, and brain worm disease caused by ingesting snails and slugs. Over the next decade, open farmland was purchased, existing habitat was improved, surface mines were restored to grassland, food plots were created, and more research was conducted. In 1990, the Rocky Mountain Elk Foundation (RMEF) got involved and contributed money to buy land, enhance habitat, and erect electric fencing in areas with the greatest crop damage. The herd grew to 566 by 2000, and the first elk hunt in seventy years was held in 2001. The Game Commission and the RMEF continue to provide funding for habitat, research, public access, and education, ensuring a bright future.

Elk. The bull elk's antlers are fully grown by August and can weigh up to 50 pounds. The alpha bull has a harem of fifteen to twenty cows to protect. During mating season, an 800-pound bull does not eat or sleep much and can lose 150 pounds. The cows come into estrus near the end of September; on my last visit, the peak was September 30. They are receptive to breeding for only about eighteen hours, and if they are not successfully bred they will have two or three more breeding cycles every twenty-one days. As soon as the calf is born in early June, the mother will consume all byproducts of birth to prevent predators from locating the calf. She then licks the calf thoroughly. The calf can stand within twenty minutes and will begin to nurse within one hour. They instinctively know to hide and remain motionless for the next few weeks. This instinct is so strong that biologists have picked up calves and they remained stiff, never moving a muscle. Some calves are given radio collars that are elastic, to grow as the calf grows, and will fall off before the calf outgrows the collar. They are monitored several times each week. To protect the calf, the cow minimizes contact except to suckle the calf. Its spotted coat and lack of scent help reduce the odds it will be detected by a predator. They both rejoin the herd in approximately three weeks, when the calf can move with the herd and outrun predators. The average life span of elk is relatively short: eight years for bulls and ten years for cows, with a few reaching twenty years.

NC5 Parker Dam State Park, Clearfield County

Parker Dam SP is a beautiful park—just the right size and amenities for quiet relaxation. The park is surrounded by the vast wilderness of Moshannon SF. Within the park's 968 acres is a network of trails providing access to a forest of mixed hardwoods, swamp meadows, pine plantations, and a 20-acre lake. The trails also serve as connections to long-distance trails in the SF, such as 73-mile Quehanna Trail. The park is conveniently twenty minutes from I-80 and only forty minutes from the center of elk country. It is possible to see elk wandering through the park. In 1930, the state began buying land at $3 an acre, and three years later the CCC set up camp to plant trees and build roads, bridges, a beautiful stone dam, and cabins.

Windstorm Preserve. On May 31, 1985, an outbreak of tornadoes touched down in Pennsylvania and ripped through 27,000 acres of forest. The F4 tornado that hit both sides of the state park's Mud Run Road traveled 69 miles in ninety minutes, with wind speeds up to 250 mph. The only people in the park at the time were two fathers and their three young boys, who were very fortunate to be staying in a sturdy, eight-sided log cabin built in the 1930s. At 7:45 p.m., the tornado took less than two minutes to destroy the northern section of the park, including every tree within hundreds of yards of the cabin. Miraculously, the cabin suffered only minor damage. The boys and their fathers walked out of the park that night by climbing over downed trees in the dark. Salvage timber cuts were made

Parker Lake, Parker Dam SP

The fallen trees of the 1985 tornado as seen in 2008. The 4-inch saplings are the next generation.

By 2016 the saplings were 10 inches, and many smaller trees had died from lack of sunlight.

The stonework by the CCC throughout the park system is quite impressive; Parker Lake Dam.

A beaver's strategy is puzzling sometimes. Why two large trees at once?

east of Mud Run Road. The west side was left virtually untouched for visitors to witness how the forest recovers naturally. Sadly, the mountainside had many old trees. The Trail of Giants was repaired and renamed the Trail of New Giants. As time goes on it becomes harder to see the damage. Trees are rotting away and some are gone. A few giants are still standing, but many have fallen in recent years, crushing stands of young trees. Mounds and depressions on the forest floor are evidence of uprooted trees that have completely decomposed. The small trees that I saw in 2008 are now 6 to 7 inches in diameter.

Trails. The 1-mile-long Trail of New Giants begins at Cabin Colony Road and loops up and back to Mud Run Road. As you hike up the mountain, notice that all of the tornado-downed trees fell in the same direction, and as you hike down the mountain, all the trees are lying in the opposite direction. At the highest point on the trail, a steep side trail climbs to an impressive vista overlooking the lake and an endless forest. The 2.3-mile Beaver Run Trail follows Mud Run in the park and SF land through beautiful lowlands where beaver have dammed the stream, creating a long chain of ponds, making navigation easier. Bring binoculars, walk to a good vantage point, and sit quietly to watch the beaver repair their dams, haul branches, fell trees, and work as a team. They are one of nature's most amazing creatures. Take Gas Well Road or Abbot Hollow Trail to a remote valley with beaver dams along Abbot Run. This area was also devastated by the tornado. There are plenty of multiuse trails for mountain biking, hiking, and cross-country skiing. Backpackers should register at the park office and may start their hikes in the park but must camp in the SF. While hiking the fourteen trails in the park and adjacent state forest, look for deep-forest species of birds and wildlife, such as warblers, wood thrush, redstart, bobcat, porcupine, coyote, deer, and black bear.

Recreation. The modern campground has 110 sites ranging from sunny to full shade. There are organized camping areas and sixteen rustic cabins with a kitchen and bathroom. More than 400 picnic tables and seven pavilions are scattered throughout the park. Along the lake is a nice sandy beach with a food concession and camp store during the summer months. Boating is restricted to electric- or human-powered boats. Kayaks, canoes, and paddleboats can be rented during the summer months. The lake and streams are stocked with brook trout, and the lake has largemouth bass, bluegill, and catfish.

The park also has guided walks, evening programs, environmental education, and interpretive programs. On weekends in March, visitors can watch

Beaver Run Dam, Quehanna Wild Area

View of a wet meadow from the Beaver Run observation blind

demonstrations of the maple-sugaring operation. In October, visitors can see how apple cider is made. Winter activities include ice skating, ice fishing, sledding, snowmobiling, and cross-country skiing on several groomed trails.

NC6 Quehanna Wild Area, Natural Areas, and SGL 34; Elk, Cameron, and Clearfield Counties

The Quehanna Wild Area is the DCNR Bureau of Forestry's first and largest designated wild area. In fact, it is more than three times the size of Manhattan. It is also one of the state's most rugged and remote areas. The 48,186-acre wild area has no permanent residents and is composed of Moshannon SF, Elk SF, Marion Brooks NA, Goddard Wykoff Run NA, and State Game Lands 34. Quehanna Highway, which is actually a two-lane road, crosses the region's plateau on the highest elevations. Along both sides of the highway, small streams begin their descent through steep canyons lined with boulders and rhododendron. The few roads in the wild area follow these streams down to civilization. Before visiting the area, order or pick up the DCNR's "Quehanna Shared-Use Trail Map."

History. The land received the same logging and wildfire abuse as other forested sections of Pennsylvania. In 1955, Curtiss-Wright Corporation bought 80 square miles to test nuclear-powered jet engines. They used two relatively small areas: one at the southeast perimeter and another near the center of what is now the wild area. Five years later, after building their facilities and conducting research, they decided to leave. Other tenants moved into the buildings and continued to contaminate the site. The state reacquired the entire area between 1963 and 1967. Cleanup took eight years and cost $30 million. Today, the developed site and new buildings serve as a state correctional boot camp and minimum-security prison.

Gorges. Four streams with headwaters on the plateau carved deep canyons. Lost Run Road provides access to Mosquito Creek, which flows south through a 500-foot-deep gorge. On the north side of Quehanna Highway,

A large stand of white birch approaching maximum age of ninety years old, Marion Brooks NA. Forty years earlier the stand was nearly 100 percent white birch.

View from the rock outcrop along Lincoln Trail

Red Run Road descends along beautiful Red Run in a spectacular 900-foot-deep canyon. If you are adventurous, park just past the bridge at the hairpin turn and hike along the mountain stream to view the dense rhododendron, boulders, pools, and small waterfalls. Jerry Run Road follows Upper Jerry Run, and Wykoff Run Road parallels Wykoff Run—the largest stream in the wild area—through incredible canyon scenery for 10 miles. It must have been extremely difficult to log the sides of any one of these canyons.

Nature. On Memorial Day in 1985, the most powerful of the seventeen tornadoes that hit Pennsylvania passed through Quehanna WA. The F4 tornado crossed Quehanna Highway at the border of Elk and Clearfield Counties, flattening thousands of trees. The trail map shows the location of the "Tornado Zone." If the timbering, forest fires, and tornado were not enough, the forest has been attacked by blights and insects. In the early twentieth century, between 25 percent and 50 percent of the Quehanna forest was American chestnut trees. By 1925, the chestnut blight wiped out every tree. From the late 1960s to the 1980s, larvae of the oak leaf roller moth, pit scale insects, oak leaf tier, and gypsy moths defoliated 884,000 acres in Elk and Moshannon SFs, causing moderate to large-scale tree mortality. Today, the wild area is 84 percent hardwood forest, and the rest is conifers, mixed forest, and open meadows. The forest also has large thickets of mountain laurel, rhododendron, blueberry bushes, and huckleberry bushes. The wild area is home to elk, coyote, bobcat, black bear, fisher, and deer, and rattlesnakes are occasionally seen. In 1995, twenty-three fishers were released along Wykoff Run. This once-extirpated species has successfully spread throughout the region. The area's diversified habitat, including the regenerated forest in the tornado zone, was designated an international bird area and is home to 102 species of birds. Most of the streams have native brook trout, and some streams are stocked with brook, rainbow, and brown trout.

Marion Brooks NA & Goddard Wykoff Run NA. The 917-acre Marion Brooks NA encompasses the largest stand of white birch trees in the eastern US. The 32-acre almost pure stand of white birch began growing years after the Quehanna area was logged and subsequent fires damaged the soil's organic material. (Stands of white birch develop because their roots deposit a toxin in the soil that inhibits other types of trees from growing.) Many of the trees are reaching their maximum ninety-year age limit. To truly appreciate the stand, park in the small lot along the highway and follow the faint trail into the forest. You will find that the densest section is near the road. The 1,215-acre M. K. Goddard Wykoff Run NA is a plateau with the highest elevation in the wild area. The headwaters for Red Run and Wykoff Run originate in the NA, and Old Hoover Trail is the only trail traversing it.

Beaver Run Dam & Hoover Farm. The Beaver Run area, managed by the Game Commission, featured a shallow impoundment surrounded by wetlands. In 2017, the fear of a possible breach in the dike necessitated the GC to open a section of the dam to permanently drain the lake. Now wetland vegetation covers the lake bed and the snags remain standing. An old osprey nest can be seen in one of the dead trees. Below the dike are large open meadows. Park in the lot along Beaver Run Road and hike down the grass road. Overlooking the wetlands is a large, covered observation blind tucked into the woods. Look for marsh and grassland birds. Beaver Run is still one of my favorite locations in Quehanna WA. Visit early morning on a weekday or during the off-season and the sensation of being alone in the wilderness will envelope you. The Hoover Farm Viewing Area is an old farmstead with open meadows and a viewing blind. Several trailheads are located here. It is certainly a picturesque place to watch wildlife moving through the meadows early in the morning or at the end of the day.

Trails. The oval-shaped, 75-mile-long Quehanna Trail loops around the entire wild area and Moshannon SF to the west. The trailhead is in Parker Dam SP. You can design your hike by using either the West Cross Connector or East Cross Connector to make shorter loops and avoid car shuttles.

The Lincoln Loop Trail loop was recommended to me by the gentleman who maintains it. The maintenance of most trails in the wild area is assigned to individual volunteers from the Quehanna Area Trail Club. I was also warned about staying alert for abundant rattlesnakes found in sunlit rocky areas. Keep in mind that they are very rarely seen and will avoid contact if possible. For a great view, take a five-minute walk on the Lincoln Trail to the rock outcrops at the edge of the plateau. This is the only vista that is close to the Quehanna Highway. The view into Red Run Canyon is excellent. The trail continues through a gap between the huge rocks and then follows the edge of the plateau and connects with Teaberry Trail. Two more vistas are along this second loop trail.

At the Yellowsnake Camping Area, north of Piper, each of the six equestrian sites has a covered horse stall, picnic table, and fire ring. Most types of camping require a free permit. Backpackers should register for their own safety. Contact either of the two state forest districts for trail information, maps, and permits.

NC7 Sinnemahoning State Park and Elk State Forest, Cameron and Potter Counties

Sinnemahoning SP is a picturesque park protecting a 9-mile valley along the First Fork of Sinnemahoning Creek. The 1,910-acre park was created after the state built the George B. Stevenson Dam for flood control. The lake, stream, food plots, wild meadows, riparian habitat, and deciduous forests attract the park's abundant wildlife.

George B. Stevenson Dam. The huge dam spans 1,918 feet across the entire valley and was built high enough to hold a tremendous amount of water during flood events. The normal lake elevation is 921 feet, and the spillway is 1,026 feet—a difference of 105 feet. The 142-acre lake would become 1,470 acres and flood the entire park. This actually happened once. After Hurricane Agnes dumped record amounts of rain, the lake rose to the top of the spillway but did not flow over it. The dam is one of four operated by the DCNR but is regulated by the Army Corps of Engineers during flood conditions. The dam is definitely worth visiting. You can park in the lot along Route 872, walk across the bridge over the spillway, and then walk along the top of the dam for a view of the scenic mountains and valley. Another roadway leads to the 211-foot-high control tower, which houses two 37-ton control gates. Several kiosks provide information. I was surprised to see how high the dam is, as well as the large area of mowed lawns below the dam.

View from the impressive George Stevenson Dam, Sinnemahoning SP

Visitor center at Sinnemahoning SP

Square Timber Lookout on Ridge Road, Elk SF

Recreation. A boat launch, mooring spaces for forty-five boats, fishing pier, picnic area, and the park office all are in one area on the northern end of the 1.3-mile-long reservoir. Boats with electric motors or human-powered boats are allowed on the lake. The lake has both cold- and warm-water fish, including brook, rainbow, and brown trout; smallmouth and largemouth bass; and pickerel, perch, crappie, tiger muskie, catfish, and panfish. The beautiful creek flows for 7.5 miles from the north end of the park to the lake. A 2.5-mile section of the creek has special regulations for fishing.

The park has two main trails that pass through different habitats. The 4-mile Low Lands Trail uses the old railroad bed and leads to the wildlife-viewing platform. The 1-mile Red Spruce Trail travels through an old field converted to a spruce plantation, which happens to be good habitat for small rodents and predatory hawks, owls, and snakes. Forty Maples Day Use Area is a great spot for picnics, fishing, or simply relaxing. It is named after the maple trees planted by one of Pennsylvania's most famous and fascinating woodsmen, Chauncey Logue. The modern campground has thirty-five sites for tents and large campers. It is in a grove of mature pines, so the sites have limited privacy. Two-story Brooks Run Cabin is available to rent all year. Snowmobiling and cross-country skiing trails connect with the state forest trails.

Nature. The large, rustically designed visitor center opened in 2011; it houses nature displays and historical photographs. Park rangers provide information and conduct environmental programs, hikes, and workshops. The wildlife-viewing platform is an excellent location for bird watching. The raised observation blind overlooks wild meadows and cultivated fields of clover managed by the Game Commission as an enhanced wildlife program. Elk are sometimes seen between the Forty Maples picnic area and the observation area, and eagles are often perched above the lake, looking for a meal. Eagles have nested in the park since 2000 and are currently nesting in a large pine across the lake from the boat launch.

Elk Forest Vista. To really appreciate how rugged the mountain terrain is near the park, I recommend driving on gravel forest roads to several vistas in Elk SF. From Route 872 in Sinnemahoning Park, take Brooks Road up the mountain through an amazing steep-sided canyon for 4 miles. You will pass a couple of cabins that were squeezed into small pockets of almost level ground. At the top of the mountain, turn right onto 21-mile-long Ridge Road. Three vistas are within the first 2 miles. Use the Elk SF map to find your way in these mountains.

NC8 Sproul State Forest, Wild and Natural Areas, Clinton County

Remote and wild is how I would describe 305,000-acre Sproul State Forest. It is the largest state forest in Pennsylvania, and because it is one contiguous block of land, it occupies one of the smallest overall areas of any state forest (the other state forests are spread out or segmented). The land is a rolling plateau, with steep, narrow canyons created by stream erosion. The remote 450-square-mile southern tract is surrounded on three sides by the West Branch of the Susquehanna River and has no permanent residents, electricity, or cell phone service. A 30-mile section of Route 144 bisects the southern tract, so I assume it beats the Quehanna Highway as the longest wilderness road in Pennsylvania. Sproul SF has some of the most inaccessible areas imaginable. The three designated wild areas are Russell P. Letterman, Burns Run, and M. K. Goddard WAs. The three designated natural areas are Tamarack Swamp, East Branch Swamp, and Cranberry Swamp NAs. Within Sproul SF are four state parks: Bucktail, Kettle Creek, Hyner Run, and Hyner View. There are also a number of excellent vistas in the state forest. The district forest office is on Route 120, a few miles west of Renovo.

Russell P. Letterman Wild Area: Four tributaries in the 4,715-acre wild area merge to form Fish Dam Run, which flows into the West Branch of the

View of the Russell P. Letterman WA at an overlook along Route 44, Sproul SF

Vast stands of mountain laurel thrive in East Branch Swamp NA in June.

Old tree stumps from the early 1900s are scattered throughout Cranberry Swamp NA.

The remains of a giant hemlock, East Branch Swamp NA, Sproul SF

Susquehanna. Each tributary has carved its own steep ravine. The wild area is 3 miles wide along Route 144 and 5 miles in length to the Susquehanna River. The infamous tornado of 1985 destroyed a wide swath of forest from Slash Dam Hollow to Dennison Fork. The best way to see the path of destruction is to visit Dennison Overlook along Route 144 during the winter, with snow on the ground. The Chuck Keiper Trail is the only trail that traverses the WA. It enters from Route 144 at 2,200 feet and then drops down into the Fish Dam tributary ravine at 1,450 feet and climbs back up to 2,200 feet. The river elevation at the mouth of the stream is 672 feet.

Burns Run Wild Area: This designated wild area is smaller than but very similar to adjacent Letterman WA. It is a roadless second-growth hardwood forest with several streams that cut steep ravines in the plateau. They merge to form Burns Run, which flows into the river. The tornado also caused extensive damage here. The wild area has individual and groves of white pine trees from the late 1800s. The streams in both wild areas hold native brook trout. The only trail in the wild area is Keiper Trail, which follows Burns Run as it gradually descends 1,000 feet until it merges with Owl Run. At the streams' juncture, the trail changes direction by following Owl Run up a steeper ravine to the plateau.

Cranberry Swamp Natural Area: The 144-acre swamp is different than almost all of the swamps, bogs, and wetlands that I have explored in Pennsylvania. On one July visit I could actually walk out into the swamp by stepping on hummocks without getting my feet wet. Small pines are scattered across the wetland, and an island of pines is in the middle. The swamp is the headwaters of Cranberry Run, a black-water stream with areas of open water toward the outlet. Lots of hundred-year-old stumps are visible in the swamp. Before the large trees were cut, the ground was probably drier because the

Benjamin Road was an effective firebreak during the large Benjamin Fire.

trees transpired a tremendous amount of water. From Route 144 take Pete's Run Road for 2.8 miles, turn right onto Benjamin Run Road for 0.5 mile (check out the obvious signs of the Benjamin Fire), and then turn right on Cranberry Road for 0.4 mile. The road goes downhill and enters the forest, with parking 100 feet before the gate. The wet areas around the swamp always make access difficult, so visit when conditions have been dry. If the weather has been rainy, a small section of swamp is visible if you walk down the pipeline to the wet inlet area. Otherwise, it is better if you hike on the road 100 yards past the gate and bushwack at a slight angle toward the swamp and away from the pipeline. Pick your way into the swamp. The map shows a trail around the swamp, but it is poorly marked or not marked at all.

East Branch Swamp Natural Area: One way to locate the trail around the natural area is to park at the bottom of Coon Run Road near East Branch stream. From here you can hike the trail on either side of the swamp; I chose the west side. Down the dirt lane on the right is what remains of the base of a giant tree more than 4 feet wide that fell and burned a long time ago. The trailhead is past the cabin and blazed yellow. Along the trail the forest floor is covered with ferns, and below the trail is one of the largest stands of mountain laurel I have ever seen. They bloom during the last two weeks of June. Most of the old-growth hemlocks were knocked down by the 1985 tornado, and the few remaining are hard to reach.

Tamarack Swamp Natural Area: This 267-acre natural area is actually a nonglacial bog with boreal conifers typically found in Canada. It is along Route 144, approximately 5.5 miles north of Renovo. The swamp was named for the tamarack tree, the only deciduous conifer tree in Pennsylvania. To have black spruce, balsam fir, and tamarack together in one area is unusual in Pennsylvania. It has been designated an important bird area by the Audubon Society. Species include golden-winged warbler, great crested flycatcher, alder flycatcher, black-billed cuckoo, and northern waterthrush. Three plants are listed as rare, and Hooker's orchid is one of two plants that are endangered. During the 1990s, the Western Pennsylvania Conservancy purchased more than 9,000 acres to add to the state forest, including a third of the bog. Land development and oil and gas extraction threaten the natural area. A gas pipeline runs through the middle of the swamp.

Recreation. The two main trails are the 50-mile double-loop Chuck Keiper Trail south of Route 120 and the 90-mile Donut Hole Trail north of Route 120. The western loop of Keiper Trail bisects the 9,600-acre Two Rock Run Fire area, where 90 percent of the trees died. Paddling on the West Branch of the Susquehanna River from Karthaus to Keating is superb. There are a number of kayak and canoe access areas along the river, and commercial companies have rentals and shuttles. Mountain bikers and horseback riders can ride on any trails and forest roads except Keiper and Donut Hole trails. Eagle Mine Camp Trail, 21 miles long, is a shared-use trail designed for mountain bikers, and there is a 15-mile equestrian loop trail from Kettle Creek SP. Other activities include hunting, fishing on 400 miles of cold-water streams, cross-country skiing, and snowmobiling. State forest map and trail maps are essential in this rugged region.

NC9 Hyner View State Park and Hyner Run State Park, Clinton County

Hyner View SP—famous for its view—is the best hang-gliding location in Pennsylvania and one of the best in the eastern US. The view from the large, stone retaining wall is breathtaking. This 6-acre park is surrounded

Winter scene from Hyner View SP. Winter access is difficult or impossible on the 4-mile, unplowed road; 3 inches of snow at the bottom of the road increases to 10 inches at the top.

The West Branch of the Susquehanna River
1,300 feet below

by Sproul State Forest and is 1,300 feet above the West Branch of the Susquehanna River. The trees at the vista were removed to open the entire spectacular view of the undeveloped mountains and steep valleys of Sproul SF on the other side of the river. There is a 20-mile view in both directions of the river valley, which Bucktail SP NA partially protects. Driving the 4.4-mile Hyner View Road, with its steep drop-offs and hairpin turns, is a mini-adventure in itself. The road widening and recently installed guardrails have tamed it somewhat. The road is not plowed in the winter, which is understandable but unfortunate, because the view of the mountain ridges and valleys is accentuated with snow on the ground.

At the top are a small picnic area, parking, a large viewing terrace and wall, a bronze monument to the young men of the CCC who built the park's structures, and a stone monument to the dedicated state forest fire wardens. On one of my visits, a park ranger was conducting a class on raptors and owls. Every year hundreds of trail-running enthusiasts enter the 25K or 50K Hyner View Trail Challenge. Athletes run through the forest on a single track and must endure major climbs, descents, and stream crossings to complete the course within nine hours.

Hang Gliding. Standing next to flyers as they take flight with their hang gliders and watching two or three soaring overhead is an awesome spectacle.

Sisters watching the sunset

Hang gliders launch from the lookout area and, if conditions are right, will soar for hours.

A black-phase timber rattlesnake slithers across the path next to the lookout.

Behind the campground at Hyner Run SP

On nice weekends or holidays, spectators line the wall. The flyers, with assistance from friends, carry their gliders down to the takeoff area below the stone wall. When safety checks are completed, they run downhill for no more than 30 feet, and as soon as they are airborne, they zip their legs into what looks like a sleeping bag. After that they are free as a bird. By adjusting their grip on the control bar they can change direction and air speed. Normally, flights last an hour or two, and then fatigue sets in. If thermals are just right, some flyers have stayed aloft for up to five hours and reached altitudes of 10,000 feet. They like to drop down into the valley and then maneuver toward the mountain to pick up thermals or winds blowing up the mountain and over the viewing area. If conditions are not ideal they still take off and descend gradually to the grassy landing strip, where they execute a controlled landing on their belly. Every year the Hyner Club holds five fly-in events with camping at the landing zone and nearby Hyner Run SP.

Hyner Run SP. Hyner Run SP is a quaint 180-acre park surrounded by Sproul SF. It was the site of a CCC camp in the 1930s and opened as a state park in 1958. The park has a thirty-site modern campground with tall pines and a rhododendron-lined stream. There is also a large two-story cabin, a picnic area with two pavilions, and a beautiful swimming pool with a separate kids wading pool. Scenic Hyner Park Trail starts from the campground, heads toward the picnic area and pool, and then follows the stream through the pine forest. The trailhead for long Donut Hole Trail is in the park.

NC10 Black Moshannon State Park, Centre County

Black Moshannon SP is a beautiful 3,394-acre park on a high mountain plateau. The park's long, narrow lake is fed by springs and small streams from five separate wetlands. A large wetland area was designated by the DCNR as Black Moshannon Bog Natural Area; the bog is the largest restored wetland in Pennsylvania. The name "Moshannon" is believed to be the English

Before sunrise at the southern end of the Bog
Trail, Moshannon SP

version of the Native American name for "moose stream," and "Black" was added to describe the color of the swamp's tannin-colored water. The park and adjacent parcels of private land are surrounded by Moshannon SF.

History. During the timber era, Beaver Mill Lumber Co.—one of the largest lumber companies in Pennsylvania—operated four mills and lumber towns. The remains of the company's Star Mill, built in 1879, can be seen along the Star Mill Trail. After the timber was depleted and the mills were closed, the pond remained a local picnic area. Between 1933 and 1937, the Civilian Conservation Corps established a camp and built the park's cabins, pavilions, dam, trails, and roads and planted trees. All the structures are still in use and are listed on the National Register of Historic Places. The state park opened in 1937, and relatively small Mid-State Airport, along the park's southwest border, was opened in 1942.

Nature. The park, with a lake elevation of 1,900 feet, is on the eastern edge of Allegheny Plateau, near the transition to the Ridge and Valley Appalachians. Unlike typical glacially created bogs, Moshannon's bog and lake are in a natural basin. This basin also traps cold air that sinks from the surrounding higher elevations, creating seasonal temperatures that are comparable to locations far to the north. The bog's low-nutrient soil, highly acidic water, and cool climate create an environment conducive to

The view looking northeast from the Bog Trail

specialized plants and shrubs. Three species of carnivorous plants, arctic cotton grass, and an incredible seventeen different orchids are found in the park's bogs. The 1,992-acre natural area is also host to cranberry, blueberry, viburnum, and leatherleaf shrubs.

The park was designated an important bird area. With its diversified habitats and location along the Allegheny Front, it is not surprising that 175 species of birds have been recorded. An abbreviated list of waterfowl includes common loon, greater and lesser scaup, hooded and red-breasted mergansers, tundra swan, pied-billed and Slavonian grebes, northern shoveler, American wigeon, and many species of ducks. Migrating raptors and shorebirds include golden and bald eagles, osprey, northern harrier, greater and lesser yellowlegs, and three species of sandpipers. Six species of hawks, barred owls, Virginia rail, sora, northern waterthrush, alder flycatcher, and numerous species of warblers and vireos have been observed nesting in the state park and forest.

Sections of the Star Mill Trail follow the lake shoreline through a forest of hemlock, oak, beech, varieties of spruce, and a red pine plantation. At the southern end of the trail is a stand of balsam fir, with the largest only 5 inches in diameter and 40 feet tall. The 40-foot trees, along with trees less than 12 feet tall, indicate that the stand is a planted population that is naturalizing. Near the trail is a small stand of old-growth hemlocks and two 100-foot-tall red oaks with girths of 9 feet.

Black Moshannon Lake from
the bridge near the beach

The boardwalk through the bog

This angler had the entire
lake to himself. October

Trails. The park and state forest have more than 20 miles of multiuse trails for hiking, mountain biking, horseback riding, cross-country skiing, and snowmobiling. My visits to the park usually include an easy hike on both of the bog loop trails. The half-mile Bog Trail is a raised boardwalk, enabling visitors to walk through the bog and view its wildlife, insects, and unique plants. For those who enjoy solitude in a wilderness environment, the Blueberry Trail and 7.7-mile Moss-Hanne Trail are ideal. The 1-mile Blueberry Trail passes through a wetland of tall shrubs. The parking area is on the left side of Airport Road, before the airport fence. Several points of access to the Moss-Hanne Trail allow shorter out-and-back hikes. The Shingle Mill Trail follows the Black Moshannon Creek through the scenic valley downstream from the dam. Due to colder winter temperatures, the lake is the region's first to freeze thick enough for ice fishing, and the cross-country skiing trails have more and longer-lasting snow. Some of the most popular trails for cross-country skiing are Hay Road Trail, Indian, Seneca, and Sleepy Hollow.

Recreation. The modern campground has seventy-two sites, twenty-one cabins of three different types, and an organized-group camping area. The park also has eight pavilions and four picnic areas, and a white-sand swimming beach where the lake narrows in a picturesque setting. Boating, fishing, and bird watching are popular activities on the gorgeous 250-acre lake. To preserve the serene setting, only human- and electric-powered boats are allowed. Four boat launches and a fishing pier provide convenient lake access. The warm-water fishery has largemouth bass, perch, pickerel, northern pike, muskellunge, crappie, bullhead catfish, and panfish. Rainbow and brown trout are stocked in Black Moshannon Creek. Hunting is permitted in the state forest and certain areas of the park.

NC11 Bald Eagle State Park, Centre County

This 5,900-acre park is a popular recreational destination, with plenty of diverse habitat for wildlife and nature lovers. It is only 10 miles from I-80, in a broad valley that was formerly farmland. The 1,730-acre Sayers Reservoir—the central feature of the park—is 8 miles long and has 23 miles of shoreline. The flood-control dam was built in 1969 and is operated by the Army Corps

The meadows along Main Park Road near the recreation area, Bald Eagle SP

Pontoon boats are popular on Foster Sayers Lake.

The park quickly changes character after Labor Day weekend (mid-September).

of Engineers. Bald Eagle SP opened in 1971, with the recreational facilities operated by the Pennsylvania DCNR in a cooperative effort with ACE. Another distinguishing feature of the park is its stunning fields and meadows, which for birders are some of the best in the state. The DCNR manages the fields to maintain an extensive variety of plants and habitats.

Lake Activities. Boating, fishing, waterskiing, and tubing are popular activities on the lake, but be aware of the lake's boating regulations. The huge marina has 369 slips for seasonal rental, plus additional slips for daily rental. The boating concession rents several types of fishing boats, pontoon boats, and jet skis during summer months and fall weekends. Six boat launches and one canoe launch are on the lake's north shore, and one launch is on the south shore. Anglers fish for large and smallmouth bass, perch, tiger muskellunge, crappie, channel catfish, and walleye. All boat launches have twenty-four-hour access. A fishing pier is next to the Winter Launch.

Recreation. The huge recreational area at the north shore point has a 1,200-foot curved, sandy beach, food concession, and shower facilities. There are also five picnic areas, nine pavilions, playgrounds, and volleyball nets. The modern campground has ninety-seven sites, two yurts, and three cottages. Trees have been planted, but bring your own shade. The primitive campground is wooded and near the south shoreline. It has thirty-five walk-in sites and thirty-five sites for camping vehicles. Hunting is permitted on 4,900 acres of the park, plus Game Lands #323, which borders the park. Winter sports include ice fishing, skating, and sledding in designated areas. Several trails and unplowed roads are available for cross-country skiing.

Habitat & Wildlife. According to the Audubon Society, Bald Eagle State Park has one of the largest bird species lists of all sites in Pennsylvania. The park is situated between Allegheny Plateau to the northwest and

View from the Nature Inn, the state park system's first inn

Ice fishing on the lake

Ridge and Valley Province to the southeast. Bald Eagle Mountain, rising 1,100 feet above the lake, is the farthest west of the Allegheny Mountains. The DCNR manages the habitat to include mowed fields, grasslands, wildflower meadows, wild shrubland, pockets of woods, a pond with wetland vegetation, and forestland. A four-year research project was conducted to learn what type of shrub habitat is preferred by the increasingly rare golden-winged warbler and the worm-eating woodcock. Their numbers in the northeastern US have plummeted at a yearly rate of 20 percent due to loss of habitat. We no longer have major forest fires, floods, or abandoned farm fields, and invasive shrubs are competing with native species. The Bureau of Forestry is now working to improve that type of habitat in parts of thirty counties.

Birding & Trails. The park was designated an important bird area for its large numbers of migrating birds that stop to rest and feed. It also has an impressive number of nesting species. Eagles can be spotted all year because the lake has open water in the winter. One pair of eagles is one of the most productive in the state, fledging two or three eaglets regularly every year. Preparations begin in January and February, when they diligently add more sticks to their expanding nest. At the end of F. J. Sayers Road you can watch their activity on their nest across the lake on the south shore. Another good spot to look for eagles is the lookout near Pavilion #5.

The park has nine named trails and many other trails that connect recreational areas. One of the best nature trails is the 1.25-mile Butterfly Trail, which meanders through more than a dozen gardens and fields with plants that butterflies need for each phase of their life. The trail also passes the Frog Pond and its wetland, which attracts migrating waterfowl. The Skyline Trail is a relatively easy 2-mile hike through forest and areas of dense shrubbery, and a good place to look for migrating wood warblers. More than thirty warblers have been recorded in the park. A popular trail for viewing waterfowl, gulls, terns, shorebirds, and wading birds is the 1.75-mile Woapalanne Trail, which begins at Pavilions 6 and 7 and heads east along the shoreline. Blue Bird Trail transects an area where sixty bluebird boxes were installed. Both blue birds and swallows occupy the boxes.

Before you go bird watching you should consider visiting the eBird Trail Tracker kiosk at the Nature Inn to learn what birds have been reported by previous bird watchers and where and when they were observed in the park. You can also add your own bird observations (for online information about the eBird program, go to www.birds.cornell.edu/is/ett). Environmental-education specialists conduct nature programs, hikes, and other activities.

Nature Inn at Bald Eagle. The DCNR made the bold decision to build this beautiful inn, the first in the state park system. The modern stone-and-wood inn on high ground has sixteen rooms and suites overlooking the fields and lake. It also has a breakfast room with an adjoining deck, and a patio for outdoor cooking. A nesting pair of eagles can be seen from the inn. It is a popular destination, especially in the summer and fall, so make reservations (814-625-2879) months in advance.

NC12 Snyder-Middleswarth Natural Area and Bald Eagle State Forest, Snyder County

Within 500-acre Snyder Middleswarth NA is a 250-acre, half-mile-long virgin forest of mostly hemlock trees. It is in the valley between Thick Mountain and Buck Mountain, with Tall Timbers NA to the west and Middleswarth Picnic Area to the east. Until the early 1990s, Snyder Middleswarth was a state park, and Tall Timbers was a Bald Eagle SF natural area; now they both are SF natural areas. It is not known why this stand of old-growth trees was passed over by the timber companies.

One of many old-growth trees along Snyder-Middleswarth Trail

Old-growth forest from the Hemlock Trail above Swift Run

The giant hemlocks are dying due to the microscopic hemlock woolly adelgid.

Speculation that it was too difficult to haul the timber or that the trees were less desirable hemlock does not make sense because the entire forest surrounding the old-growth trees was cut. In 1902, the state bought 14,000 acres, including this natural area, and gave it protection. A sign at the trailhead commemorates the forest as a national natural landmark.

Rock Springs Picnic Area is a half mile downstream, along Swift Run Road. A trail from this picnic area leads down to a small tributary waterfall with inclined rock outcrops on each side. Approximately 2 miles west, the vista on Locust Ridge Road provides an awesome view of the valley between Jack's Mountain and Thick Mountain.

Driving across the mountains of the Ridge and Valley Physiographic Province can be daunting at times, but one of the many pleasures of traveling to remote places in this region, or any remote area in Pennsylvania, is witnessing rural life and culture. The isolated farms and communities in Pennsylvania project a peaceful, simpler, grassroots way of life. It is hard to resist taking photographs every mile or so of the beautiful Amish farms.

Trails. The Swift Run Trail and Hemlock Trail form a 1-mile loop through the natural area, starting from the picnic area. Most visitors hike up the valley on Swift Run Trail, which stays close to the stream on the right side. The trail is well worn, but because it is at the bottom of the V-shaped ravine, sections of the trail are rocky and up and down and can be wet. After a half

A typical hemlock grows straight as an arrow.

This nontypical hemlock adjusted to surrounding conditions as it grew.

mile and a 250-foot gain in elevation, turn left onto a short trail with a bridge that crosses the stream and connects with Hemlock Trail for the descent back down to the parking area. The Hemlock Trail hugs the mountainside 50 to 75 feet above the stream. From here the perspective is different; you are looking level at the treetops instead of up. The trail goes through areas where it is obvious that several big trees were knocked down, and in the new sunlight dense thickets of young birch or white pine have staked their claim. Near the parking area, the trail crosses a small stream called Swift Run, which originates from a separate valley.

Nature. The size and number of these trees was impressive, but this is a forest of trees of all ages with a dense understory in many areas, especially along the stream. I had hiked only 50 yards when a sharped-shinned hawk took off and landed on a low branch a short distance ahead. Each time I proceeded farther up the ravine the hawk did too. Eventually, it had enough of me and flew out of the ravine. Apparently this place was its meal ticket. In the distance I heard a pileated woodpecker squawking and tapping at tree bark, searching for insects. Besides hemlocks, there are a few yellow birch and white pine along the trail. On the mountainside and ridge you will find old-growth black birch, chestnut oak, and pitch pine. The shaded forest floor is covered with ferns. Along the stream and trail is a healthy but chaotic-

The view from Locust Ridge Road, west of
Snyder-Middleswarth NA

looking environment of saplings, ferns, moss-covered boulders, trees of
every size, and some fallen old trees. The stream itself is choked with wood
debris. The debris might not look picturesque, but it performs an important
function, creating pools for native brook trout, amphibians, and insects, and
habitat for rodents, such as masked shrews, short-tailed shrews, mice, and
chipmunks. Mink, fox, weasels, birds—including the hawk I saw—and other
forest creatures depend on rodents as a food source.

Strong winds and heavy rain have toppled several old trees within the
past three years. I am surprised and alarmed how often it occurs in almost
all of our old-growth forests. The forest floor is littered with moss-covered
trees that decompose and contribute organic material back into the soil.
Ferns and young trees have the ability to start life directly on the fallen trees.
Unfortunately, another characteristic that Snyder Middleswarth NA shares
with other stands of ancient hemlock in Pennsylvania is the invasive insect
hemlock woolly adelgid, which is killing the hemlocks. Some of the trees in
the natural area are dead but still standing, and others look like they will
be dead within a few years. It seems the first to die are usually the larger
and older trees. On a positive note, more than half the hemlocks looked
healthy and unaffected. The tallest trees are more than 150 feet high and at
least 40 inches in diameter. The oldest trees are estimated to be between
350 and 400 years old. The growth rings on one fallen tree revealed it was
347 years old. The width of the tree rings implies that they grew at a faster
rate when they were young and their growth gradually slowed down, but
in reality as they age, their annual gain in mass actually increases.

South-Central Region

SC1 Rothrock State Forest Natural Areas, Huntingdon County

The 96,956-acre Rothrock SF is in the rugged Ridge and Valley Province of central Pennsylvania. Within the state forest are six natural areas, two wild areas, and four state parks. The natural areas in the northern portion of the state forest are Bear Meadows, Detweiler Run, and Alan Seeger. All three are surrounded by or adjacent to Thickhead Wild Area and have a substantial number of old-growth trees.

State Parks. All four state parks are in the SF's northern region and offer a wide range of activities and facilities. Penn-Roosevelt SP is a quiet, isolated park with a primitive campground, small lake, and extensive CCC stonework at the dam and raceways. On a recent off-season visit, I was the only person camping in the park. Greenwood Furnace SP was originally an eighteenth-century iron-making industrial community. The lovely park has a lake, beach, concessions, and modern campground and conducts tours of the preserved historic buildings. Scenic Reeds Gap SP is along beautiful Honey Creek. It has a large swimming pool, concessions, modern shower buildings, and a secluded camping area. Wipple Dam SP is a very popular day-use park. The lake has separate sections for recreation and nature, a large beach, boat launch and rentals (nonpowered only), and concessions.

Bear Meadows NA. Within the spectacular 890-acre Bear Meadows NA is one of the largest bogs in the eastern US. The 320-acre boreal bog was designated a national natural landmark in 1965. The wetland, with an elevation of 1,820 feet, is surrounded by forested mountains ranging between 2,200 and 2,400 feet. Just above the bog's upper end, springs provide a steady low-volume source of acidic groundwater to the bog. The other source of water is slightly acidic rainwater. Sinking Creek's dark-colored tannic water flows out of the bog through the only opening in the bowl. For thousands of years, the bog, which began as a lake, has gradually filled with sediment and decaying sphagnum moss. Compressed layers of peat are now 8 feet thick. Trees and shrubs have encroached into much of the bog.

This high-altitude environment shares similar characteristics with Canadian boreal forests. Fortunately, many of the perimeter trees were never logged. Old-growth species include hemlock up to 350 years old; black birch; black gum; red, white, and chestnut oak; white pine; spruce; poplar; and balsam fir. Their growth is slow due to low-nutrient soil, acidic water, and relatively cold climate. A spruce measured only 15 inches in diameter and 71 feet high, yet its core sample proved it to be 223 years old. Another unique characteristic of this natural area is that it is one of the few sites in Pennsylvania where six different conifer species are growing

Bear Meadows NA and surrounding ridge, Rothrock SF

The spring-fed west section of the bog

naturally in the same location: hemlock, pitch pine, white pine, red spruce, black spruce, and balsam fir. The bog's unique habitat supports several species of orchids and Pennsylvania's three carnivorous plants. Bears frequent the bog in mid- to late summer for highbush blueberry shrubs.

The well-worn, rocky, and sometimes wet 3.5-mile Bear Meadows Trail circumnavigates the bog. Parking is near Sinking Creek bridge, and the trailhead is 100 feet south. The trail's orange blazes are somewhat far apart. Along the south side of the bog the trail goes through one of the tallest and most dense stands of rhododendron I have ever seen. One interesting observation was that nothing, including rhododendron, grew directly under large hemlock trees. The only place along the trail that provided easy access to the bog was at the far western end through a stand of hemlocks. I did see signs of bear and beaver along the trail. One 16-inch tree was chewed halfway through by beavers, then for some mysterious reason it was abandoned. The bog provides winter habitat for northern birds such as pine siskins, redpolls, and red- and white-winged crossbills. Hemlocks and rhododendron thickets provide nesting habitat for many warblers and other deep-forest birds. In the fall, the berries of the black gum trees are a favorite food for migrating birds. The trail ends at North Meadow Road. Turn right and walk 0.25 miles to Bear Meadow Road and another small parking area. Turn right and walk 0.6 miles to your starting point. The natural area offers solitude and a beautiful and an interesting environment, with only the sounds of birds singing and leaves rustling.

Detweiler Run NA. Detweiler Run NA is one of the most rugged and least visited of the state's natural areas. This 463-acre, 2-mile-long natural area encompasses a steep ravine, an old-growth forest, and headwaters for Detweiler Run. The parallel ridges have an average elevation of 2,200 feet, and the bottom of the ravine descends from 1,700 feet to 1,300 feet. The forest in the ravine was never harvested because two logging operations

Detweiler Run NA's old-growth hemlocks, Rothrock SF

The trail through Alan Seeger NA's old-growth forest, Rothrock SF

disputed ownership of 45 acres. Old-growth hemlock and white pine are the dominant species near the stream. Deciduous trees such as chestnut oak, red oak, black gum, yellow-poplar, black and yellow birch, and pitch pine are scattered along the stream and up both mountainsides. Thick stands of ancient rhododendron grow 20 feet high along Detweiler Run and make it almost impossible to see the stream. The water is shaded and cool for native brook trout. One tree expert found a hemlock with a girth of 13.4 feet and an estimated age of more than 500 years. He also found one of the state's tallest pitch pine.

Two parallel trails—Detweiler Run Road and Mid-State Trail (MST)—can be combined with the blue-blazed Axeman (connector) Trail to form a loop through the natural area. For a longer loop, use the pipeline at the northeast boundary as the connector trail. Park where Detweiler Run Road intersects Bear Meadows Road. From the yellow gate, take the orange-blazed Mid-State Trail into the ravine, then upstream along babbling Detweiler Run. The trail is surprisingly well maintained and is cleared fairly wide. You might encounter one or two fallen trees. The trail becomes more rugged and rocky the farther upstream you hike, but the scenery is gorgeous. Detweiler Road starts at the gate and runs parallel, but well above the stream. You will see several old springhouses and open areas of rocks and talus.

The NA was designated an important bird area, as well as an amphibian/reptile protected area. Be aware that this area is a haven for rattlesnakes, but the odds are very low that you will see one. The natural area is also a top location for butterfly enthusiasts. An abbreviated list includes spring azure, morning cloak, red and white admirals, tortoiseshell, red spotted purple, and great-spangled fritillaries. Many deep-woods birds breed here. This habitat is also ideal for many species of mammals. In fact, it is believed that the Detweiler Valley region was home to some of the last wolves in Pennsylvania. Not far from Detweiler Run NA, on Wampler Road, is a vista

The dense stands of rhododendron make this a rare view of Detweiler Run.

Mid-State Trail parallels the stream through most of the NA.

The branchless main trunk of an old but healthy hemlock

worth visiting. The road is rough, and the drop-off along the road is one of the steepest slopes I have encountered in Pennsylvania

Alan Seeger NA. The 390-acre natural area encompasses 118 acres of virgin forest, considered to be one of the finest in Pennsylvania. The old-growth trees include eastern hemlock, white pine, chestnut, red and white oaks, yellow-poplar, red maple, black gum, white ash, and cucumber trees. Some of the hemlocks are believed to be more than 500 years old, and one has a girth of 11 feet. Results of extensive surveys list the height of a yellow-poplar and white pine at 137 feet. The most likely reason this stand of trees was spared is that ownership of the land or its timber was disputed. The State Forest Commission preserved this area as a forest monument in 1921.

The best way to view the natural area is by hiking the 0.8-mile Alan Seeger Trail, which is an open-loop trail. Two small parking areas and a picnic area are along beautiful Detweiler Run. The trailhead, if hiking counterclockwise, is approximately 50 yards past the second parking area, on the left side of Seeger Road. The trail is not marked but is well worn. It follows Standing Stone Creek and tunnels through a dense stand of ancient 20-foot-tall rhododendron. Tall hemlocks are everywhere, but sadly many are either dead or dying due to the invasive hemlock woolly adelgid. After crossing several small bridges and reaching the halfway point, you will notice a distinct change in the forest. This section of forest has fewer old hemlocks, and the forest understory is more open. Interestingly, the second section has a lower percentage of dead and dying old-growth hemlocks than the first section. The trail ends on Stone Creek Road.

Breeding birds include many species of warblers, ovenbird, flycatchers, pewee, Louisiana waterthrush, and wood thrush. The damp, cool forest is also great habitat for a long list of mosses, fungi, and mushrooms that serve an important function by breaking down the fallen trees into light organic material called duff. The second-generation forest along Stone Creek Road is an unusually dense stand of tall, perfectly straight hemlocks with patches of rhododendron as the open understory. It looks magical in the warm glow before sunset.

SC2 Raystown Lake Recreation Area, Huntingdon County

Raystown Lake Recreation Area is an exceptional destination for boaters, anglers, mountain bikers, and everyone who enjoys outdoor recreation. Raystown Lake—the largest lake within the state's borders—was created when the Army Corps of Engineers built a dam across the Raystown Branch of the Juniata River. The project's mission is to control flooding, generate hydroelectric power, and provide recreation. The dam was completed in 1972, just in time for the lake to be filled by Hurricane Agnes and prevent an estimated $60 million in damage to the valleys below. The park attracts 1.5 million visitors annually, but you can always find places to escape. On weekdays in the off-season the park feels deserted.

The 8,300-acre reservoir is surrounded by 21,000 acres of forested mountains and old farm fields. Adjacent to the Raystown Project are Rothrock SF, Trough Creek SP, and state game lands. The 30-mile-long (straight-line distance) lake is actually much longer, because it lies in a serpentine valley with more than twenty bends. The shoreline, with its countless coves, inlets, and peninsulas, is 180 miles long. At normal lake level the maximum depth is approximately 190 feet, with an average of 80 feet. One especially attractive feature of the property is the vast amount of natural habitat surrounding the lake. The mountains on the lake's eastern shoreline rise 1,000 feet above the lake, and numerous large cliffs rise nearly vertical from the shore.

Habitat. Raystown Project's great diversity of habitat includes wetlands, mudflats, shallow ponds for waterfowl, meadows, fields planted with warm- and cold-season grasses, crabapple and fruit orchards, shrublands, 200 acres of food plots, and old fields that are now early successional woodlands. The lake's depth allows a fishery both of warm- and cold-water species. The mission of the fishery management program is to add structures, stock fish, conduct research, improve shoreline vegetation, and reduce erosion.

Wildlife. Eagles thrive at Raystown Lake because there are many miles of shoreline with trees for perching. The lake has a healthy fishery, and parts of the lake never freeze. Eagles also benefit from the high-quality

Hawn's Overlook provides an excellent view of Raystown Lake.

stream and habitat below the dam; as many as nineteen eagles have been recorded during annual winter surveys. The four best places to spot eagles are at the northern end of the lake, along the stream, at Aitch Recreation Area, and at Tatman Run. Near Tatman Run, winter sightings of fifteen to twenty eagles are not unusual.

The best areas to find migrating waterfowl, gulls, shorebirds, and wading birds are in the long inlets on the west side of the lake. Occasionally waterfowl can be seen on open water. A partial list of waterfowl includes three species of mergansers, three species of grebes, common loon, American scooter, and more than a dozen species of ducks. Ring-billed and herring gulls are commonly seen at the Aitch Boat Launch, and Bonaparte's gulls are often observed at the lake's northern end. Solitary and spotted sandpipers, killdeer, and other birds work the mudflats, while bitterns and green and blue herons wade in the shallow water. The lake's marshy wetlands also provide habitat for some of the state's rarer birds. Other birding locations are Ridenour Lookout, the Hilltop Picnic Area, Weller Road fields, and the ponds in the Game Commission's Aitch Propagation Area, which is closed during nesting season. With some luck, you might see river otters at the north end of the lake. They like to lie on large rocks but are often overlooked because their dark fur blends in with the shadows, and they quickly disappear underwater and can swim as far as a quarter mile before resurfacing.

One morning in late October, in the Weller Road area, I had the pleasant experience of walking into the middle of a flock of more than 1,000 cedar waxwings. They ignored me as they gorged themselves on red berries,

Early-morning sun lights up a forest of vines and a lone great blue heron.

The new bike park is across the road from the park office.

moving from tree to tree in groups of fifty to one hundred. Hundreds of birds were perched in nearby trees, patiently waiting their turn. Another memorable moment occurred later that day, when I was watching a beautiful sunset from Hawn's Lookout. Immediately after the sun disappeared, I was serenaded for ten minutes with the unmistakable calls of a loon and screech owl.

Boating. Raystown Lake is one of the top boating destinations in Pennsylvania. You will see every type and size of boat on the lake, including 70-foot houseboats and luxury boats. Even sea planes are permitted to land on the lake. Many houseboat owners enjoy spending the night anchored in a secluded cove. Unlike most large lakes, Raystown's coves, inlets, and no-wake zones provide an infinite number of quiet and safe places for kayakers and anglers. The park has six boat launches. Full-service Seven Points Marina—the largest in Pennsylvania—has dockage for 946 boats with various leases. The marina rents a wide range of boats, from kayaks to large houseboats, and is the home port for the double-deck tour boat *Princess Lake Cruiser*.

Fishing. The lake is famous for its excellent fishery, which includes muskie, lake trout, Atlantic salmon, striped bass, largemouth and smallmouth bass, walleye, brown trout, crappie, perch, channel catfish, carp, and bluegill. The state record (53 lb., 12 oz.) striped bass was caught here. Every year anglers catch 40-pound muskies, 15-pound walleye, and huge stripers. Fishing from shore or Aitch RA's pier can be productive, especially at night. The river below the dam is also a great place to fish. To maintain the excellent fishery, most anglers practice "catch and release" fishing.

Hiking Trails. The park has more than 70 miles of hiking trails. The 0.5-mile Hillside Trail winds through overgrown fields and woodland past a pond and provides a scenic view of Seven Points Bay. Riverside Trail begins below the dam, parallels the Raystown Branch stream, and passes through

Racing to his favorite fishing spot

wetlands to an observation platform, then through successional forest and fields that support woodcock, ruffed grouse, and turkey. The 29-mile Terrace Mountain Trail is a popular backpacking trail that passes through the remote and scenic forests along the eastern edge of the lake.

Mountain Biking. Raystown Project's Allegrippis Trail System (ATS) is a premier single-track trail system built by the International Mountain Biking Association in 2009. The twenty-four trails totaling 36 miles were laid out in stacked loops and were designed for riders of all levels. The ATS has become a renowned destination and hosts major events such as the annual Dirt Rag Dirt Fest, which draws 3,000 bikers. A 5-acre bike park in front of the visitor center opened in 2016. The wide dirt track sits below the road, providing spectators with a complete view of the track. Its three skill level circuits on rolling terrain incorporate wood and dirt bridges, berms, jumps, and high-banked turns.

Recreation. The modern Seven Points campground has 261 sites in six areas near the marina and beach. Some sites are on the water. A great place for kayak or canoe camping is primitive Susquehannock CG—at the end of a long peninsula—with sixty-one mostly shaded sites, including some that are on the water. Near the CG, but now underwater, professional archeologists excavated the famous Sheep Rock Shelter and found 12,000-year-old human remains. For a real escape, rustic Nancy's Boat-to-Shore CG is accessed by boat only. The park's vistas are always worth visiting. Hawn's Overlook—my favorite—is an easy 300-yard walk from

The trees were filled with nearly 1,000 cedar waxwings migrating together.

the lot to the end of a ridge with a sheer cliff to the water. The sunsets are magnificent, but photography is better in the morning. Hunting is permitted in designated areas. The park has two beautiful, large, sandy beaches: Seven Points Beach has showers and food concession, and Tatman Beach has more-primitive facilities. The lake's clarity also attracts scuba divers.

SC3 Trough Creek State Park, Huntingdon County

Trough Creek State Park is a 541-acre scenic gorge with unique geologic and historical features. Beautiful serpentine-shaped Great Trough Creek cuts its way through the gorge and empties into a cove in Raystown Lake. In this relatively small park, you get the feeling of being in a remote and isolated location because it is surrounded by thousands of acres of Rothrock SF and the Army Corps of Engineers' Raystown Lake Project. There is only one road through the park, and it is a dead end. On weekdays in the off-season the park has few visitors.

The gorge was created over millions of years by the erosive force of the stream and rainwater seeping into cracks in the rock and expanding when it froze. Rocks broke apart and fell from cliffs to the bottom of the gorge, where the stream carried them away. Evidence of these geologic processes is seen in the park at Copperas Rock, Rainbow Falls, Balanced Rock, Raven Rock, and the boulder fields above the Ice Mine.

Paradise Furnace. Near the park office are the preserved buildings and structures of Paradise Furnace, which was built in 1827 and is listed on the National Register of Historic Places. Paradise Furnace was built and operated by "ironmaster" Reuben Trexler. Iron making required a vast acreage of forests to make charcoal, a stream for waterpower, and a close source of iron ore. It also required housing, a mill, and farm fields for food and grain for the teams of horses. The collier and his assistants made charcoal, and a large labor force cut timber. The preserved buildings at Paradise Furnace include the ironmaster's mansion, the remains of the stone furnace, and the log home for workers, built in the late 1700s. The buildings are not open to the public, but the ironmaster's home is available

Balanced Rock high above Trough Creek

to rent. By 1840, new furnaces were using anthracite coal and gradually switched to coke made from bituminous coal. Shipping raw materials by the new railroads meant new furnaces could be built near population centers. Most of the rural charcoal furnaces did not modernize and were closed by 1870.

Copperas Rock. Copperas Rock is a stream-cut cliff named for its copper-colored stains. Groundwater seeping out of the rock carries ferrous sulfate that leaches from a small pocket of coal. This mineral is one of the main pollutants in the drainage of abandoned mines, but the small quantity at Copperas Rock does not harm the stream. The stream's power to cut into rock is obvious here.

Balanced Rock. On top of a high cliff undercut by the stream is a huge rock precariously balanced on the edge of the cliff. It looks as though it could roll over the edge at any moment, but it has been in this position for thousands of years. The overhanging sandstone block broke from rock that has been eroded away. The underlying softer rock also eroded, leaving this block in its current position.

Ice Mine. The ice mine is actually a short shaft dug into the hillside by early prospectors searching for iron ore deposits. Years later, railroad workers discovered that the shaft's entrance was covered in ice as late as June and July. The mountainside above the shaft is a boulder field several feet deep covered

Ice hanging from Copperas Rock in late February

Water laden with minerals creates the orange stain at Copperas Rock.

by a layer of dirt, leaves, debris, and trees. The coldest winter air sinks into the voids between the lowest boulders, where it is stored. From late spring to midsummer, when the outside air is warm and humid, the cold, dry air in the boulders begins to sink downhill into the shaft. Melting snow and higher humidity freezes at the entrance to the shaft when it meets the frigid air. After July, the air in the boulders warms up and the downward air flow stops. In the 1930s, the CCC built walls around the ice mine and stairs. Today, little ice builds up because the enclosure inhibits the warm- and cold-air dynamics. Between May and July is the best time to feel the ice mine's colder air.

Trails. There are a dozen trails throughout the park. The most popular hike is to Balanced Rock. Park along the road, cross the stream on a suspension bridge, and turn right. The trail was cut into the steep mountainside along the stream and is lined with old rhododendron. The next small bridge crosses Abbot Run below Rainbow Falls. Stone steps help your ascent to the right turn onto Raven Rock Trail and then uphill to Balanced Rock and the scenic view. On a visit after a recent snow, I saw the fresh tracks of a bobcat that had come down the mountain and walked halfway across the suspension bridge. The cat decided to turn around and headed down to the stream to hunt, then bounded back up the steep mountain to its den in the rocks. Another beautiful hike starts at Pavilion #5, crosses the stream on the wooden bridge, and turns right onto Terrace Mountain Trail. Follow the old roadbed past the remains of the stone dam. Go around the gate and follow the trail along the scenic stream, through hemlock and deciduous trees, to the cove at Raystown Lake.

Recreation. The rustic campground has twenty-nine sites with electric that are somewhat open among the tall trees. Hunting is permitted in an area near Raystown Lake property. Great Trough Creek provides fishing for trout and smallmouth bass. A great place to picnic is the area at the eastern end of the park. This large, grassy area with tall trees, tables, restrooms, and pavilion is near the amazing stonework of the old dam and bridge crossing the stream.

Trough Creek

SC4 Hemlocks Natural Area AND Tuscarora State Forest, Perry County

The 120-acre Hemlocks Natural Area is an old-growth forest of mostly hemlock trees in a steep, narrow, rocky ravine. The top of the ravine has a sizable number of old-growth deciduous trees and is the headwater for Patterson Run. Hemlock Road provides access and a great view of the forest. This section of forest was never logged by Perry Lumber Company because of the terrain, the expense of transportation by oxen to the railroad, and the fact that most of the trees were less valuable hemlock. In 1921, the Pennsylvania Forestry Commission preserved the ravine as a forest monument. In 1972, it was designated a national natural landmark.

Eastern Hemlock. The property's environment is more than just natural: it is virgin, pristine, and remote and has a diversity of trees and wildlife. Unfortunately, many of the hemlock trees have died and the entire ecosystem is dependent on the hemlocks. The destruction was caused by the hemlock woolly adelgid, an invasive insect that arrived in the NA in 1999. Since then, 65 percent of the hemlocks have died, mostly in the center section. Many of the dead trees are still standing with their bark and most of their limbs gone, and the trunks' wood has bleached to the color of bone. I see them as the forest's soldiers that fought gallantly but lost an unjust battle. The old-growth hemlocks that have been saved are still vulnerable because they are now more exposed to damaging winds. Also, young hemlocks do not compete well with fast-growing, sun-loving birch trees because the birch's fibrous root systems absorb more nutrients and water than the hemlock's roots.

The tiny adelgid's nymphs insert a stylet into the end branch and inject toxic saliva to suck out the tree's sap. Without sap the needles die and eventually drop off. The following season, new growth will again be food for the adelgid. After approximately four years the tree stops growing and the adelgids die with it. A few trees somehow survive and get healthier for a few years, only to have new adelgids start the cycle again. This cycle

The view across the ravine at
Hemlock NA, Tuscarora SF

Standing reminders of the
past; many more have fallen.

One of the healthy old hemlocks
that was saved from the hemlock
woolly adelgid

can last up to fifteen years before the hemlock finally dies. It has been my
observation that the oldest hemlocks in a ravine are generally the first to
die. It is also interesting that the adelgids do not kill the hemlocks in a
wave pattern. Instead, they spread in a somewhat random pattern because
they are primarily transported by sticking to birds' feet.

The Pennsylvania Bureau of Forestry and agencies in other states are
trying to find a solution to this problem. Genetic research is being conducted
on the western hemlock, which is resistant to the adelgid. Spraying from
the air does not adequately soak the branches. In 2003, predatory beetles
were released, but that experiment failed. Later that year, forestry personnel
laboriously injected a systemic insecticide into the soil around the roots
of all the old-growth hemlocks, with the exception of test trees. Repeat
applications are given every four years, and the results have been successful
but expensive. Another solution must be found.

Nature. The largest hemlock and poplar trees are in the upper section.
The lower section has younger hemlocks with larger canopies, and some
of the largest black gum trees in the state. The more impressive hemlocks
have girths of 10 to 12 feet and heights above 130 feet, with the tallest at

138 feet. Besides hemlock, the list of old-growth species includes American basswood, black and yellow birch, black gum, black locust, cucumber, red and sugar maple, white ash, and chestnut and red oak.

The NA provides deep-woods habitat for scarlet tanager, four species of flycatchers, red-eyed vireo, three woodpeckers, common raven, sharp-shinned hawk, and numerous wood warblers, such as Louisiana waterthrush and black blackburnian warbler. As fewer numbers of dense-forest birds nest here, other species with different requirements will take their place. Bear, bobcat, fisher, deer, and other deep-woods mammals are found here, as well as brook trout in Patterson Run. The area also has a healthy population of timber rattlesnakes and northern copperheads. Ferns are prolific and the understory is becoming dense, so if you hike down the ravine, be mindful of your immediate surroundings.

Trails. Three trails enable visitors to explore the NA. The Hemlock Trail—marked red—begins at the upper parking lot and follows Patterson Run, crossing the stream five times. To hike shorter loops, take either of the two side trails that provide exits out of the ravine to Hemlock Road. The yellow-marked Rim Trail and the orange-marked Patterson Trail stay on the higher elevations of Rising Mountain and provide views into the ravine. For many years, while the hemlocks were dying, the trails were not maintained and visitors were discouraged from hiking in the ravine due to safety concerns. In 2016, forestry managers determined that the situation had stabilized, and the huge job of clearing the trails began.

SC5 Colonel Denning State Park and Tuscarora State Forest, Cumberland County

Colonel Denning SP—one of Pennsylvania's hidden gems—is a remote 273-acre park tucked into a narrow, dead-end valley where Blue Mountain doubles back on itself. It is small and off the beaten path, but it is surrounded by Tuscarora SF, has all the recreational activities of many larger parks, serves as the trailhead for several popular trails, and is a tranquil place to enjoy nature. Doubling Gap Run and the 3.5-acre lake are the prominent natural features. The park was named after Col. William Denning, who served in the Revolutionary War as a sergeant. He is recognized for his improved canon design and manufacturing for the Continental army. In 1930, the land became a state recreational area. Six years later, a CCC camp was established to make major improvements to the park. Their stonework can be seen throughout the park, especially at the dam and spillway.

Recreation. The lake is fed by the clean water of Doubling Gap Run and has a deep, sandy beach and food concession during the summer months. Paddlers

The beach and lake at Colonel Denning SP

and anglers can enjoy the lake from a canoe or kayak, except from the first day of fishing season to the Friday before Memorial Day weekend. Trout are stocked in the stream and lake. A gazebo near the dam spillway provides a scenic spot for photos, or simply relaxing. A large picnic area with a pavilion, grass playfield, volleyball court, and playground is in a wooded area above the beach. A second picnic area is along the road, below the dam.

Near the park entrance is the log cabin nature center, with exhibits, an amphitheater, and a small frog pond. Environmental-education programs and campfires are held during the summer season. The primitive campground has fifty-two sites in three loops. Almost all the sites have electric and shade. The sites on the outside of the upper loop are large, with the most privacy. On busy weekends, most if not all sites are filled. The exception might be one of the six secluded walk-in sites. Other activities include hunting, cross-country skiing, orienteering, and hiking.

Trails. The 1.5-mile Double Gap Trail is a fairly level loop trail that starts at the parking lot above the west end of the dam. It follows the lake shoreline, then runs along the stream, and past the connector trail. The woodland trail passes a few potential old trees and an area of wetlands along the stream. At the turn it crosses the stream on a wooden bridge and heads back to the connector trail or straight to the beach. The 2.5-mile out-and-back Flat Rock Trail starts at the nature center footbridge and ascends the steep, rocky mountainside in Tuscarora State Forest to Flat Rock Lookout, 1,200 feet above the trailhead. At the approximate midpoint, called Wagon Wheel

The frog pond at the education center

The tranquil setting at the spillway

The view from Hickory Ridge Overlook

Laurel Run, Tuscarora SF

Junction, Flat Rock Trail joins Tuscarora Trail and three other trails. The trail continues, crosses the headwaters of Wildcat Run, and then heads up a moderate grade to Flat Rock, with a spectacular view of Cumberland Valley.

One note worth mentioning is that in this mountainous Ridge and Valley region, northern copperheads favor forested mountainsides in partially open areas with rock outcrops and talus slides. The timber rattlesnake's preferred habitat is high elevations on rocky ridges with south- and southwest-facing slopes. On a visit at the end of the summer, I was informed that one of the places rattlesnakes are seen is on the lower ledges of Flat Rock Lookout. Also, only one rattler was found in or near the park that year, and it was run over by a car outside the park. Odds are infinitesimally small that you will see either a rattlesnake or a copperhead. Stay on the trails and watch where you step and place your hands. If you do see one, enjoy the special moment from a safe distance, then go your separate ways in peace.

SC6 Waggoner's Gap Hawk Watch, Perry and Cumberland Counties

Waggoner's Gap Hawk Watch (WGH), purchased by Audubon Pennsylvania in 2001, is one of the best sites in the eastern US to watch migrating hawks, eagles, osprey, falcons, merlins, vultures, and other migrating flyers. The site is a large, rocky outcrop on Blue Mountain's ridge, 100 yards east of Route 74. It is one of three hawk migration viewing sites along Pennsylvania's 200-mile section of the Kittatinny Corridor, where daily counts of raptors are recorded. WGH records approximately 20,000 raptors each year—more than any other site in Pennsylvania.

The corridor is used by tens of thousands of raptors during their migration south because the mountain provides air currents that birds use to glide without expending much energy, and the corridor's land is protected forest. It is also the eastern front of the Appalachian Ridge and Valley Province and is separated from the nearest ridge by 14 miles. The Pennsylvania corridor was designated by Audubon as one of the state's largest and highest-priority important bird areas. The Appalachian Trail follows this corridor with 229 miles in Pennsylvania.

Site & Trails. The site itself is exceptional because visitors have an unobstructed view out both sides of the ridge without moving. Also, birds will come in low and circle directly overhead on thermals created by the site's rocks, which absorb solar energy and release thermal heat. The parking lot is on the east side of Route 74, 200 yards north of the crest of the gap. The gate to the lot is closed at night. Hawk Watch Trail—blazed with orange falcon silhouettes on the rocks—is a fifteen-minute hike to the main viewing area. Song Bird Trail begins at the far corner of the lot and is marked with yellow songbird silhouettes. The trail leads to the smaller East Rocks Overlook and then parallels the ridgeline to the main viewing area. The trail between the lookouts is over jumbled rock and is very difficult to negotiate.

Birds. On a brief visit on October 6, I saw sharp-shinned, cooper's, red-tailed, and red-shouldered hawks; several osprey; and at least four bald eagles. One eagle was probably three and a half years old because it had less than half of its white feathers. Each species has a specific time frame when they migrate. Generally the earliest to migrate are broad-winged hawks, peregrine falcons, and ospreys, which fly as far as South America. Some species, such as golden eagles and red-tailed hawks, migrate late in the season because they fly only as far as the southern states, and some individuals no farther than West Virginia.

The best time to visit is during optimum weather conditions and peak migration. For sheer numbers, the peak time for broad-winged hawks is the third and fourth week in September. At WGH, winds from the northwest produce the highest number of birds. With south winds, birds tend to fly low along the ridge, but you will see fewer birds. Photographers often come

when a south wind is in the afternoon and the sunlight is behind the camera, lighting up the bird as it approaches. Northern cold fronts and stormy weather will drive huge numbers of birds south. In the morning, if conditions were good the previous evening and are still good, acceptors, osprey, and eagles will start flying at sunrise. In the afternoon, acceptors will usually stop flying by 3:00 p.m. to hunt for food. Most sites, including WGH, have an owl decoy on a pole planted out in the rocks to draw the birds in closer. Raptors such as falcons, sharp-shinned hawks, and cooper's hawks consider owls to be a threat and will frequently attack an owl when they see one.

Bird Counters. A group of dedicated volunteers take turns at the WGH site identifying birds and recording the time and species. A bird is considered to be migrating when it passes a certain designated point. If it circles back it is subtracted from the list. The site has a counter—weather permitting—from sunrise to early evening every day from August 1 to December 31.

The site on the ridgeline provides viewing on both sides of the mountain.

Waggoner Gap Hawk Watch is on this Blue Mountain ridge north of Carlisle.

Northwest view from the ridge

This local resident is a fence lizard.

The data are entered every evening into a national database operated by the Hawk Migration Association of North America (HMANA). Their website, called HawkCount (www.hmana.org), has current and past daily and monthly totals for WGH, and more than 275 other sites in the US.

To be able to sit on a pile of boulders for hours, you need to be comfortable. The following is a general list of items to bring: binoculars, bird book, a cushion (or even better, a folding stadium seat), water, food, brimmed hat, sunglasses, sunscreen, and layered clothing, preferably a dark, drab color.

SC7 Cowans Gap State Park, Fulton County

The 1,085-acre Cowans Gap SP is in a lovely forest valley between Tuscarora Mountain and Cove Mountain and is surrounded by Buchanan SF. The park was named for the adjacent wind gap on Tuscarora Mountain. The lake, swim beach, trails, and camping are the park's main attractions.

History. Two iron furnaces—Mount Pleasant (1783–1835) and Richmond (1865–1885)—operated in the area and depleted much of the forest by clear-cutting sections every twenty to twenty-five years. Soon afterward, Kalbach and Company bought 4,800 acres and built a rail line made with wooden rails into the gap to log the remaining timber until they closed in 1907. The mountains were covered with treetops and brush that burned in massive fires set by sparks from passing locomotives. Between 1933 and 1941, the CCC built roads, bridges, fire and hiking trails, cabins, pavilions, and the dam and planted trees on thousands of acres. The pavilions are some of the nicest in the state park system. The park opened in 1937.

Lake. Cowans Gap Lake is fed by Little Aughwick Creek, which receives most of its water from a half-dozen springs. The 42-acre lake and stream have excellent trout fishing, in addition to the lake's largemouth and

Cowans Gap Lake

smallmouth bass, perch, crappie, and panfish. There are two boat launches for electric- and human-powered boats only. The boat rental concession has kayaks, rowboats, and paddleboats.

Recreation. The day-use area is one of the nicest in the state. It has a 500-foot-long sandy beach with concession and shower buildings, terraced gardens, horseshoe pits, sand volleyball, a nature center, an amphitheater, beautiful pavilions, lots of picnic tables, and well-maintained gravel trails. Two separate modern campgrounds at opposite ends of the park have a total of 201 sites and seven walk-in tent sites. The sites are filled on holiday weekends. An overnight boat-mooring area is provided for registered campers. Ten three-room rustic cabins with plenty of privacy are available seasonally. The cabins were built by the CCC and are registered on the National Register of Historic Places. Hunting is allowed on over 600 acres. Bird watching is good along the lake and stream above and below the lake. Winter activities include ice fishing, ice skating, cross-country skiing, and snowmobiling in the state forest.

Trails. Twelve trails total 11 miles within the park. A combination can make loop trails of varying length. The most popular trail is the 1.5-mile Lakeside Trail, which circles the lake shoreline. Plessinger Trail follows Aughwick Creek upstream for 1.1 miles and is used by fishermen and bird

The popular swim beach

Boat rentals, with the campground at the far end of the lake

One of the CCC pavilions

watchers. A section of the 110-mile Tuscarora Trail follows the ridge north to the gap, where it enters the beach area, crosses the dam and bridge, and then heads north again along the stream. It eventually connects with the Appalachian Trail. Standing Stone Trail—voted best in the state—is a difficult 76-mile trail that joins the trails at Greenwood Furnace SP. From the dam, take Tuscarora Trail to Horseshoe Trail and up the steep mountain to Standing Stone Trail at the ridge. A parking lot is designated for equestrian riding on Horse Trail, Knobsville Road Trail, North Logging Trail, and other state forest trails on Cove Mountain. Mountain biking is also allowed on these trails, as well as a few others in the park.

SC8 Kings Gap Environmental Education Center, Cumberland County

Kings Gap EEC is one of the DCNR's four state parks dedicated to environmental education. The 2,531-acre park provides programs for students, teachers, and the general public to increase their knowledge and appreciation of our preserved land and the natural world. The park's 4-mile-long road winds through the forest to the top of South Mountain and to the former estate that now serves as the park's office and training center. From the expansive terrace, visitors have a commanding view of the Cumberland valley. The park is divided into three different day-use areas: Mansion, Pond, and Pine Plantation. A park trail map, bird guide, and garden guide are available at the park office.

History. The forests were cut several times to provide wood to make charcoal for the region's iron furnaces. Fires and erosion had increased the degradation of the land when in 1908, John Cameron, a wealthy businessman from Harrisburg, built a thirty-two-room stone mansion for his summer retreat. He stayed at his Kings Gap home from May to October and eventually acquired 2,700 acres. After his death in 1949, the C. H. Masland Carpet Company purchased the mansion and 1,430 acres of land. Their improvement projects included planting 30,000 pine trees and building a pond along the mountain road. In 1973, the state, working with the Nature Conservancy, purchased the estate and opened the Kings Gap EEC in 1977. The Nature Conservancy purchased an additional 1,077 acres, most of which was part of the original estate.

Mansion Day-Use Area. The mansion was converted to offices and a training center with facilities for meals and overnight lodging; it may be reserved for various functions. The Ice House—built above- and below-ground—was used to preserve garden vegetables. Ice was cut and hauled from nearby lakes until 1931. The Carriage House had stables and living quarters. Its unique features included a bay for an automatic carriage wash

The mansion at the top of the mountain, Kings Gap EEC

View of Cumberland Valley from the mansion

This frog blends into its surroundings at Kings Gap pond.

The Pine Plantation Area at the bottom of the mountain

and a large, hand-operated equipment elevator. The Generator Building housed gasoline engines that generated electricity for the house. The caretaker lived year-round in a two-story brick home. Spring water was pumped 0.75 miles up the mountain to a 10,000-gallon wooden water tank mounted on top of a brick tower. It supplied gravity-fed water to all the buildings. Today a well provides the source of water, but the basic system is still in use. A walk through the mansion garden and the butterfly garden is an enjoyable educational experience. The garden is divided into three separate sections: an herb garden, a native habitat garden, and a shade garden. Most plants are identified.

Pond Day-Use Area. This area probably has the most diversified habitat. The spring-fed stream and pond feature wetland habitat with sphagnum moss, skunk cabbage, and wildflowers. The pond supports turtles, frogs, salamanders, snakes, and aquatic insects. The stream and pond reveal the sandy composition of the mountain. The 0.3-mile-long White Oaks Trail is a paved ADA-accessible trail with interpretive exhibits. Hiking on the 1.9-mile Watershed Trail is more difficult, since it follows both forks of the stream to make a loop.

Pine Plantation Day-use Area. The 42-acre plantation of white pine, Douglas fir, and tamarack is near the entrance to Kings Gap. It was planted in the early 1950s as an experimental tree farm. During the winters of

1995–1997, the Bureau of Forestry thinned the dense plantation to ensure that the trees remained healthy. The 0.3-mile Whispering Pines Trail is paved and has interpretive signs. The 0.6-mile Pine Plantation Trail is an easy loop, with signs explaining the techniques used to thin the trees. Areas that were recently opened up to sunlight now have stands of young white pine.

Nature. Chestnut oak dominates the forest, with additional sections of black gum, maple, white oak, and oak/pitch pine. The primary understory is blueberry, mountain laurel, and huckleberry. Kings Gap provides ideal habitat for reptiles, including painted and box turtles and the five-lined skink. Copperheads and rattlesnakes are occasionally seen near the garden's stone walls and other rocky areas. Several vernal ponds are found on the property and support spotted salamanders, spring peepers, wood frogs, and aquatic insects.

Recreation. Visitors can hike seventeen marked trails from the three day-use areas. I recommend using a trail map, compass, and sturdy footwear. The 6-mile Buck Ridge Trail traverses Michaux SF to connect with Pine Grove Furnace SP. The park has three orienteering courses of varying degrees of difficulty. Course maps are available, and the center conducts orienteering courses for beginners. Kings Gap Hollow Area is available for group camping, with a capacity of thirty people. Hunting is permitted on 1,860 acres, with an additional 633 acres open for deer hunting during the regular two-week season. Contact the center's office about hunting, group camping, and environmental programs (717-486-5031).

SC9 Pine Grove Furnace State Park and Michaux State Forest, Cumberland County

Pine Grove Furnace SP occupies a narrow, 3-mile-long section of forest valley with South Mountain flanking the western side and Piney Mountain to the east. The 696-acre park has two lakes and is surrounded by Michaux SF. In addition to the picturesque setting, natural features, and recreational activities, the park has two other distinguishing features: the beautifully preserved iron furnace and buildings in the national historic area and the park's location, which is famously positioned at the halfway point of the Appalachian Trail.

Historic Sites. Between 1764 and 1897, this valley supported a thriving industrial community that produced cast-iron ingots and finished products such as stoves, fireplace backs, and heavy military items. The furnace was close to an iron ore deposit where Fuller Lake is now located. Charcoal was made from timber extracted from the company's 18,000 acres of forest. Mountain Creek was the source of water and power. The ironmaster's brick mansion was completed in 1829. In 1830, Laurel Forge was built to

Pole Steeple overlooking Pine Grove Furnace
SP, Michaux SF

convert cast-iron ingots into wrought iron. The Laurel Lake dam supplied power for the new forge. In 1895, new technologies used by larger, more-efficient mills forced Pine Grove Furnace to close after 131 years. The state purchased the furnace, buildings, and 17,000 acres in 1913.

Many of the original buildings are still in use. The ironmaster's home is used as an American youth hostel by thru-hikers on the Appalachian Trail and as an educational facility. The stables were converted to the well-known general store, and the gristmill is now the visitor center. The inn is used for the park office. The furnace, clerk's office, and some residences are also in excellent condition. Raceways behind the campground and a few charcoal hearths are still evident. Pine Grove Cemetery is similar to many old rural cemeteries; the flat rocks placed upright at each grave have been lost over the years. The visitor center has exhibits featuring wildlife, geology, and the history of the area. The best way to view the historic sites is to walk the 1.25-mile self-guided interpretive trail.

Appalachian Trail. Approximately one mile of the 2,186-mile Appalachian Trail runs through the park. The trail's halfway point is just south of the park, in Michaux SF. When thru-hikers reach the midpoint milestone, they traditionally celebrate by eating a half gallon of ice cream at the general store. Many of the hikers you meet at the store are completing the trail in segments. The park is also a traditional place for family members to spend time with thru-hikers before they head back on the trail. The Appalachian Trail Museum is in the historic area. Fascinating displays and artifacts tell the history of the trail, the dedicated pioneer trail builders, and the early hikers. The primitive hiking equipment used in the 1940s and '50s provides a new perspective on what we think is required today. The museum will be expanding in the future.

Recreation. Both 1.7-acre Fuller Lake and 25-acre Laurel Lake have a white-sand beach and a food concession / shower building. Boating (electric or human powered) is permitted only on Laurel Lake, which has boat rentals, a boat launch, and mooring. Anglers can fish for pickerel, perch, bass, panfish, and stocked trout at both lakes. Mountain Creek has brown,

View of Laurel Lake from Pole Steeple

rainbow, and brook trout. Only 75 acres at the southern end of the park are available for hunting. The modern campground has seventy wooded sites, with some that are large and fairly private. Behind the campground are old-growth trees, the old raceway, and 0.5-mile Creek Trail, which passes vernal ponds and a stand of beautiful white pines. Biking is allowed on all park roads, including the 2-mile rail trail. Use caution, since these roads are also used by vehicles and pedestrians. Winter activities include snowmobiling on miles of SF roads, with parking south of the park; cross-country skiing on the rail trail and SF trails; and ice skating and ice fishing on Lake Laurel only.

Trails. The 1.4-mile, yellow-blazed Mountain Creek Trail follows the stream through forests and wetlands, and Swamp Trail—only 0.25 miles long—circles a forest swamp. Both are good for viewing wildlife. The 1-mile, yellow-blazed Koppenhaver Trail follows Toms Run and Mountain Creek past rock outcrops, then loops back through stands of hemlocks and pines.

Michaux SF. The 85,000 acres of forest is home to the state's first forestry school. Established in 1903, Mont Alto was only the second forestry school in the country, and the year before, the state's first tree nursery was established. Within the SF are three state parks and four natural areas. The region is in the Ridge and Valley Province and is the northern terminus

The park's general store, where Appalachian Trail thru-hikers celebrate the halfway point

The old stone mill near the general store houses the Appalachian Trail Museum.

of the Blue Ridge Mountains. The ridges—1,000 feet above the valleys—have numerous outstanding vistas along forest roads and trails. Visit the SF website for information about recreation and trails.

I highly recommend hiking the 0.75-mile, blue-blazed Pole Steeple Trail to Pole Steeple Overlook. The trailhead is along Biker Hiker Trail road, at the parking area near Laurel Lake. The trail climbs steep Piney Mountain to the quartzite outcrop. Switchbacks and rock steps definitely help make the hike less strenuous. The view from the 80-foot-high outcrop is spectacular. Laurel Lake and the beach can be seen 500 feet below. The outcrop is also a popular destination for rock climbers.

In 2008, I took photos along Ridge Road, in Michaux SF, of what I thought at the time was a controversial forestry practice. It was a large, clear-cut area where nearly every tree branch was chipped and hauled away, leaving mostly bare ground, exposed rock, and a few pitiful, scraggly trees. I was dumbfounded that they would still clear-cut the forest after all we know about the previous century's destructive logging methods. When I revisited the clear-cut area in 2017, it took a while before I was 100 percent convinced that I was in the right place. The log-loading area is now an open area of grass, and the clear-cut has transformed into an impenetrable, surprisingly diversified stand of 10- to 18-foot trees and shrubs. Fortunately, a mountain bike trail runs through the stand, providing the only access. The trees included white and black oak, white and pitch pine, red maple, sassafras, hickory, quaking aspen, black gum, mountain laurel, and blueberry bushes. As I was leaving I thought, "This is just one more example of the amazing wonders in the natural world."

Water snakes are sharing a log peacefully with painted turtles while the snakes mate.

Notice the heads of two smaller males resting on the female.

In 2008, this area along Ridge Road in Michaux SF was logged and brush was removed.

My 2016 return was shocking; the area was impenetrable, with trees more than 12 feet high.

SC10 Mt. Cydonia Ponds Natural Area, Michaux State Forest, Franklin County

Mt. Cydonia Ponds NA is a collection of approximately sixty vernal ponds in a deciduous forest between Mt. Cydonia and Little Mountain. The ponds range in size from 20 feet across to 0.5 acre, and like all vernal ponds, they have no tributary inlet or outlet and are typically dry by August. Several species of amphibians—called vernal-pool indicators—breed only in vernal ponds because the ponds cannot support predatory fish. The Nature Conservancy took samples of sediment from depths to 9 feet and found pollen from spruce trees, which have not grown in that area for thousands of years. Another sample from a pond nearby was dated to 15,210 years before present.

The Mt. Cydonia Ponds support three of Pennsylvania's four indicator salamanders (spotted, marbled, and Jefferson), both indicator frogs (wood frog and eastern spadefoot), and fairy shrimp. Marble salamanders breed and deposit their eggs in the fall. The Jefferson salamander breeds in early March, followed by spotted salamanders, and then by red-spotted newts in late spring. Wood frogs breed in early March. Spring peepers arrive at the ponds in mid-March, and American toads show up in May. The one objective that all amphibian hatchlings must accomplish is to grow quickly, so they can leave the pond before it dries up. In addition to the indicator species, the ponds support spring peepers, gray tree frogs, green frogs, red-spotted newts, waterfowl, turtles, many insects, and associated prey animals, such as snakes, green heron, raccoons, skunk, and red fox.

Marbled Salamander. Mt. Cydonia's three indicator salamander species are classified as mole salamanders because they spend the majority of the year feeding in subterranean tunnels in the woodlands near the ponds. They eat worms, slugs, insects, and just about anything else they can fit in their mouths. The marbled salamander is the only one that breeds in the fall on the bottom of the dry pond. The female will lay 40–200 eggs under a log or leaves and will remain to guard the eggs until the pool begins to fill with water. She then leaves for her winter dormancy in the woods. The embryos hatch soon after their nest is inundated with seasonal water during the winter. The larvae begin growing before other salamanders lay their eggs in the spring. They are also the first to complete their larval development, a process that takes 4.5 months. When they become terrestrial adults, they leave the pool for the woods. Nearly all salamanders will return to breed in the pool where they were born.

Spring Peepers. Spring peepers are the beloved harbinger of spring and breed in vernal pools and permanent wetland habitats. The male frogs are less than an inch long, and the females are about 1.5 inches—the smallest of Pennsylvania's frogs. Only the males make the familiar high-pitched call soon after stirring from their winter dormancy. Arriving at the pond before the females, their calling frequency increases while they defend a small 4- to 16-inch territory. During peak breeding season, their extremely loud call occurs about once every second, and as often as 4,500 times during the night. As you can imagine, a vernal pond packed with peepers can be deafening. Females will select a male that is larger than average and has the ability to call at a faster rate. She will release approximately 800 eggs, which are immediately fertilized. The breeding season can last a month or more, with members of both sexes arriving at the pond in staggered numbers. The eggs hatch within a week, and the tadpoles begin grazing mostly on algae. As one of nature's most amazing feats, they metamorphose by absorbing their tail, growing limbs, changing their breathing from gills to lungs, and altering their digestive system from vegetarian to carnivorous. In November, they burrow to the bottom of leaf litter or under a log and become dormant. Their bodies will freeze, but a glucose-based compound causes the ice to form in the spaces between their cells, protecting their cells from damage. In early March, they emerge and the cycle of life begins again.

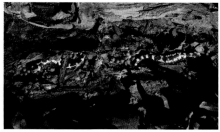

One of Mt. Cydonia's vernal ponds is almost dry in early November.

Two dormant marbled salamanders with their eggs. Their protective log was gently returned.

To visit the ponds, take Cydonia Road south, past the sand quarry. Park at the only area cleared for parking along the right side of the gravel road. From the parking area, an unmarked trail becomes an old forest road. Stay on this road, avoiding the many side trails. You will pass about seven ponds within the first twelve minutes of hiking. On an October visit, I found two marbled salamanders with their eggs under a small piece of wood in a dry pond. They never moved. After a few photos, I carefully replaced their protective cover. I also found several ponds that still had water.

SC11 Cordorus State Park, York County

Cordorus SP is a picturesque 3,500-acre park surrounded by farms near the border with Maryland. The 1,275-acre Marburg Lake is the park's main feature, but the developed recreation is what attracts large numbers of visitors. The lake was created as a result of a cooperative program between the state and Glatfelter Paper Company. The company uses approximately eleven million gallons of water each day and needed a more reliable source of clean water. By offering to build and manage the 109-foot-high dam, the borough would have a better supply of water and the state would manage the land as a state park. The dam was completed in 1966, and the park was dedicated in 1970.

Lake. Lake Marburg—one of the cleanest in Pennsylvania—has 26 miles of shoreline with seven boat launches, including one in the campground area. The motor limit on the lake is 20 horsepower. The marina has seasonal and daily mooring for lease, as well as boat storage. Pontoons, motorboats, canoes, kayaks, and paddleboats are available to rent. A second boat rental area, with nonpower boats, is at the swimming-pool area. Scuba diving is permitted in Sinheim Cove with a permit. The lake is a warm-water fishery with the following species: largemouth bass, yellow perch, crappie, northern pike, muskellunge, tiger muskie, and catfish. Cordorus Creek is stocked with brown and rainbow trout and is a good stream for fly fishing.

Recreation. The modern campground has 185 sites for tents and RVs, fifteen walk-in tent sites, and a boat launch and shoreline mooring. Yurts and cottages are also available. The campground is conveniently located near the swimming pool via a walkway. The pool is one of the largest in the park system and overlooks the lake. It has a separate spray area for kids, a large slide, and grassy areas around the pool. Raised patios provide seating, and a food concession is open during the summer. On summer holidays and some weekends the pool and campground reach their maximum capacity, which for the pool is 1,600 people. The park has three picnic areas with 750 tables, two pavilions, and restrooms.

The Cordorus Disc Golf Course is rated as one of the nicest and most challenging in the state. Fifty-four holes with paved tees wander through rolling woods and fields and provide views of the lake. There is also a nine-hole mini disc course for children. Hunting is permitted on 2,800 acres with shotgun, muzzleloader, or bow. Waterfowl hunting is popular, with fifteen duck blinds awarded by lottery. Winter recreation includes snowmobiling on 6.5 miles of trails, cross-country skiing, sledding, and ice skating at Chapel Cove, and ice fishing anywhere on the lake except Chapel Cove.

Trails. The park has dedicated 195 acres near the office to mountain biking, hiking, and cross-country skiing. More than 6 miles of marked trails wind through the forest. Also, 8 miles of equestrian trails, with trailer

Lake Marburg, Codorus SP

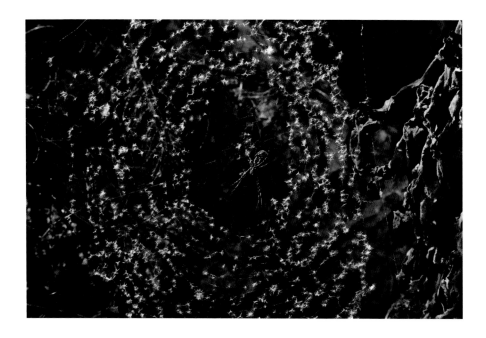

A spiderweb with wind-blown seeds

parking near the Main Launch, take riders through forests and fields and along the shoreline. Ranger Lookout's benches and hitching posts make it a pleasant place to rest. The trails are also available to hikers. There are two trails restricted to hiking only. The 3.5-mile Mary Ann Furnace Trail uses a boardwalk through the wetlands at Black Rock Flat. The 1.5-mile LaHo Trail follows the shoreline of Wildasin Flats, which is another wetland that is an excellent area for bird watching.

Wildlife. The visitor center has excellent displays of mounted fish and mammals and a collection of bird eggs. The park's diversified habitat of mixed hardwoods, stands of pines, wetlands, overgrown fields, meadows, mudflats, and the lake are credited for the long list of more than 240 species of birds recorded in the park. An active eagle nest can be seen from the classroom building overlook. Osprey also nest in the park, and large numbers of migrating waterfowl and shorebirds are common visitors. Volunteers manage about 175 bluebird boxes. Turtles, muskrats, kingfishers, herons, and wood ducks live in the wetland areas. The woodlands are home to scarlet tanagers, rufous-sided towhees, kinglets, ovenbirds, and numerous warblers.

The scenic lake has lots of coves for fishing, kayaking, and exploring.

The park's visitor center has excellent displays of nature.

Eastern Pennsylvania

Northeast Region

NE1 Salt Spring State Park and Woodbourne Forest and Wildlife Sanctuary, Susquehanna County

Both Salt Springs SP and Woodbourne Preserve are small gems with wonderful natural features that include old-growth forests. They are not well known, partly because their location is in a less-traveled area of the state. Both preserves are operated by nonprofit organizations.

Salt Springs SP. The 405-acre Salt Springs SP's main feature is the Falls Brook NA. Within the natural area are three waterfalls in a steep canyon, an old-growth hemlock forest on both sides of the canyon, and a mineral spring. This is one of the few state parks that is managed and maintained by a local nonprofit organization, the Friends of Salt Springs SP. Their office, gift shop, park information, and displays are in the Wheaton Home. The Friends also own 437 acres adjacent to the park's southern border and conduct a variety of educational programs. The old-growth hemlocks were probably spared the axe because this area was a popular recreational attraction as far back as 1810. Since approximately 1840, the land had been a dairy farm owned by the Wheaton family. The state acquired the land, two historic homes, and the carriage barn in 1973.

The first of three falls at Salt Springs SP

Mom and her two children take a break below
the second falls.

There are two ways to see the canyon's falls and ancient trees. You can
take the Hemlock Trail up and back, but you will see the stream only from
a distance. The second option, if conditions permit, is to hike up the Fall
Brook Trail. The trail is actually the rock streambed, which means climbing
the rock ledges on the left side of each of the 10-foot-high waterfalls. At the
top of the third waterfall, climb the left bank to return on the Hemlock Trail
through the forest. It is not too difficult, but be careful climbing the falls.

A wooden observation deck near the top of Hemlock Trail provides a
view into the canyon and the lower two falls. Hemlock Trail continues on
a boardwalk along the edge of the canyon's steep drop-off. The scenery is
outstanding and the trees are impressive. A large rock—called Penny
Rock—is where people have traditionally placed pennies between the
rock's thin layers. It seems odd that every penny is bent down. The trailhead
is near Salt Spring. When I visited, the mineral water was not flowing, but
methane gas was bubbling out. The gas is created by organic matter
breaking down deep underground in the sedimentary rock.

The prime habitat of mixed hardwood forests, grasslands, overgrown
fields, and wetlands is home to more than 150 species of birds, deer, black
bear, bobcat, coyote, red fox, porcupine, raccoon, and beaver. A small rustic
camping area with twelve sites is along Silver Creek. Nearby is a grassy
area with two one-room camp cottages. Both streams are stocked with
trout, and 800 acres are open for hunting.

Hemlock Trail's old hemlocks grow on the edge of the steep ravine.

Penny Rock, where people traditionally wedge pennies in the rock's cracks

Woodbourne's wetlands and bog

Woodbourne Forest & Wildlife Preserve. The main features of the 648-acre preserve are the old-growth forest, the 16-acre alder swamp, and Cope's Pond. The 200-acre stand of ancient trees is the largest in northeastern Pennsylvania. In 1956, the property was donated by the Cope family to the Nature Conservancy, making it the conservancy's first preserve in Pennsylvania. Its remote location is somewhat difficult to find; use their website's directions, not the listed address. Also, it is easy to miss the preserve's sign and entrance to the small parking lot situated below the road. A trail map is essential, but you will not find one on the conservancy's website; instead, plastic maps can be borrowed at the parking-lot shelter.

From the lot, the trail winds through fields and into the woods, where it splits: a spur trail leads to an observation platform overlooking the large, open-water swamp. Beavers have raised the level of the lake with their very impressive dam. The yellow-blazed, 0.75-mile Swamp Trail heads to the right along the wetlands and through the old-growth forest. At the beaver dam the trail loops back to itself. Across the small stream is the connection for the orange-blazed, 3-mile Woodruff Hill Trail. This loop trail continues through the old-growth forest and follows a tributary stream. The blue-blazed, 4.5-mile Cope's Ramble Trail begins to the left of the platform, hugs the wetland, then makes a wide loop around the property.

The giant trees create a cool, shaded environment with open views. Woodbourne's old-growth trees include white pine, hemlock, oak, ash, and maple. The preserve is a quiet place that attracts more than 180 species

The preserve has the largest old-growth forest in northeastern Pennsylvania.

of birds, of which ninety species nest on the property. The wetlands also support nine species of salamanders and several species of frogs and reptiles. More than eighty-five species of plants live in or around the wetland. Forest mammals include deer, bear, coyote, mink, snowshoe hare, river otter, and southern bog lemming. I was very impressed with the number of giant trees. I also enjoyed seeing a mother beaver leading the way for her one youngster.

NE2 Worlds End State Park and Loyalsock State Forest, Sullivan County

Worlds End SP is a 780-acre forest plateau with countless ravines and picturesque Loyalsock Creek flowing through a deep gorge. Most of the park borders Loyalsock SF, with elevations ranging between approximately 1,065 and 2,000 feet. All of the park's facilities and most recreational activities are on the few level areas along the stream. When the park's land was purchased in 1929 and 1931, it was a jungle of briars and brush growing on previously logged and burnt land. Between 1933 and 1941, the CCC built the dam, swim area, trails, roads, pavilions, and cabins. The cabins, made from local stone and timber, are listed on the National Register of Historic Places.

Recreation. The modern campground has seventy sites along Route 154 and the Loyalsock. Downstream is the entrance to the office, parking, and concessions. Across the bridge are the three group sites, and nineteen rustic cabins with fireplaces and porches or patios along the stream. The popular cabins are frequently rented well in advance. Loyalsock Creek has been stocked with native populations of trout. The shallow creek can be floated, but most people float it by starting well below the park. Sones Pond and Bear Wallow Pond offer excellent flat water for kayaking in a scenic setting. The park also has several great overlooks. Famous Loyalsock Canyon Vista provides a stunning view of the gorge 800 feet below and the surrounding mountains. Behind the overlook is Rock Garden Trail, which winds through

Canyon Vista overlooks Loyalsock Creek
(mid-October).

a group of large, square-shaped boulders that used to be a single rock outcrop. Three waterfalls—Dry Run Falls, Jacoby Run Falls, and Angel Falls—can be reached after a short walk. Other activities include hunting, fishing, horseback riding, cross-country skiing, and snowmobiling. Pick up a state forest map to visit additional scenic locations and vistas.

Trails. The 59-mile Loyalsock Trail is one of Pennsylvania's most outstanding and well-known trails. It was developed in the early 1950s, making it one of the oldest in the country. The trail, for the most part, follows Loyalsock Creek and travels through forests and deep ravines past ponds, wetlands, waterfalls, and vistas. There are also plenty of opportunities to see wildlife. Two SP trails that follow above the stream and climb a moderate elevation to a vista are 2.5-mile-long Butternut Trail and 1-mile-long High Rock Trail. The 3.5-mile Canyon Vista Trail starts at the campground and ascends the mountain to Canyon Vista and the Rock Garden. Worlds End Trail climbs to a vista above the beach and into the SF to connect with Loyalsock Trail.

One of my favorite hikes is to the unique Haystacks on Loyalsock Creek. The Haystacks is an area of large, rounded quartzite boulders strewn across the stream where it drops in elevation. From the parking area off Route 220, take the trail at the west end of the lot downhill to the old railroad bed. Turn left (west) and follow the old road to the stream. Then follow the trail

The smooth-layered rock at Loyalsock Creek looks like an old lava flow.

Boulder-strewn, pristine Loyalsock Creek

Sones Pond, Loyalsock SF

downstream to the Haystacks. At 200 yards above the Haystacks are large slabs of flat rock that extend out into the stream—perfect for resting and soaking in the scenery. Make sure you have a trail map.

One late afternoon, I was standing on rocks below the Haystacks, preparing to take photos, when I saw a mother bear and her three large cubs just 15 feet above me. They were making their usual stream crossing by hopping from haystack to haystack. When the mother saw me, she stopped and contemplated whether to continue or turn around. After a few seconds, she turned around and huffed. The three cubs instantly climbed the nearest trees. Thirty seconds later, she grunted and the cubs climbed down and followed her upstream along the trail. Ten minutes later I watched them in the distance, crossing the stream where the water is shallow. The bears' communication skills and reaction times were amazing.

Nature. The park and SF are home to deer, black bear, coyote, bobcat, fisher, otter, turkey, and rattlesnakes. Bear sightings in and near the park are common. The hemlock valleys, hardwood mountains, and a few wetlands create habitat for 200 species of birds. The park is an Audubon important bird area. Birds include blue-headed and red-eyed vireos, least and Acadian flycatchers, many species of warblers, Swainson's thrush, grouse, and bared, great horned, and saw-whet owls.

The Haystacks

A long exposure captures the light of the full moon reflecting off the stream.

Loyalsock SF. The SF's designated natural areas are 774-acre Kettle Creek Gorge NA, a remote wild valley; Tamarack Run NA, a 234-acre boreal conifer wetland; and Devil's Elbow NA, a 404-acre emergent, shrub, and forested wetland with carnivorous plants. The SF's designated wild areas are 7,500-acre McIntyre WA, which has several tributary streams with cascading waterfalls, and 2,600-acre Kettle Creek WA, which protects adjacent Kettle Creek Gorge NA.

NE3 Ricketts Glen State Park, SGLs 13 and 57; Sullivan, Wyoming, and Luzerne Counties

Ricketts Glen SP is one of the most beautiful parks in Pennsylvania. The highlight of the 13,050-acre park is the spectacular Glens Natural Area, with twenty-two waterfalls and approximately 2,000 acres of old-growth trees. The 2,845-acre Glens NA comprises four glens: Ganoga Glen and Glen Leigh, two branches of Kitchen Creek; Ricketts Glen, a 1.8-mile section of Kitchen Creek; and Boston Glen, below Route 114. Glens NA was designated a national natural landmark and a state park natural area. West of the state park is 49,528-acre SGL 13, a rugged forest with clear mountain streams and numerous waterfalls. On the park's eastern border is 45,986-acre SGL 57, a forested, high-elevation plateau with several shallow lakes and wetlands. The three properties preserve a total of more than 108,000 acres.

Geology. The park encompasses the Allegheny Plateau and the Allegheny Front, which drops 1,000 feet in 2.5 miles. Kitchen Creek is unique compared to other streams along the Front because its gradient is abnormally steep for its rate of water flow. For millions of years, Kitchen Creek had a small watershed area, and not much erosion occurred. After the Wisconsinan glacier retreated, the watershed expanded by 7 square miles.

History. In the early 1850s, the Ricketts brothers bought 5,000 acres and built a stone lodge and tavern on Lake Ganoga, just north of the park (Lake Ganoga is the highest natural lake east of the Rockies). Amazingly, the famous waterfalls were not discovered until 1869, when two guests explored Kitchen Creek during a fishing excursion. One of the sons, R. Bruce Ricketts, eventually owned 80,000 acres, and between 1890 and 1913 he leased his land to a lumber company. He never allowed logging in the glen. In 1913, Ricketts opened the falls to the public and charged one dollar for parking. After his death in 1919, the family sold 48,000 acres to the Game Commission. The remaining land was approved as a national park site, but the Depression and WWII ended the plan. The state bought the land and the park was officially opened in 1944.

Waterfalls. Every year, tens of thousands of visitors hike Falls Trail to see and hear the magnificent waterfalls. The trail is recognized as one of the best in the eastern US. Ten nearly continuous waterfalls between 11 and 94 feet high are on the left fork of Kitchen Creek. On the right fork are eight falls from 16 to 60 feet high and four bridges. Below the fork at Waters Meet are three more falls with heights from 16 to 36 feet. Below Route 118 is beautiful 36-foot Adams Falls, which carves its way through large sections of exposed rock. On top of the plateau, scenic Highland Trail connects the two branches of Falls Trail to form a 3.2-mile V-shaped loop. Highland Trail passes through stands of hemlock trees and Midway Crevasse, a gap through large blocks of glacial rock. Falls Trail is an amazing engineering feat, but it is still wet, slippery, steep, and potentially dangerous. To photograph the falls and avoid traffic on the trails, I highly recommend visiting during early morning on a weekday, and preferably in the off-season. Photographing the falls is best on a slightly overcast day and after a hard rain.

Ancient Forests. Glens NA also harbors one of the largest stands of old-growth trees in Pennsylvania. Many of the trees are more than 500 years old, and the rings on one fallen tree proved it to be 900 years old. Some of the fifteen species of old-growth trees include American basswood, black and yellow birch, black cherry, black gum, chestnut oak, eastern

The 94-foot Ganoga Falls—the tallest in the park

hemlock, white pine, sugar maple, yellow-poplar, and white ash. Along Boston Run, near Kitchen Creek, are hemlocks and 5 acres of what might be the second-oldest and tallest stand of white pines in the state. Forest Cathedral, in Cook Forest SP, is rated number one. The tallest pine was measured at more than 144 feet. A half mile upstream from Route 118 is a 127-foot white ash—one of the state's tallest—and some large hemlocks, with one measuring 11.7 feet in circumference and 121 feet tall. Farther upstream is a 138-foot tulip tree and a 101-foot yellow birch, the tallest in the state park system.

Recreation. The 245-acre Lake Jean, at an altitude of 2,224 feet, is the center of recreation in the park, with a 600-foot-long beach, food concession, and boat rental. Electric- or human-powered boats are allowed on the lake. Anglers can fish for trout and warm-water species. The two modern campgrounds have 120 sites along the shoreline of Lake Jean. At some sites you can beach your kayak. Ten large, modern cabins and one group area are also available. Hiking on the park's eleven trails—totaling 26 miles—is the best way to see the park. Winter sports include cross-country skiing, snowmobiling, ice fishing, ice climbing, and winter camping.

A close-up at the top of Adams Falls

A section of Adams Falls

Nature. The state park was designated an important bird area and an important mammal area. Lake Rose and Lake Leigh were formerly manmade lakes that are now wetlands, adding diversity to the park's habitat. The park has a healthy population of deer, bear, turkey, coyote, bobcat, fox, mink, and numerous other small mammals. Thirty-nine fishers were released in the adjoining game lands and have successfully expanded their

Mom is watching her mallard ducklings at Lake Jean (mid-June).

The 30-foot-high Sullivan Falls, SGL 13

territory. The park and nearby game lands are ideal for breeding populations of American bittern, bald eagles, four species of flycatchers, two species of waterthrush, Swainson's thrush, northern goshawk, northern harrier, and many of the twenty-three species of warblers identified in the park.

Game Lands. Numerous waterfalls are in SGL 13, along the East Branch of Fishing Creek, Sullivan Run, Pigeon Run, and Heberly Run. To visit Sullivan Falls—the most photogenic and easiest to access—take Bear Run Road (Jamison City Road)—just north of the park entrance—for 2 miles to the parking area near the stream (East Branch Fishing Creek). Follow a short trail to the falls. The best view of Sullivan Falls is from the pool, but do not miss the deep stream cut into the rock above the falls. Walk farther upstream to appreciate one of the most beautiful streams in Pennsylvania. Ten other falls are upstream and five falls are on Heberly Run, but all are difficult to access.

SGL 57 is a vast wild plateau dotted with many ponds, lakes, and wetlands. From Route 487, about a mile north of the park, turn right onto Fish Commission Road. The road is about 5 miles long and passes Wild Fowl Pond and the Meadows. A left turn leads to Beech Lake and two other shallow lakes. If you continue straight, you eventually reach Mount Spring Lake (recently drained) and Ice Dam No. 1 (abandoned long ago). A topographic map is necessary if you plan on hiking in either game land.

NE4 Promised Land State Park and Bruce Lake Natural Area, Pike County

Promised Land SP is on the Pocono Plateau at an elevation of approximately 1,800 feet. The park's 3,000 acres are surrounded by 12,464 acres of Delaware SF. The main features are 422-acre Promised Land Lake and 173-acre Lower Lake. Two unusual aspects of the park are that there are

224 private cabins that lease land from the DCNR, and the village of Promised Land is private property within the park. Despite the fact that it is in a very rural area, its proximity to I-84 and major population centers only two hours away brings lots of visitors.

History. The land was originally purchased by a religious group called the Shakers. After their attempt to farm the land failed, they moved on. The land was repeatedly timbered and was mostly briars and scrub when the state began purchasing the land in 1902. The price varied from eighteen cents to $2.00 per acre. Three years later, Promised Land became the commonwealth's fourth state park. In 1933, the CCC made major improvements, including all the fine stonework that is still evident today. I recommend visiting the Masker Museum, the state park system's largest museum. It covers the area's natural history and life in a CCC camp, with impressive displays of mounted butterflies, insects, waterfowl, and mammals. They also have a native plant garden, bird-feeding station, environmental programs, and guided hikes.

Recreation. The park has four separate campground locations. Pickerel Point has seventy-five modern sites, a beach, and boat rental. Deerfield has thirty-four rustic sites, the Pines has fifty-eight rustic sites, and the Lower Lake Campground has more than 217 modern sites in four areas: Beachwood, Northwood, Rhododendron, and the Equestrian Camping Area. Twelve rustic cabins built by the CCC are also available. The large day-use area has a beach, concession, boat rental, and expansive grass areas with picnic tables. Electric- and human-powered boats are allowed on the lakes, which have five launches.

Foggy sunrise at Promised Land Lake

Scenic Little Falls and trail at the western end of the park

The park's beach area

Two friends playing in the falls

The park has a large nature center with excellent displays.

Boat rentals are also available on Lower Lake and Pickerel Point. Anglers fish for large and smallmouth bass, pickerel, muskellunge, perch, sunfish, and catfish. A few other activities are biking, horseback riding, hunting, cross-country skiing, and snowmobiling in the park and SF.

Trails. The park and surrounding SF have sixteen trails totaling 50 miles. Little Falls Trail is a scenic 1-mile loop trail that follows the East Branch of Wallenpaupack Creek. Hike along the shaded stream past cardinal flowers and other wildflowers to the modest waterfalls. Cross the footbridge to return on the opposite side of the stream. The Conservation Trail is a self-guided nature trail. Use the trail guide, which describes the island's natural features, such as the 18-foot-high rhododendron.

Wildlife. An observation station is on the north shore of Lower Lake, where you can view the wetlands, waterfowl, blue herons, and an eagle's nest on the far side of the lake. The eagles visited the park for the first time in 1995, fledged their first eaglets in 2000, and have been coming

The view from the east side of Bruce Lake

back to raise at least one eaglet every year since then. Promised Land Lake is home to river otters, which are sometimes seen at Big Inlet and Burley Inlet at sunrise. The deer population is held fairly low because of the large population of black bear that prey on young fawns that instinctively remain motionless instead of fleeing. Pike County has one of the largest populations of bear in Pennsylvania. It also has some of the largest black bear in North America. Bear over 600 pounds are harvested every year, and several bear weighing over 800 pounds have been documented.

Bruce Lake NA. This natural area has the feel of being in the lake region of Ontario, Canada. The 2,845 acres encompass 42-acre Bruce Lake, a 20-foot-deep glacial lake; 47-acre Egypt Meadow Lake, which was created by the CCC; 300-acre Balsam Swamp, the tributary of Egypt Meadow Lake; Long Pond Swamp, near the eastern border; and many other wetlands. Egypt Meadow Lake and Bruce Lake are beautiful, remote lakes that have very few visitors. I was the only person there on a sunny weekday in early October. Beavers and otters are well established at the two lakes. All three carnivorous plants—pitcher, round-leafed sundew, and bladderwort—as well as rare and threatened plants are found at Bruce Lake. Bald eagles, osprey, turkey, grouse, twenty-two species of warblers, and many other species of birds nest or stop to feed here. The natural area is also home to seventeen species of amphibians and twenty-one species of reptiles, including the timber rattlesnake.

Egypt Meadow Lake from the bridge over the narrow neck between the lake and wetlands

Three parking lots along Route 390, north of the park, provide access to many of the SF trails. To reach Bruce Lake, park at the lot on Route 390 near I-84 and take Egypt Meadow Trail (EMT) clockwise around Egypt Meadow Lake. The trail connects with Bruce Lake Trail east of the bridge. Check out the gorgeous scenery from the bridge, then head east on the wide Bruce Lake Trail for 1.4 miles. There are two separate campsites (permit required) along the shore of the lake. At this point the trail becomes a long footpath that circles the entire lake and large swamp at the southern end. Most people retrace their steps back to the bridge. I hiked the trail a half mile past the campsites, then bushwhacked to the lake. It was exhausting walking through the thick understory. To return, hike 150 yards west from the bridge on Bruce Lake Trail, and at the post turn right onto Egypt Meadow Pass, which is rockier and harder to follow than the trail coming in, but very scenic. It takes you back to the EMT, where you turn left and head back to your starting point.

NE5 Shohola Lake and Waterfalls, SGL 180, Pike County

The Game Commission's 1,137-acre Shohola Lake and Waterfowl Management Area was created within 11,493-acre State Game Land 180 to provide a habitat for waterfowl. Similar to other GC projects, it is prime habitat for many other species of wildlife, most notably bald eagles. Recreational activities include visiting Shohola Falls, fishing, hunting, birding, hiking,

The splash pool and canyon below Shohola Falls

The fall's layers, plenty of water, and blue skies created perfect conditions for this image.

The strange configuration of green grass reminds me of Salvador Dali's clock painting.

and wildlife viewing. The lake is long, narrow, and shallow, with a maximum depth along the submerged creek bed of approximately 8 feet. The lake's southeastern side and southern end transition into extensive wetlands and flooded stands of timber. Two large propagation areas protect wildlife from human encroachment. The refuge is surrounded by forested rolling terrain, wetlands, and small streams typical of the Pocono Plateau.

Shohola Falls. The most popular attraction within SGL 180 is beautiful Shohola Falls. The photogenic stream tumbles over numerous horizontal ledges and a shear drop into the dark plunge pool. The pool's vertical rock walls divert the water down a narrow rocky canyon. The steep sides are

anchored by hemlocks, creating a moist, shady environment perfect for moss, ferns, and wildflowers that grow on the shale and siltstone rock. The fall's character is improved with larger volumes of water. To visit the falls, take the narrow gravel road next to the parking lot along Route 6 for 0.3 mile and turn right at the T. The trail follows the fall's descent to the plunge pool. To access the viewing platform on the west side of the falls, park in the lot along Route 6. Walk on Route 6 to cross Shohola Creek, then follow the well-marked trail upstream to the falls.

Shohola Lake near the kayak launch   Snags are still standing in the shallow lake.

Hunting & Fishing. Another popular activity is fishing. Species include largemouth bass, yellow perch, chain pickerel, black crappie, bullhead catfish, and panfish. At times the bass can be difficult to catch, but the prospect of catching a bass weighing more than 5 pounds provides plenty of incentive for anglers to return. The only places you can fish from shore are the main launch, the kayak launch area, and the falls parking area. Only electric- and human-powered boats are allowed on the lake. During the winter, the roads and parking lots are maintained for ice fishing and viewing the falls. Shohola Creek is stocked with trout above and below the lake. The land is open for hunting deer, bear, turkey, snowshoe hares, woodcock, and ruffed grouse.

Kayaking. Shohola Lake is a fantastic place to kayak in a near-wilderness setting. The best area to see wildlife is the southern section of the lake, which has islands and a forest of dead snags in the lake and wetlands. The locations of the refuge's two propagation areas are clearly identified on maps, and access is prohibited. During the summer and fall, the channel of the old serpentine-shaped stream remains weed free. Paddle quietly, then sit patiently to watch eagles flying or perched on one of the snags, looking for fish.

Birding. The Audubon Society of Pennsylvania designated SGL 180 as a Pennsylvania important bird area for nesting and migrating birds. Resident eagles and ospreys are the main attraction for most bird watchers. Climb the observation tower along Willis Hill Trail to view the eagle nest on the opposite side of the lake. A second viewing area is along Spring Brook Road, approximately 3 miles from Route 6, but the view is not nearly as good because it is too far from the lake. A few of the many birds that nest on or near the lake include bald eagle, osprey, wood duck, black duck, hooded merganser, and screech owl. Other birds commonly found in the wetlands include blue and green heron, common merganser, greater scaup, northern pintail, ring-necked duck, common goldeneye, bufflehead, horned and pied-billed grebe, common loon, and cormorant. The wetland habitat also attracts nesting and migrating shorebirds. The woodland, with its swamps and wet meadow habitat, supports turkey, roughed grouse, woodcock, numerous species of warblers, American redstart, indigo bunting, eastern towhee, willow and Acadian flycatchers, vireo, scarlet

An immature eagle dries its wings in the sunlight.

tanager, rose-breasted grosbeak, and northern oriole. One noteworthy species that nests in SGL 180 is the golden-winged warbler, whose numbers have drastically decreased. The Game Commission actively manages the bird's preferred habitat of overgrown fields, young forests, and wet meadows.

Bald Eagles. By the 1970s, the number of bald eagles had declined to such a degree that they were added to the list of endangered species. Loss of habitat, a diet of fish living in polluted waters, and the eagle's weakened eggshells from DDT contributed to their decline. In 1980, the only three nest sites in Pennsylvania were in Crawford County. In 1982, the Pennsylvania Game Commission began a seven-year Bald Eagle Restoration Program. The recovery team captured young eagles from Saskatchewan, Canada, and transferred them to Haldman Island, on the lower Susquehanna River, and Shohola Lake. Hacking towers were built, where volunteers fed the eaglets without direct human contact until they fledged. Several of the eighty-eight eagles returned to Shohola as adults to raise their own young. In 1990, there were eight active nests in Pennsylvania; forty-eight nests were found in 2000, and in 2013, more than 270 nests were in fifty-eight of the state's sixty-five counties. The bald eagle was removed from the endangered and threatened lists but is still protected by state and federal laws.

NE6 Seven Tubs Natural Area, Luzerne County

Seven Tubs NA is one of the more picturesque wonders in Pennsylvania. The 527-acre site contains Wheelbarrow Run, which tumbles down the mountain into much-larger Laurel Run. Wheelbarrow Run flows through deep rock channels and circular cuts, called tubs or potholes. Laurel Run also tumbles through a canyon and over layers of rock, but it never had the right ingredients to carve channels into the rock. The property is within SGL 292 but is separately owned by Pennsylvania's DCNR. It is a bit tricky to find. From the turnpike, take Route 115 north for 2.6 miles. From the left lane, turn left onto Bear Creek Boulevard. Look for the brown sign, which is easy to miss. Drive 0.3

A deep tub carved by swiftly running water carrying abrasive material

The slot and one of the tubs in the Seven Tubs NA

Trails are close to the edge on both sides of the carved slot and falls.

miles past two parking lots and park in the lot on the right, before the road curves downhill to the right. Walk across the road to the paved trail that leads to the bridge over Wheelbarrow Run and marked trails.

The natural area is not promoted like other comparable places but is very popular with local residents and is somehow becoming known to people from other states. Summer weekends it can become crowded, so as usual, my advice is to visit in the morning on a weekday. On my most recent visit, I arrived at 11:00 a.m. on a weekday and the lot was empty, but by 4:00 p.m. the lower lot was almost full. Interestingly, half the license plates were from other states, some as far away as Connecticut and Wisconsin.

Geology. As the most recent glacier receded, the sand and gravel in the torrents of Wheelbarrow Run cut a winding path through the sandstone and conglomerate rock in Whirlpool Canyon. The water followed the path of slightly softer rock where joints of different layers met. As the water spun around in whirlpools, it wore the rock into the tubs you see today. Resistant rock has created a few small waterfalls.

Trails. From the bridge I usually hike upstream on the right side. The 1.5-mile blue-blazed trail follows the stream in the cool shade of hemlock trees. The water flowing down in the channel is not visible from the trail, but it is certainly audible. You can view the chute at numerous locations by walking away from the trail, but be careful when you are at the edge of the channel. Wet rocks and moss are extremely slippery, and once you are in the water there are not many places to get out. Hike upstream until you arrive at a small bridge, cross over, and follow the trail downstream. Where a rock wall blocks the way, climb the steel steps providing access to the rim above. Continue down the trail, taking side trails to view the stream.

From the bridge you can hike the short distance down to the wide rockslide that empties into Laurel Run. This beautiful area is open and shaded with large hemlock trees. It is a great place for a picnic lunch, or to relax on the rocks along the stream. The 3-mile yellow-blazed trail begins here and heads upstream along interesting Laurel Run. The trail crosses under a power line, turns left, and climbs up the mountainside to just below the railroad tracks. It turns left and parallels the tracks until it connects with the upper section of the blue trail. Both trails are good places to look for birds that prefer forest habitat.

NE7 Brady's Lake, SGL 127, Monroe County

Brady's Lake is a remote lake in vast 25,527-acre Game Land 127 that is managed in conjunction with the Pennsylvania Fish and Boat Commission. The long, narrow lake is accessible by driving to the end of a 3-mile gravel road. The original dam was built in the 1800s and rebuilt in 1914, for the purpose of harvesting ice. At Brady's the ice was cut into blocks and hauled to a ramp by teams of horses. A steam engine pulled the slabs into the ice house, where it was packed with sawdust for storage. Trains with as many as 100 cars transported the region's ice to markets in the East and as far south as Florida.

Recreation. Fishing has steadily improved after the lake was lowered by 8 feet for the dam-rebuilding project completed in 2007. Game fish include largemouth bass, pickerel, catfish, and panfish. Only electric- and human-powered boats are allowed. On most nice days, three to five boats will be

One of the many beaver lodges in the shallow lake

Brady's Lake from the dam

on the water and several people will be hiking the trails. The GC manages the land for wildlife, such as black bear, deer, coyote, bobcat, snowshoe hare, turkey, and grouse. Jeep trails provide access for hunters who want to hike into this wild land to hunt or trap with few, if any, people nearby. The trails are also open to the general public for hiking and mountain biking. The lake is a kayaker's paradise—especially the northern section—but finding a place to beach a kayak in the lake's upper half is not easy. Much of the shoreline is impenetrable brush, or the water is covered with dense weeds far out from shore. When you reach solid ground the water is too deep to hop out.

Nature. The forest is mixed hardwoods of red and sugar maple, black cherry, and American beech, with areas of hemlock, birch, and aspen. The topography is slightly undulating, so swamps and wetlands are scattered everywhere. The landscape looks like what you would expect to see in a Canadian wilderness. A pair of bald eagles built a nest in a tall pine overlooking the wetland at the northern end of the lake. Beaver lodges and dams are on the upper half of Brady's Lake.

On a hike several years ago, not far from the lake, I came across an electric right-of-way with several large, wooden utility poles that were used by bears as scratching posts and to mark their territory. They had 1-inch-deep gouges from 5 to 8 feet above the ground all the way around the poles. On that same hike, I backpacked an inflatable kayak to a remote glacial lake completely surrounded by wetlands. I discovered it accidently

A curious beaver came out of his lodge several times to inspect the intruder.

Brady's Lake, one of the remote lakes in the Poconos, receives only moderate fishing pressure.

The only way into impenetrable Mystery Swamp is by following the inlet stream.

while doing aerial photography nearby. It is one of many unnamed small wetland lakes on the USGS map. The only access to open water required hacking my way down the boulder-strewn inlet stream. As I paddled through the channel and across the lake, I could not help feeling like an explorer from the 1600s, entering an unknown land. I also wondered if anyone had ever floated the lake. It was a memorable day and reminded me that we need to protect seldom-seen places like it.

Paddling on Brady's Lake, I discovered two low dams that beavers had built where a tributary enters the lake. The two dams were built to give the beavers a deeper weed-free channel to carry newly cut branches from the woods. It must have taken an incredible amount of effort to build the long,

Backpacking an inflatable kayak is the only way to float this remote lake.

horseshoe-shaped dam far from shore. At their lodge, branches were stuffed next to the underwater entrances on opposite sides of the lodge. Later that day, I paddled to another lodge and after a few minutes made a few squeaking sounds. To my astonishment, a beaver suddenly appeared behind me, checked me out, and then disappeared. I called again and he surfaced again. As I turned to photograph him, he slapped his tail and dove underwater. He came out one more time, then apparently decided his curiosity was satisfied.

NE8 Delaware Water Gap National Recreation Area, Monroe and Pike Counties

The 67,608-acre Delaware Water Gap NRA—owned and operated by the National Park Service—is the largest recreational area in the eastern US. The 40-mile-long park straddles the Delaware River and encompasses the parallel mountains in New Jersey and Pennsylvania. The Pennsylvania portion is 28,164 acres and the New Jersey portion, including land converted to state parks, is 39,444 acres. The park headquarters, facilities, and most of the recreation and natural attractions are in Pennsylvania's portion of the park. The main feature is the river, which is the longest undammed river east of the Mississippi and one of the cleanest for its size in the country. It is also one of the most floated rivers in the country. The East Branch of the river originates from Pepacton Reservoir, in the Catskill Mountains, and the West Branch originates from New York's Cannonsville Reservoir. Countless clean streams flow off the Pocono Plateau and Kittatinny Mountain. Springs provide a constant flow of cold, pure water from the base of the mountains. In 1978, the 40-mile section of the Delaware River within the park was designated a national wild and scenic river. Approximately 3.5 million people visit annually, making it one of the most visited parks in the country and in Pennsylvania.

History. Soon after the 1955 flood, which killed dozens of people and caused extensive damage, the Army Corps of Engineers proposed building the largest dam in the eastern US. The Tocks Island National Recreation Area would control flooding, supply clean water to New York City and Philadelphia, produce hydroelectric power, and provide recreation. Starting in 1960, the land was acquired by eminent domain. Fifteen thousand people were displaced and an estimated 3,000 to 5,000 structures were demolished. The public opposed the dam due to environmental impact and unfair land acquisitions. A 1974 study revealed that better options were available for flood control and water. The Delaware River Basin Commission, which had no authoritative power, voted against the project. The project would have continued anyway were it not for two new developments: the discovery that the bedrock in the proposed dam location could not support the dam, and the project's high cost. The dam project

Sunrise on the Delaware River in early February

was shelved and the land was turned over to the National Park Service. Also worth mentioning is the Shawnee-Minisink archeological site, which revealed stone tools, seeds, bones, and postholes dating back 10,000 years. In 1968, a 12,000-year-old mastodon skeleton was excavated from a peat bog near the park. It now resides in the state museum in Harrisburg.

In 1996, the flooded river cut high into the steep mountainside on the New Jersey side. The 16-inch-deep ground was so saturated that an avalanche of dirt, trees, and rock slid down the mountain into a massive tangled mess in the river. All that remained was bare bedrock. Within a few years, everything in the river was washed away. Today, 8-foot pine trees and other vegetation grow in cracks on the bare bedrock. In 2010, an earthquake in the Washington, DC, area probably caused a section of ground along Route 209—including a trail—to drop 17 feet. The main road in the park was closed for many months while it was rebuilt.

Natural Habitat. The park's habitat is extraordinarily diverse, and what makes this park unique is that most of the habitats are relatively narrow strips—20 to 40 miles long—that run parallel to the river. The six ecozones in order are the river, with its small rapids, riffles, and long pools; the wide riparian woodland; the fertile agricultural fields, grasslands, and meadows; the deciduous and white pine mountainside forest; rocky cliffs; and the relatively flat plateau with ponds and wetlands. Two other habitats are

Sunrise above the river at the top of a cliff

the steep hemlock-shaded ravines with streams that pour off the plateau, and low-elevation wetlands. One interesting note is that the park leads the National Park system in the number of acres that are farmed: 3,000 acres are leased to approximately ten farmers who plant crops and maintain grasslands under strict wildlife management and environmental guidelines.

Some of the more inaccessible areas have old-growth trees. The tallest—a white pine—is nearly 170 feet high. Other tree species in the hemlock ravines include white pine, sweet birch, yellow birch, white oak, sugar maple, sycamore, and rhododendron. Unfortunately, the hemlock woolly adelgid entered the park in 1998 and has killed some of the hemlock trees. Work is being done to save the larger hemlocks. A positive note is that along Hornsbeck Creek are five American chestnut trees from 10 to 41 feet tall (top half is dead). The area also has a 117-foot hemlock and a 108-foot sugar maple. Surveys reveal that the ravines' plant species include 122 wildflowers, twenty-four different ferns, and 123 mosses. The high rock cliffs harbor unique colonies of lichen, and prickly pear cactus are found on the dry, rocky ridges. The riverbanks and meadows have a profusion of wildflowers during summer months.

Waterfalls. Approximately twenty spectacular waterfalls are spread out along the northern half of the park's Pocono Escarpment. Raymondskill Falls, at 180 feet, is the highest in Pennsylvania and only 4 feet shorter than Niagara Falls. The upper parking lot provides easy access to the area at the top of the falls. Notice that the large boulder on the other side of the falls has rolled on its side. Follow the trail down to the viewing area at the bottom of the upper falls (easy access from lower parking lot). Access below this point is restricted to protect the hemlocks on the steep slope. The access to 130-foot Dingmans Falls, the second-highest in Pennsylvania, is on a boardwalk that crosses the stream, and passes 80-foot Silverthread Falls, through an ancient stand of rhododendron. A trail continues to the viewing platform at the bottom of the falls. Approximately 250 steps help you climb to the top of the falls. My favorite area is Childs Recreational Site. The wide, cindered trail takes you past hemlocks nearly 3 feet wide to cascading 17-foot-high Factory Falls. Farther down the trail is 55-foot Fulmer Falls. To reach 30-foot Deer Leap Falls, continue on the trail across the bridge and down to a second bridge with a nice view overlooking the falls and the plunge pool.

The 3.5-mile trail for Indian Ladders Falls has tremendous scenery and few people. You pass four major falls, many smaller falls, plunge pools, and 12-foot-deep cuts through rock, and you are always within hearing distance of the roaring stream. Park at the small lot on Emery Road and take the trail next to Hornsbeck Creek. At the bottom of the second major falls, cross the stream and continue down the mountain. The 60-foot Pinchot Falls is on the Grey Tower Estate. I highly recommend visiting the other undeveloped falls, which are not promoted and require more effort

The cliff's unique environment supports cedar trees, prickly pear cactus, mosses, and lichen.

to find and access. They are inherently more dangerous, have beautiful natural scenery, and have far fewer, if any, people. They include Tumbling Waters (two falls, highest is 70 feet), Spackmans, Adams, and Hackers Falls. When visiting any falls, wear sturdy footwear and do not take risks.

Wildlife. The Delaware has more than sixty species of fish, including smallmouth bass, walleye, and muskellunge. Migratory fish that leave the ocean and travel 200 miles up the Delaware River to spawn include American eel and shad. The river is also home to otters, beavers, and crayfish. Native brook trout live in the shaded ravines. Bears, with males weighing up to 700 pounds, leave their paw prints on the river's sandy shoreline at night. Within the park are fourteen species of snakes, eight turtles, and two lizards. The venomous copperhead and rattlesnake prefer high-elevation, rocky terrain and are seldom encountered. Both the lowland and plateau wetlands are prime breeding locations for spring peepers, wood frogs, spotted and Jefferson salamanders, and spotted newts. Near the park office, the Park Service closes a 5-mile section of River Road on rainy nights in late March and early April so thousands of amphibians can travel safely between their forest home and their breeding ponds.

The surprisingly high 249 species of birds identified in the park is due in large part to the proximity of the Delaware River and Kittatinny Mountain

Both falls, called Tumbling Waters, have
beautiful splash pools.

Deer Leap Falls, George W. Childs
Recreational Site

migration corridors. During the spring migration, at least thirty species of warblers have been recorded. The river, ponds, and wetlands support shorebirds, waterfowl, herons, osprey, and eagles. The hemlock ravines are home to black-throated green and blackburnian warblers, arcadian flycatchers, and hermit thrush. The grasslands support bobolink, grasshopper sparrow, and turkey. The deciduous forests are preferred by ruffed grouse, woodpeckers, owls, and warblers.

The Delaware River supports a large population of nesting eagles. Nests are usually built in large white pines near the river and are used by the same pair every year. Eagle watching has become a major tourist attraction. More than 100 eagles spend the winter along the ice-free sections of the upper Delaware and Lackawaxon Rivers, including ten to twenty in the park. The cliffs at Delaware Water Gap's Mount Minsi are closed to hikers and rock climbers between late January and early August to protect nesting peregrine falcons.

Recreation. Float trips down the river are extremely popular. Approximately 200,000 people float the river every year, of which commercial companies average 170,000 annual clients. For those with their own equipment, Pike County provides free shuttle service every half hour between access locations during the summer (you should verify in advance). The

Early-morning fog looms over the Pennsylvania side of the river.

View of 1,463-foot Mount Minsi from 1,527-foot Mt. Tammany, Delaware Water Gap (mid-October)

A female eagle is getting her nest ready so she can lay eggs (mid-February).

Boardwalk to Dingmans Falls

A good example of nature speaking volumes: the tracks of two coyotes chasing a deer

A beautiful pair of bald eagles on their perch above the river

park has six river access sites, of which four have ramps for boaters. The river is extremely scenic and offers great fishing for smallmouth bass and walleye. Almost the entire length is away from roads, buildings, and noise. Designated campsites are available for multiday float trips.

The park's rustic Dingman's Campground has 133 sites and is operated by a private company. Smithfield and Milford are the park's two swim beaches. Fourteen trails on the Pennsylvania side of the park and the Pocono Environmental Education Center's six trails provide hiking to vistas, ponds, waterfalls, a fossil quarry, and every type of habitat. The 32-mile McDade Trail is surfaced with packed gravel for biking, hiking, and cross-country skiing. Six miles of the Appalachian Trail run through Pennsylvania's side of the water gap. The park's cliffs provide some of the best rock climbing in Pennsylvania. A mowed grassy area is dedicated to flying radio-controlled model airplanes.

PEEC. The Pocono Environmental Education Center in the park is one of the largest and most comprehensive EECs in the eastern US. Their 38-acre campus with two lodges, cabins, dining hall, and education building hosts conferences, retreats, and meetings and provides programs and guided hikes.

First of four Indian Ladder Falls, 0.8 miles
from Route 209

NE9 Hickory Run State Park and Natural Areas, Carbon County

The 15,990-acre Hickory Run SP—one of the largest in Pennsylvania—is the only SP with three designated state park natural areas: Boulder Field, Mud Run, and Mud Swamp. Boulder Field is also designated a national natural landmark. Adjacent to the park are SGLs 149, 129, and 40 and Lehigh Gorge SP, which add another 16,000 acres of protected land. This huge park supports a long list of wildlife, plants, trees, and natural features.

History. Early European settlers called this vast forest of pine, hemlock, oak, and maple the Shades of Death. Beginning in the 1830s, the upper section of the Lehigh Canal was completed. Loggers moved in and mills were erected on Hickory Run and Mud Run, and the town of Hickory Run was established. When the stagecoach road between Bethlehem and Wilkes-Barre was completed, the town of Saylorsville was established. In 1849, one of many floods swept through both towns, killing at least seven people. The Great Fire of 1875—the largest of several—destroyed mills and homes. By the late 1880s, the forests were cut and the citizens moved on. In 1918, Harry Trexler, an Allentown businessman who made his fortune in the cement and logging industries, began buying the land to establish a public recreational area. After his death, his estate trustees donated 12,908 acres

Sunset at Boulder Field NA, Hickory Run SP

Aerial view of the largest boulder field in Pennsylvania

The long loop road through the park

Black Creek (SGL 40) adjacent to the park

A wild turkey chick sits motionless with its head down, waiting for mother to return in Mud Run NA.

to the National Park Service. Improvements were made, and in 1945 the recreational area was transferred to the commonwealth as a state park.

Boulder Field NA. Boulder Field Natural Area is a level area of boulders 0.25 miles long, 400 feet wide, and approximately 12 feet deep. The red sandstone and red conglomerate sandstone boulders vary in size, but most are 2 to 6 feet, with some up to 24 feet long. This field is the largest in North America and is unique because boulder fields are usually in steep-sided valleys. The boulder field was created by several processes during the most recent Wisconsinan glaciation. The rock outcrops on the parallel ridges were gradually broken apart when water seeped into cracks during the day and froze at night. The boulders, along with glacial silt and sand, were washed across the frozen ground by torrents of glacial meltwater. The final step occurred when large amounts of water washed away the sand and silt, leaving just the boulders you see today. An additional bonus for visitors is the old-growth spruce forest around the field's perimeter. For an unknown reason, loggers decided not to cut the virgin spruce trees, which are now rarely found in Pennsylvania. The 6-mile loop road to the boulder field will definitely give you an idea of the large size of this park.

Mud Run NA. Mud Run—a pristine mountain stream—flows through a stunning, remote, steep-sided canyon until it reaches the Lehigh River Gorge. The middle section of the stream is within the 1,335-acre natural area, where the two side ravines of Hawk Run and Panther Creek enter Mud Run. Mud Run has a native population of brown and brook trout. There are three ways to access Mud Run; stop at the office for a map and information. A remote access is achieved by parking along Route 534, on the east side of the turnpike, and hiking the unmarked trail downhill through a dense stand of rhododendron to Mud Run. Hike downstream for 1.4 miles until you reach private property. Wildlife abounds in this remote canyon, and I doubt you will run into other people.

Mud Swamp NA. Mud Swamp is a remote emergent wetland with spruce trees and rare plant species of concern. This wetland is similar to habitat found in northern boreal areas. The 152-acre NA in the extreme southeastern corner of the park has no established trails or roads.

Recreation. The campground is huge, with 381 sites, three cabins, and a camp store. The park also has thirteen organized group tent camps and two group cabin camps that hold 124 and 149 people. Hickory Run, Mud Run, Hickory Run Lake, and the CCC dam are stocked with brown and brook trout. The sandy beach and concession are at Sand Spring Lake. Enjoy a scenic hike to Hawk Falls and along Mud Run. Other activities include hunting, disc golf, cross-country skiing, snowmobiling, and environmental-education programs. Twenty-three maintained trails provide scenic access to every type of habitat, natural feature, and recreational area.

NE10 Lehigh Gorge State Park and Glen Onoko Falls, SGL 141, Carbon County

Lehigh Gorge is a premier scenic destination for whitewater rafting and kayaking on the river, and hiking and biking on beautiful 26-mile Lehigh Gorge Trail. The 6,107-acre state park and SGL 141 protect both sides of the Lehigh River from the Francis Walter Dam at the northern end to Jim Thorpe at the south end. There are only three main access points to the river and the trail: White Haven, at the north end, has parking only. Rockport, in the middle, and Glen Onoko, near Jim Thorpe, have parking, water, and restrooms. The river from White Haven to Rockport is 8.7 miles long and from Rockport to Glen Onoko is 12.2 miles.

A view of Lehigh River Gorge from high above

Lehigh Gorge Trail. The easy-to-ride trail runs parallel and above the Lehigh River and passes close to several waterfalls and historic stone ruins of old canal locks. One side of the trail drops steeply to the river, with the sound of the rapids always present. The upper side is partially lined with large rhododendron, wildflowers, and sections of cut rock. Since Glen Onoko is near the tourist town of Jim Thorpe, it might be the most popular place to start for those who are riding out and back. The lower section of the gorge is the deepest and has the most cliffs and river bends. The upper section is more shaded and scenic. Along the trail, just north of Rockport, is Buttermilk Falls, an impressive series of rocks carved by the stacked falls. Concessioners take bikers to Rockport or White Haven to ride one-way downhill. At Glen Onoko, you can walk through the old railroad tunnel to the sheer cliff where the track used to continue on a bridge over the river. Drive across the bridge and park in the main lot if you are hiking to Glen Onoko Falls.

Whitewater Boating. The Lehigh River is a great place to go for an exhilarating float trip, with plenty of whitewater through the beautiful gorge. If you do not have your own gear, four commercial operators run trips from April to October, as long as there is enough water flowing. The

Buttermilk Falls along the bike path, 0.2 miles north of Rockport

The Lehigh River has class I–III rapids and is fairly shallow and rock filled.

Rafting is very popular, especially on water release days.

A skilled kayaker in a duckie faces upstream with little effort by using the river's hydraulics.

Two lovers behind Glen Onoko Falls

character of the class III river changes dramatically depending on the flow rate. The Army Corps of Engineers operates Francis Walter Dam and controls the amount of water released into the river. Twenty-four water release days are scheduled in advance by the Army Corps.

Glen Onoko Falls. Glen Onoko Run, on SGL 141, is a swift-flowing stream that drops 875 feet in one mile and empties into the Lehigh River. Three falls are at the top of the steep ravine: Chameleon Fall, a 25-foot cascade, Glen Onoko Falls, a 60-foot drop over an undercut ledge, and, near the top, Hidden Sweet Fall, a 10-foot cascade. The best time to visit is when there is plenty of water flowing. Equally impressive is the stream itself, which tumbles over boulders on its way down the hemlock- and rhododendron-filled ravine. Falls Trail is one of the most scenic and challenging trails in Pennsylvania, and the view at the top is spectacular. The well-worn, 1.4-mile hike to the top parallels the stream straight up the mountain, with two boulder crossings, but it is difficult to maintain. The Game Commission does not promote the falls as a tourist attraction, and there are few trail improvements. A less strenuous orange-blazed trail leads to the top by circling out away from the ravine. From the bottom of Glen Onoko Falls you can hike to the right around the rock outcrop to reach the top. Look at the view, but do not get near the edge of the falls!

A yellow-phase timber rattlesnake over 5 feet long at Rockport

The rugged trail up the steep ravine parallels and crosses the gorgeous Glen Onoko Run.

The view from a safe position at the top of the falls

To find the two trailheads from the main parking lot, walk past the restrooms and at the river turn right. Walk under the bridge and uphill to the right to the warning sign. To the left is Falls Trail and to the right is the orange trail. If you hike both trails as a loop, I recommend hiking up Falls Trail and back on the orange trail. More injuries occur hiking down the rugged trail than up. Wear proper hiking boots, do not get near the edge of any drop-off, and do not bring young children or dogs; the trail and rocks are slippery. In fact, more injuries and deaths have occurred at this trail and waterfalls than probably any other outdoor site in Pennsylvania. Between 1977 and 2016, at least twelve people have died from falling. Dozens more were severely injured or lost, requiring massive rescues from local EMS and fire departments. At minimum, countless hikers have hobbled down the mountain with sprained ankles. Thousands of people enjoy the trail and falls every year without incident, so use caution and enjoy nature's beauty.

NE11 Penn Forest Land and Reservoirs, Carbon County

Both the 480-acre Penn Forest Reservoir and the 304-acre Wild Creek Reservoir are within a watershed of pristine and protected land. The approximately 12,000-acre property is owned by the Bethlehem (Water) Authority. They also own a second, extremely valuable 10,000-acre property 8 miles away called Long Pond (see NE13). Two fundamental characteristics of the Penn Forest property make it unique and increase its environmental value: first, it is not promoted for recreation, unlike almost all other preserved properties in Pennsylvania; second, public access is very limited. The land is open to the public for hiking, mountain biking, bird watching, cross-country skiing, and nature study. With the exception of a few hunters (hunting is not open to the general public) and water authority personnel, you will probably be the only person there. Both reservoirs are surrounded by fencing and public access is not permitted. There are no designated parking areas, marked trails, maps, or restrooms. It is patrolled daily to prevent the use of four wheelers and snowmobiles. The lack of recreational development on such a large block of land has created high-quality and secure habitats for wildlife and a place for humans who seek solitude in a natural environment.

Description. The land encompasses the Pocono Plateau in the northern section, with an elevation of 2,000 feet, the Pocono Escarpment, and the Ridge and Valley Province in the southern section, which has an average elevation of 1,000 feet. Call Mountain rises to 1,500 feet. The City of Bethlehem bought the former farmland seventy years ago and let it revert back to a forest. Conifers line the reservoirs' shoreline and blanket steep Hell Hollow ravine. The rest of the forest is a mix of northern hardwoods. The crystal-clear streams are shaded by dense thickets of rhododendron, and a few wetlands are on the property. Only one paved road is open all year. One gravel road, called Hell Hollow Road, is open to the public but is not maintained during winter months. Parking is permitted along the shoulder of Hell Hollow Road and at the entrance to forest roads as long as you do not block gates or roads. Adjacent to the Bethlehem Authority's land is another 3,800 acres of protected land owned by DCNR's Department of Forestry, Lehighton Water Authority, and two hunting clubs.

In 2011, Bethlehem Authority entered a long-term conservation easement with the Nature Conservancy's Northeast Pennsylvania office. The protection of Penn Forest's and Long Pond's 22,000 acres was accomplished through the Nature Conservancy's Working Woodlands

Wild Creek Reservoir and Penn Forest Reservoir

Both reservoirs are surrounded by forests in a self-contained watershed.

This scene is near the pump station on Bethlehem Authority's Long Pond land.

Program. This program encourages landowners to participate without direct monetary exchange. Instead, the landowner receives a modest revenue source through forest carbon credit payments and forest certification, which is guided by a detailed forest stewardship plan and inventory.

Wildlife. Wildlife abounds on this property. Bald eagles and osprey nest in the white pines at the reservoirs and, along with otters, take advantage of the abundant native fish in the reservoirs and streams. Other wildlife include black bear, deer, bobcat, coyote, and turkey. On rocky higher elevations— especially Hell Hollow—is one of the healthiest populations of rattlesnakes in the state. Herpetologists conduct rattlesnake surveys every other year. Several expert birders consider this property to be one of the most valuable bird habitats in northeastern Pennsylvania. The Lehigh Valley Audubon Society conducts birding tours during migration and nesting seasons.

One morning, I parked off the road below Penn Forest Reservoir and took a ten-minute walk to an area I had never seen before. As I headed toward the stream, I passed a stand of huge hemlocks. A dozen warblers and other small birds were flitting and singing high above me in the hemlocks' branches. When I reached the babbling creek, a bald eagle was perched in a tree, looking for its next meal. In the clear water, brook trout darted for aquatic insects.

NE12 Beltzville Lake State Park, Carbon County

Beltzville SP is a popular 3,002-acre day-use park with a 949-acre lake. The park was created in a cooperative effort by ACE, DCNR, and the GC. ACE built the high dam for flood control and recreation, and the state park opened in 1972. The recreational pool level is 628 feet, but the lake level fluctuates depending on rainfall. The parallel south ridge slopes steeply uphill to 1,000 feet, and on the north side the land slopes gently uphill. Wild Creek and Pohopoco Creek are the two main tributaries entering at the east end of the long, narrow lake. More than 500,000 people visit the park each year, and on a busy holiday the number can approach 8,000 visitors.

Beltzville Lake from the dam

Boating & Fishing. Boating is very popular, especially in the summer for waterskiing, fishing, and simply cruising. There is no horsepower limit on the lake, but there are designated areas for waterskiing and no-wake zones. A boat launch is on each side of the lake. The 170-foot-deep lake holds a large number of species of fish, including largemouth, smallmouth, and spotted bass; walleye; crappie; chain pickerel; lake trout; striped bass; and three types of catfish. Fishing success is notoriously difficult, but there are plenty of large fish. A mounted 43-inch, 37-pound striped bass is displayed in the park office. Pickerel up to 24 inches are common, and largemouth bass up to 7 pounds are caught each year. Many anglers fish the dam spillway and stream below for stocked trout.

Recreation. The main recreational area has a sandy beach, food concession, and bathhouse. A boat rental concession is near the beach. An interesting activity at the beach is looking for ancient fossils. The fossils are molds of small creatures that lived in a shallow sea 350 million years ago. Crinoids were animals but had flower-shaped heads and segmented stems anchored to the seafloor. Impressions of branchiopods look like small clamshells. Look for fossils along the shoreline of the beach and to the right side of the beach, but fossils may not be removed from the park.

Check out ACE's informative displays and vista near the dam. I was surprised at the size of the emergency spillway and dam. The park's diversified habitat of fields, wetlands, ponds, lake, and forests attracts many species of birds. On April 1, 2017, one bird watcher saw forty-six species, including Wilson's snipe, common loon, horned grebe, long-tailed

Fishing in Pohopoco Cove

This small fish is a chain pickerel that a kingfisher caught and dropped while flying.

The waterfalls along Falls Trail

Kayaking in a quiet cove

duck, green-winged teal, white-winged and surf scoter, bald eagle, fish crow, palm and pine warbler, and several other waterfowl.

Waterfalls. Wild Creek Waterfall is a hidden gem in a secluded hemlock- and rhododendron-filled ravine. It seems almost out of place in this somewhat tame park. Take the wide trail from the back of the parking area straight for 300 yards. Turn left and walk downhill and across the bridge over the stream's 5-foot-deep hole. The scenery is beautiful. The blue-blazed Falls Trail loop starts here. Head upstream to the gorgeous falls. The stream flows between exposed rock walls and over large boulders with rhododendron on both sides. You can either turn around or follow the loop trail through the forest to a pipeline, where the blazes end. Turn right and walk downhill until you come to a faint trail and stony wash. Turn right and follow the wash to the stream and then turn right, back to the bridge. You can also view the falls and stream from high ground on the west side. From the lot, take the trail until you enter the woods. Turn left and walk 100 yards through a stand of large hemlocks to the cliffs above the stream, then walk upstream to the falls.

I found this 350-million-year-old crinoid and a mix of shells and stems at the beach. Note: fossils can no longer be removed, but you can still look for them.

Trails. Saw Mill Trail is a double-loop trail below the dam. The trail passes the historic ruins of a mill, a raceway, gateways, ponds, wetlands, a stream, and an old slate quarry dating back to the 1700s. Pick up a trail guide at the park office. Christman Trail is a favorite for cross-country skiers. One of my favorites is Preachers Camp Trail, which starts at Trachsville Hill Road and follows the cove's south shore to Preachers Camp Boat Launch. Park at the hidden lot on the east side of the road, next to the bridge. Cross the road and find the trail. The trail rises and falls along the hillside as it crosses five small tributaries in steep ravines. Access to the beautiful cove is easy from certain parts of the trail. You might see kayakers and fishermen back here. On one hike I watched a fisherman catch a large pickerel within 20 feet of where I was standing.

NE13 Long Pond Preserve, SGLs 38 and 318, Monroe County

Surrounding the hamlet of Long Pond are 17,000 acres of scrub oak–pitch pine barrens, heath barrens, wetlands, glacial lakes, and several types of forests. Located on the Pocono Plateau at an elevation of 1,800–2,000 feet, Long Pond Preserve is nationally recognized for its diverse habitats. More than thirty-two rare and imperiled plants and insects—the most in Pennsylvania—inhabit the only mesic till barren community in the world. Normally barrens are found on dry, nutrient-poor soil. The Long Pond barrens are on moisture-holding, fertile, 130,000-year-old Illinoian glacial till. It is the largest undisturbed deposit in the northeastern US. Also, a climate data station near Long Pond recorded the lowest average summer temperature and the most precipitation of the 161 stations in Pennsylvania. Historically, fires regularly sweep through the fire-tolerant barrens and have prevented other species from becoming established.

Landowners. The land is basically two separate habitat areas. West of Kuhenbeaker Road is Long Pond Preserve. Here the land is so flat that Tunkhannock Creek transitions into a wide channel and a lake that are lined by huge wetlands, heath barrens, and boreal forests. East of Kuhenbeaker

Aerial view of the serpentine channel in late November. Notice the yellow tamarack trees.

The shoreline along the open lake

One of Long Pond's grass areas

Road the elevation is slightly higher but still relatively flat, with thousands of acres of scrub oak–pitch pine barrens, swamps, glacial lakes, the headwaters of Tunkhannock Creek, and various types of forests. In the eastern section, Bethlehem (Water) Authority owns about 5,000 acres, and SGL 38 and Big Pocono SP add an additional 5,300 acres. In the Long Pond section, Bethlehem owns about 4,000 acres, and the rest is owned by the Nature Conservancy, Wildlands Conservancy, the Game Commission (SGL 318), and the township. The Nature Conservancy's northeast office is at their Hauser Nature Center in Long Pond. Their mission is to manage existing natural habitat, preserve additional environmentally valuable land, conduct research, and educate the public.

Along the channel, far from the nearest access

Rhodora—an uncommon heath shrub well known for being prolific in the barrens. May 21

Two young brothers feeding early in the morning

Long Pond. The channel begins at the bridge on Kuhenbeaker Road and ends at the bridge on Long Pond Road. This approximately 5-mile section of waterway is bordered by vast wetlands, with only a few isolated places where dry land meets open water. Kayaking and canoeing are strongly discouraged for liability and environmental reasons. Access is very limited. The channels can be clogged with weeds, and if a kayak tipped, swimming to dry land is rarely possible. Unfortunately, Pocono Raceway shares a 1-mile border with Long Pond and can produce a lot of noise. One positive note is that all of the raceway's electric use is generated by their solar panels, and they do not pollute the air by mowing the panels' grassy area. Instead, a shepherd brings his flock to feed on the grass between May and September.

The heath barrens on Bethlehem (Water) Authority land

A woodcock looking for worms before sunrise at Long Pond Preserve

Pink lady slipper orchid near Grassy Lake in early June

Trails. On the entire 17,000 acres, the terrain is relatively flat with few reference points, so it is easy to get lost. There is only one named or marked trail, with no signs, trail maps, or restrooms, and only one established parking area at the Kuhenbeaker Road bridge. Deep within the eastern section are numerous interconnecting trails that can be very confusing. Bikes should stay on the trails. Hiking off trail should be avoided or minimized, but certainly done with great caution to avoid stepping on fragile plants. Cherish it for what it is. I strongly recommend that you do not hike far into the eastern section without a topo map and a GPS device. I have hiked here for thirty years, but I still got temporarily lost one time by taking a side trail that petered out, and it is not something I want to experience again.

The two trails from Hypsy Gap Road are excellent for hiking and mountain biking. The first jeep trail passes scrub oak barrens and two types of forests at Grassy Lake, then continues north. The second jeep trail goes through scrub oak and pitch pine, then splits into three trails that head north to various habitats. North of I-80, a 1-mile hiking trail on SGL 318 provides access to one of the three glacial lakes. At the Kuhenbeaker Road bridge, a jeep trail heads east and ends at Route 115. Along the trail, two footpaths split off to the right toward the wetlands. The 1.7-mile Cathy's Trail is a loop that begins behind the Hauser Nature Center and takes you through a boreal conifer swamp, a boulder field, red spruce forest, and a northern hardwood

Wolf Swamp Lake, SGL 38

forest. A map of this trail is available at the center. A few guided trail hikes are conducted by Monroe EEC and Jacobsburg SP.

Flora. The Nature Conservancy and the GC have employed prescribed burns on several thousand acres with successful results. You will notice that trees that are not fire resistant have died while the pitch pine was unaffected, other than blackened bark near ground level. The scrub oaks and other shrubs have returned with renewed vigor, including lowbush blueberry, chokeberry, sheep laurel, mountain laurel, huckleberry, rhododendron, and rhodora. Deciduous trees include American beech, yellow birch, red maple, black cherry, five species of oak, two species of aspen, and black gum. The conifers that prefer drier ground are black spruce and white pine, and in the wetter areas there are hemlock, tamarack, balsam fir, and red spruce. The remote wetland and lake area north of I-80 contains one of the state's largest stands of red spruce. Adams Swamp Preserve, in the western section of Long Pond, is the largest undisturbed boreal conifer swamp in Pennsylvania. The shrub understory in Long Pond's heath barrens includes Labrador tea, sweet bayberry, leatherleaf, meadowsweet, rhododendron, sheep laurel, cranberry, blueberry, and rhodora. In late May, the barrens and wetlands come alive with the pink blossoms of the rhodora azalea. Long Pond has the only barrens in the northeastern US where rhodora is one of the dominant shrubs.

Within the preserve is one of Pennsylvania's largest collections of imperiled plants, including two species of orchids, all three of the state's carnivorous plants, four species of sedges—of which a community of variable sedge is the largest in the world, five species that are endangered in Pennsylvania, and at least six plants classified as rare. A short list of rare plants at Half Moon Lake includes bog sedge, yellow cowlily, Labrador tea, and northeastern bulrush, which is close to extinction. Sixteen rare moths have been discovered in the barrens, and Long Pond is the only location in Pennsylvania where seven of the moths have been found. Numerous species of rare butterflies and dragonflies are also found here. The dense habitat is perfect for bear, beaver, otter, snowshoe hare, coyote, bobcat, deer, grouse, turkey, and other deep-woods animals. Of course amphibians and reptiles, including the timber rattlesnake, thrive here. Long Pond is also designated as an important bird area and is a great place for birders.

NE14 Tannersville Cranberry Bog Preserve, Monroe County

Tannersville Cranberry Bog is a fascinating environment that has not changed much for thousands of years and has characteristics similar to the boreal forest region in Canada. As the southernmost low-altitude boreal bog along the Eastern Seaboard, it was designated a national natural landmark. The original 62 acres—purchased in 1957—was the second property purchased by the Nature Conservancy. Today, the conservancy owns millions of acres around the world. The preserve is now more than 1,000 acres and is managed by the Nature Conservancy, Monroe County Conservation District, and volunteers. Visitors must sign up for a scheduled tour led by a naturalist from the Monroe County EEC (570-629-3061).

Environment. Like most boreal bogs, Tannersville Cranberry Bog was created when a large block of ice broke off the retreating Wisconsinan glacier. Meltwater delivered silt and rock debris around the block of ice. With the ice sheet gone the land rebounded, except under the block of ice. The water-filled depression is also called a kettle lake. A true bog relies on rainwater as its only source of water. Tannersville is actually an acid fen because it receives some groundwater flow, but the nutrients in the water are negligible and the plants are similar to those found in a true bog. The main ingredient in a bog is sphagnum moss, which initially spreads out from the shoreline, forming a dense, floating mat. As sections of moss die they sink, decay into peat, and release tannic acid. Since there is almost no freshwater exchange, the bog's water contains very little oxygen. Bacteria, which breaks down organic material, is almost nonexistent in the acidic environment. Therefore, the nutrients in the organic material are not released back into the environment. By comparison, under one of

A boardwalk leads to open water at the center of the bog.

Round-leaved sundew

Pitcher plants; notice the hairs pointing down.

White Calla

your boot prints, the forest soil has up to 8,000 different species of microorganisms or bacteria. Two NASA scientists who were studying climate change took tube samples and discovered that the bog is 57 feet deep and 13,500 years old. Animals found in the preserve include black bear, river otter, coyote, bobcat, snowshoe hare, and the rare bog turtle. Bird species are typical for northern wetland regions.

Trees & Shrubs. A trail and a 1,450-foot-long floating boardwalk lead you through a succession of habitats to the bog's center. On higher ground is a forest of hemlock, white pine, pitch pine, and black, white, and chestnut oaks. Red maple, yellow birch, and rhododendron are found near the bog's edge, and a variety of ferns and wildflowers line the trail. Of particular interest are the numerous American chestnut saplings. Even though the chestnut blight killed all the trees in the US, the roots of hundred-year-old chestnut trees are still alive and have enough stored energy to send up shoots. Unfortunately, the saplings will also die when they reach about 2.5 inches in diameter, but their roots can send up more shoots. This is why the American chestnut is not on the list of extinct species.

As you enter the bog the habitat change is obvious. Shrubby thickets of heath are everywhere, including highbush blueberry, cranberry, bog and sheep laurel, swamp azalea, leatherleaf, and two of the state's rarer species, bog rosemary and Labrador tea. A boreal forest of black spruce and tamarack and a few red maples grow on the bog's peat and sphagnum. Tamarack—the only deciduous conifer—turns yellow before losing its needles in fall. Both boreal species have roots that spread out just below the spongy surface to stabilize the tree. Due to the lack of nutrients, a 40-foot tree could be 200–300 years old. It takes forty years before a black spruce produces its first cone.

Plants. The carnivorous pitcher plant and sundew plant are found in sunny areas and absorb nutrients from insects. The pitcher plant's leaves form an elongated bowl and are scented at the top edge. The inside of the leaves are slippery and have stiff hairs that point down toward the small pool of rainwater and enzymes. The insect is initially attracted to the plant's color, which they can see in ultraviolet wavelength. As the insect tries to crawl out of the bowl, the plant's cells peel off and stick to their feet. They eventually slide into the pool, where they are absorbed by the plant. The tiny sundew plant's leaves have tentacles with glistening drops of sticky enzymes. Insects are lured to the sweet nectar. Their attempt to escape triggers the tentacles to fold inward and imprison the insect. The enzymes break down the insect into amino acids and nutrients that the plant can absorb.

Several species of orchids found at Tannersville include rose pagonia, yellow lady slipper, white-fringed orchid, and grass-pink orchid. As the bog has aged, the conifers and heath shrubs have increased in density and are blocking more sunlight. Plants such as golden club, Labrador tea, Hartford fern, and orchids are becoming increasingly scarce. In 2013, the management team decided to experiment by clearing all vegetation from a strip within the bog. Results could take many years because bogs operate on a different time frame than most other habitats.

Southeast Region

SE1 Hawk Mountain Sanctuary, Berks County

Hawk Mountain Sanctuary (HMS) is a preserve with international status as the world's first sanctuary for birds of prey. Located along Blue Mountain's ridge where it doubles back on itself, it is one of the best places in the eastern US to view raptors during the fall migration. More than 16,000 raptors of sixteen different species are recorded each year. The sanctuary attracts more than 80,000 visitors and has grown to 2,600 acres. It was designated a national natural landmark, an Audubon important bird area, and an important mammal area. The HMS Association's mission is to conserve birds of prey worldwide by providing leadership in raptor conservation science and education, and by maintaining HMS as a model observation, research, and education facility.

History. In 1885, the state legislature passed the Scalp Act, which placed a fifty-cent bounty on mink, weasels, foxes, all hawks, and owls, except saw-whet, screech, and barn owls. Two years later, the law was repealed due to complaints about increasing numbers of rats and mice and the high cost of paying the bounties. Sadly, during those two years, an estimated 180,000 birds of prey were killed. In 1913, the Game Commission renewed the bounties, spending about 10 percent of its budget on claims. During the Great Depression, many families supplemented their income with bounties of $5 for each goshawk, $4 per fox, and $15 for a bobcat. In 1932, Richard Pough, a photographer and amateur ornithologist from MIT, visited well-known Hawk Mountain and witnessed gunners shooting hundreds of migrating hawks. His photographs of dead hawks lined up disturbed many people, particularly Rosalie Edge. In 1934, Mrs. Edge toured the mountain with Pough and decided that day to lease 1,398 acres for $4,000 with an option to buy. She hired a

The view from North Lookout

Two turkey vulture friends perched at North Lookout

Overlooking the river of rocks

Cantilevered rocks at Bake Oven Knob

warden and his wife, and a conservation partner, to protect the property. The shooting ended and the property was opened to the public. In 1938, Mrs. Edge purchased the property and formed the Hawk Mountain Sanctuary Association. During the 1960s, the conservation movement finally convinced legislatures to protect the goshawk, sharp-shinned hawk, Cooper's hawk, and snowy owl. The great horned owl, crow, kingfisher, and blue jay were still considered pests and were occasionally shot.

Migration. Between August 15 and December 15, volunteers are stationed every day at the North Lookout to count the number of each raptor species heading south. The sixteen species of raptors include nine species of hawks, bald and golden eagles, black and turkey vultures, osprey, merlin, and peregrine falcon. Blue Mountain—also known as Kittatinny Ridge—is 300 miles long and the easternmost ridge in Pennsylvania's Ridge and Valley Province.

With perfect conditions, raptors can fly as many as 240 miles by taking advantage of two types of air lift: winds that hit the mountain create an updraft, and warming air creates thermals that rise. Large rock outcrops at several hawk watch locations along the ridge heat up on sunny days and create their own thermals. Birds will come in low and circle above the rocks to gain altitude. A cold front moving through is one of the best times to view large concentrations of birds. Each species has specific migratory preferences, including the type of air movement for soaring, the number of days they rest and feed between flights, daily migration distance, time of year to migrate, whether to fly over large bodies of water, and how far south they migrate.

Records. Between 2012 and 2016, Hawk Mountain Sanctuary recorded an annual average of 16,737 raptors. Bake Oven Knob averaged 13,855 and Waggoner's Gap averaged 21,973 raptors. HMS's five-year annual average for broad-winged hawks was 7,244. The broad-winged record for one day is a staggering 21,448, occurring on September 14, 1978. That year also set a record for a yearly total of 40,698 raptors. Other recent

Bake Oven Knob bird-counting station

yearly averages include 4,112 sharp-shinned hawks, 2,099 red-tailed hawks, 425 ospreys, 399 bald eagles, 146 golden eagles, 173 merlin, and 59 peregrine falcons. The story of bald eagles can be told in the numbers. In 1950, 115 were counted; 1960, 22; 1970, 25; 1980, 22; 1990, 76; 2000, 174; 2010, 409; and in 2016, 522 bald eagles flew over HMS, setting a record. It is interesting that unlike all other raptors, the number of bald eagles recorded each month in 2016 did not vary. The first two were recorded on August 16, and eight were recorded on December 30. In case you were wondering about other locations, Corpus Christi, Texas, is the top US location, with more than 700,000 migrating raptors; Kekoldi, Costa Rica, records 800,000 each spring and 1.9 million in the fall; and five million raptors fly through Veracruz, Mexico, during the fall migration.

Lookouts. South Lookout is only 200 yards from the trail entrance and provides a view of the valley's River of Rocks 700 feet below. The 3,200-foot-long, 30-foot-deep boulder field was created by a process similar to the boulder field at Hickory Run SP. The hike to North Lookout, where counters are stationed, is approximately one mile. The trail gradually becomes extremely rocky and changes to a base of natural sand, which can be slippery. Two stairways make the final steep incline a bit easier. Along the trail you will pass four small lookouts. North Lookout is a large rock outcrop with various-sized boulders and a great view looking at the ridgeline.

The experienced counter is frequently the first to spot the birds and will call out the species and its location using reference names, such as distant high points or locations in the valleys. Dress in layers and bring a cushion or small bleacher seat with a back, suntan lotion, sunglasses, a hat, food, and drinks. The best spots are taken early. During September and October, I highly recommend visiting on a weekday before 10:00 a.m. If you come on a nice weekend, arrive at the parking lot before 9:00 a.m., because by 10:00 a.m. the lot might be full. Please keep relatively quiet and still.

Facilities. When you visit, do not overlook the preserve's other 230 species of birds, or the vernal ponds, bogs, streams, and nine forest trails, including a section of the Appalachian Trail. Also take time to explore the visitor center and native wildflower garden. The preserve offers numerous educational programs, lectures, guided hikes, workshops, trips, and events. In 2001, the sanctuary opened the Acopian Center for Conservation Learning, which has numerous resident and research buildings and one of the largest collections of literature about raptors. Students from locations around the world come for internships to study ornithology, biology, and environmental science.

SE2 Jacobsburg Environmental Education Center, Northampton County

Jacobsburg EEC is a popular 1,168-acre education center, historic site, and natural area with some of the best natural habitat in the region. School classes from the surrounding metropolitan area participate in a wide range of programs and field studies for hands-on experience. I have watched numerous classes wading in the stream with seine nets looking for aquatic life, and every child was totally focused on the mission and enjoying the experience. Land for the park was originally purchased by the Department of Forests and Waters in 1959 to preserve its outstanding habitats, and it was designated an EEC in 1985. When you visit, I recommend you allot some time to explore the park's less visited areas. Also at 7:00 a.m. the park is practically devoid of people, but after 2:00 p.m. on sunny weekdays and weekends it can feel crowded, so plan accordingly.

Historic buildings along Bushkill Creek

Local students studying aquatic life

What did we catch?

Habitat. Beautiful Bushkill Creek meanders through the park's forest for 2.5 miles. Sections of the stream created the slate cliffs, and the slower-moving water deposited the material to form sandbars. The most beautiful and popular area is Henry's Woods. The 1.9-mile loop trail parallels the stream through a stand of old-growth hemlock and white pine. Whenever I visit an old-growth forest, I feel joy that there are still places with ancient majestic trees, and sadness that so many were cut down. The trail continues through a stand of younger pine, over a bridge, and back upstream. On higher ground the trail overlooks the stream and Henry's Woods below. The fields are maintained in various stages of successional growth, and prescribed burns are conducted to reestablish native grasses and eliminate any encroaching trees. Bird boxes were installed and are usually occupied by late May. Across the road from the center is a wildflower garden that attracts butterflies and birds.

Recreation. When you visit, pick up a trail map and ask the staff for trail recommendations. There are 19 miles of interconnected trails in four general areas of the park, so you can design your hike accordingly. All but the Henry Woods Trail are multiuse trails for hikers, bikers, horses, and cross-country skiing. Anglers enjoy fishing the clear water of Bushkill Creek, which has excellent aquatic life and is stocked with trout. Hunting is permitted in designated areas of the park.

Birding. The personnel at Jacobsburg EEC maintain excellent habitat for wildlife, especially birds. Guided bird-watching tours are conducted seasonally by Rick Wilruat, one of the state's leading bird experts. In early May, the list of birds you will see and hear in the park is impressive. The bird boxes are monitored for species and dates of nest building, eggs laid and hatched, and young leaving the nest. On one visit a box was occupied by a pair of American kestrels. The female was sitting on eggs, and the male was perched on top of the box, resting before making his next flight to search for food to bring back to the female.

Henry's Woods Trail   Old-growth hemlocks along the trail

Boulton National Historic District. In 1792, William Henry II—the son of a famous gun manufacturer—moved to Nazareth and purchased land in Jacobsburg to manufacture guns. He also built a forge to supply the iron he needed. In 1812, to fulfill increasing demand and government contracts, he built a large manufacturing facility in nearby Boulton, which is within the park boundary. Four generations of Henrys produced guns here until the late 1800s, when mass production of interchangeable parts rendered custom-made guns obsolete. The Henry rifle was used in every conflict from the Braddock Campaign of 1755 through the Civil War. Its durability, accuracy, and affordable price made it the preferred weapon during the western frontier era. Visitors can tour the buildings and homestead, which is now the Pennsylvania Longrifle Museum. Contact the Jacobsburg Historical Society for information on hours, schedule, and tours (610-759-9029, www.jacobsburghistory.org).

SE3 Delaware Canal State Park, Northampton and Bucks Counties

Delaware Canal SP combines early American history, picturesque scenery, wildlife, and outdoor recreation. The park's 60-mile-long corridor between Easton and Bristol encompasses the canal, towpath, aqueducts, riverbank, cliffs, river islands, and six recreational areas. It also passes parks, preserves, and historic towns, bridges, and homes. The canal system, completed in 1832, is still in excellent condition. It was designated a national historic landmark as the only towpath canal in the US that is intact along its entire length.

History. In the early 1800s, Philadelphia was the political and economic center of the country and until 1825 was the largest city in North America. When anthracite coal was proven to be an efficient fuel, Carbon County and later Wyoming County were the only sources of coal in the country. Transporting coal by wagon and Durham boat was expensive and could not meet demand, so in 1817, canal construction began along the upper

Durham Aqueduct and the towpath crossing Cooks Creek; the lock is to the right of this scene.

The canal and towpath down-stream from Locks 22 and 23

A proud fisherman on the Delaware Canal

Ice climbing south of Durham in early February

Lehigh River, from White Haven to Easton. A few years later, construction on the Delaware Canal began. During the peak years, which preceded the Civil War, over 3,000 boats continually made round trips on the canals. Life for the families who lived on the boats was hard. A typical day began before 4:00 a.m. and did not end until after 10:00 p.m., when the locks were closed. A boat with 80 tons of coal would travel 30 miles a day.

Construction of the canal system was an amazing engineering feat. The canal, towpath, and berm are approximately 60 feet wide, and the canal is 5 feet deep. Trees, roots, and rocks had to be removed. It was then hand-dug by local farmers and Irish immigrants using horses. In 60 miles, the canal level drops 165 feet through twenty-three locks and ten aqueducts. Numerous bridges, lock tenders' homes, and miles of stone retaining walls up to 20 feet high were built, using large rocks perfectly cut and laid. Railroads gradually reduced canal traffic, but it was not until October 17, 1931, that the last boat delivered its cargo and ended an era. That same day, most of the canal was deeded to the state and named Roosevelt SP. In 1989, the name was changed to Delaware Canal SP. Sections of the Lehigh Canal operated until 1942.

When I ride or walk along the canal, I am struck by three amazing feats of engineering that are easily overlooked. In sections where rock cliffs dropped straight down to the river, they had to squeeze in the canal and

This wall of ice is taller than most rock-climbing routes in Pennsylvania.

towpath at heights 20 to 30 feet above the river. This required miles of blasting, filling, and massive retaining walls. Flawless workmanship is why the stone walls remain intact today. In addition, every time the canal crossed a stream they had to build an aqueduct for the canal, a bridge for the path, and huge retaining walls below. Similar to railroads, no matter what the terrain was like, the canal and towpath had to have a consistent grade.

Recreation. The well-maintained towpath is a national recreation trail. Activities include hiking, biking, fishing, bird watching, and cross-country skiing. Floating down the picturesque river by kayak, canoe, or tube is very popular, and far more scenic than you might imagine. There are large boulders in the river, islands, crystal-clear tributaries, wildflowers lining the shore, waterfowl, and a tremendous population of fish. Families picnic, swim, fish, and relax on sand or pebble beaches and boulders. Use extreme caution, because drownings occur every year. During cold winters, ice climbers scale the 300-foot-high ice-covered Nockamixon Cliffs. The river is home or spawning territory for eel, shad, smallmouth bass, walleye, striped bass, muskellunge, catfish, carp, and even sturgeon. (Surprisingly, on two occasions I inadvertently hooked into large sturgeon near Easton and fought them for over an hour until the line broke.) With the exception of shad, night fishing is best. At night be prepared for a curious beaver to

Nockamixon Cliffs

swim close and then smack its tail. I jump every time.

It is worth mentioning the many popular attractions and historic sites that are along the canal:

1. New Hope, to browse the eclectic shops and eat and drink outside and watch the street scene.
2. Bowman's Hill Wildflower Preserve, to hike their trails or take a guided tour to see the 134-acre preserve's 800 native plants, of which eighty are species of concern. It is also a great place to bird watch, or to view the Platt Collection of 100 mounted birds, 200 nests, and 600 eggs.
3. National Canal Museum in Easton, to learn how the canal was built and take a ride on a canal boat pulled by mules. The operators are dressed in period clothing.
4. Washington's Crossing Park, to learn about Washington's daring river crossing and subsequent victory during the Revolutionary War.
5. Ringing Rocks Park has an 8-acre field of boulders that when hit with a hammer ring like a bell.
6. Ralph Stover SP, 3 miles from Point Pleasant, has excellent rock climbing on 300-foot-high cliffs. There is parking and easy access to High Rocks, with views of the serpentine Tohickon Creek below. In March and November, extra water is released from Nockamixon Lake for a day of running challenging class II and III rapids. The cliffs were donated to the DCNR by well-known author James Michener.

Nature. This section of the river has slow-moving water in deep pools and modest rapids. One hole below Raubs Island is 65 feet deep. The park has two natural areas: Nockamixon Cliffs and River Islands. The cliffs face north and rarely see direct sunlight. The cooler habitat supports an alpine-arctic plant community. The cliffs are also a nesting site for several species of birds. There is a great lookout from the top. Eleven islands are protected by the DCNR and managed by nature; they provide habitat for migrating and nesting birds. When I visit early mornings and late afternoons, I usually see at least one eagle. Commonly seen birds are mergansers, gulls, ducks, grebes, cormorants, green and blue heron, kingfisher, and many species of migrating warblers and woodland birds.

SE4 Nockamixon State Park, Bucks County

Popular, 5,286-acre Nockamixon SP and its 1,450-acre lake were created for outdoor recreation primarily to serve the Philadelphia, Bucks County, and Lehigh Valley areas. The park has excellent facilities for a tremendous number of activities. It is also a surprisingly great place to enjoy nature. The lake is about 8 miles long and averages a half mile wide. The dam is 112 feet high, but the outlet is in a separate location. The water flows evenly over the 8-foot-high concrete spillway, down a series of horizontal ledges cut into rock, and into the silt pool below. The waterfall is spectacular any time of year, but especially after snowmelt or a substantial rainfall. Park along South Park Road.

History. The site consisted mostly of rolling farmland with wooded and wetland areas. It was established as part of the Department of Forests and Waters' original plan to allow every Pennsylvania citizen to be within 25 miles of a state park. In 1961, the commonwealth began purchasing a total of 290 properties. By 1972, Route 563 was relocated and the dam was built. The park opened in 1974 for boating and fishing, and the pool and marina were completed in 1977.

Recreation. The marina has a large boat launch and 648 dock spaces. Most of the boats are sailboats, with pontoon boats being a close second. Anglers can launch (20-horsepower motor limit) at one of the six public launches. Kayakers enjoy the lake's coves and 2-mile-long Haycock Cove. A boat rental concession at the day-use area has human-powered boats, motorboats, and pontoon boats during the summer. Nockamixon is a popular fishing destination. The lake's species include large and smallmouth bass, chain pickerel, muskellunge, walleye, striped bass hybrids, channel catfish, and panfish. A long fishing pier is at the day-use area. Like many lakes, fishing can be challenging, but there are large fish here. A map is available online, showing lake depths and manmade structures.

More than fourteen hiking trails take you along the lake to ponds, fields, forests, wildflowers, boulder areas, and overlooks. The south side of the lake has more than 20 miles of equestrian trails. It is open to hikers.

Mostly sailboats and pontoon boats use the 648 slips at the marina.

Nockamixon Lake's spillway falls is along
South Park Road.

A paved 2-mile bike trail begins at the marina and runs west to the Old Mill Pond and waterfall. In the woodlands east of Haycock Cove is a 10-mile trail system for mountain biking.

The pool is one of the nicest in the state park system. It is a half acre in size, with two waterslides and a children's shallow area with fountains. There are dressing rooms and a food concession with beautiful terraces and stone walls. On the busiest days the pool reaches capacity. The challenging eighteen-hole disc golf course near the marina is one of the highest-rated courses in Pennsylvania. The orienteering course is in the day-use area. Ten modern cabins are available to rent in a secluded wooded area near the lake's southern shoreline. A hostel provides accommodations for hikers and bikers. The park also conducts guided walks, environmental-education programs, and teacher workshops.

Nature. More than 250 species of birds have been recorded at the park. The fishing pier and marina pier are excellent places to look for more than twenty species of waterfowl. Large flocks of gulls stop at the lake during migration. Cormorants are common during the summer. Bald eagles and osprey are seen daily from spring to fall; they are usually spotted hunting for fish. Eagles extend their legs at the last second to grab a fish. Ospreys tuck their wings to dive and at the last second open them up and land feet first with a splash.

More than twenty nests are in the heron rookery near the north shore.

Two young eaglets in their nest along the shoreline (mid-May)

A small stream runs into the pool below the spillway.

To take off, ospreys flap their wings hard against the water and quickly lift out of the water. In a quiet area of the park, a pair of eagles have nested for several years in a tall white pine. Herons have established a rookery of twenty to thirty nests. Please do not disturb the birds or the private-property owners. Many of the old farm fields are overgrown; others have been planted with warm-season grasses to create grasslands. Wildflowers can be found almost anywhere in spring, but one of the best locations is the High Bridge Trail, starting from the hostel. One spring day, I had the pleasure of watching four fox pups come out of tall weeds and briefly play in the grass until they knew it was time to follow mom.

Ralph Stover SP is between Nockamixon and Delaware Canal SPs.

SW5 Blue Marsh Lake Recreation Area, Berks County

The 1,150-acre Blue Marsh Lake and 5,050 acres of land that surround the lake provide both recreation opportunities and natural areas for those who want solitude. The Game Commission owns an additional 2,681 acres on the north side of Route 183. The Army Corps of Engineers' 98-foot-high dam was completed in 1979 to control flooding. Summer lake elevation is 290 feet, with a drawdown of 5 feet in the winter. The narrow reservoir is almost 9 miles long. It has two coves that are 2.3 miles and 1 mile long, and it is 53 feet deep and has 34 miles of shoreline. The coves and the upper half of the lake are no-wake zones. Stop at the visitor center for a trail map, information about the lake's history and dam construction, and a great view of the lake and dam.

Recreation. The Dry Brooks Day-Use Area and lake are the main attractions during the summer months. The recreation area has a sandy beach, food concession, picnic area, sand volleyball, and a boat launch. Boats can pull up to the section of the beach that wraps around a point. Hunting is available, with the exception of two locations in the park. For bird watchers, the area produces a long list of birds. Viewing wildflowers is also popular along the edges of the fields and forests. The park has eight well-marked trails, including the 30-mile Blue Marsh Lake Trail (which circles the lake), has mile markers, and is open for hiking, biking, and horses. On weekends and after 4:00 p.m. on weekdays during the summer, the park gets very busy.

Boating & Fishing. The ACE boat launches are at the day-use area and below State Hill, which has a nice view of the lake. This launch area is large and can be packed with jet skiers and water skiers. Kayakers and paddle boarders also launch from the grass. Sheidy Launch is operated by the Pennsylvania Fish and Boat Commission and is on the upper end of the lake off Route 183. A makeshift launch for kayaks is at the end of School Lane, where the water is only 8 feet wide, but it widens within a short distance. Parking is limited, but the area is far more scenic and secluded and has wildlife. Egrets, blue heron, kingfisher, turtles, and fish jumping out of the water are common sights. Fishing is popular on the lake, which has smallmouth

Blue Marsh Lake

and largemouth bass, striped bass, muskie, walleye, crappies, panfish, and catfish. Tulpehocken Creek is a delayed-harvest artificial-lure area and is considered one of the best fly-fishing streams in southeastern Pennsylvania.

Birding. The park is on a flyway and is important for grassland birds. It is designated as an important bird area. The land was previously farmland, and some areas are still agricultural, while others are managed as grasslands. Warm-season grasses are planted and prescribed burning is used. Feeder plots are maintained and observation blinds, nesting boxes, and bird feeders have been installed. The combination of habitats attracts many species of birds. The park is also home to threatened bog turtles, red-bellied turtles, and three species of plants.

The deep lake does not freeze, so gulls are commonly seen in the winter, including black-tailed, Franklin's, glaucous, herring, great and lesser black-backed, and up to 6,000 ring-billed gulls. Large numbers of common loon, ducks, and mergansers stop during migration. Sheidy Boat Launch is a good area for cliff, northern rough-winged, and tree swallows. During winter, on the Great Oak Nature Trail you might find five species of sparrows. Blue-winged and yellow warblers nest on the Eyes of the Eagle Trail. Scarlet tanager, orchard and Baltimore orioles, great crested flycatcher, and eastern towhee are also found here. Squirrel Run Nature Trail is a great area for nesting warblers. Below the dam are eagles, osprey, ducks, blue heron,

Boats may park at the beach recreational area.

The multi-use trail circles the entire lake.

Green heron below the dam

Many local boaters enjoy the lake after work.

and green heron. Other interesting birds in the park are warbling, white-eyed, red-eyed, and yellow-throated vireos; many species of warblers; willow flycatcher; indigo bunting; Wilson's snipe; bobolink; short-eared owl; red-breasted grosbeak; and, occasionally, blue grosbeak.

SE6 Middle Creek Wildlife Management Area, SGL 46, Lancaster and Lebanon Counties

The Game Commission's 6,254-acre Middle Creek Wildlife Management Area is an outstanding achievement that combines land preservation, habitat creation, land management, wildlife protection, public recreation, and environmental education. The GC created waterfowl habitat from ordinary rolling farmland, and now 150,000 snow geese, 10,000 tundra swans, 10,000 Canada geese, and dozens of other species of waterfowl depend on the refuge for their winter layover or spring and fall migration. The numbers of snow geese and tundra swans begin to build when the first spring migrants arrive in mid-February, joining those that overwintered, and peaks around the last week in February. Exact dates vary due to weather conditions. Middle Creek has become a favorite place to overwinter because it fulfills their three requirements—rest, security, and food—but if cold temperatures freeze the entire surface of the lake or deep snow prevents their ability to find food, they are forced to leave and fly farther south. To experience the awesome sight and raucous sound of 30,000 snow geese taking flight simultaneously and twisting and turning in unison can best be described as surreal. Middle Creek WMA should be ranked near the top of everyone's list of natural places to visit in Pennsylvania

History. Middle Creek WMA was created for hunters in eastern Pennsylvania who wanted a waterfowl refuge similar to the refuge at Pymatuning Reservoir, in western Pennsylvania. In 1965, the Game Commission began to buy land, with additional state and federal funding allocated for conservation. Over the next seven years, wetlands, ponds, and potholes were built; nest boxes were installed; fields were established; and the dam, lake, and visitor center were completed. The rarity of geese in the 1960s meant the GC had to establish a resident population. Holding pens were built and the Game Commission trapped and transferred thirty pairs of geese from Pymatuning. Gradually the goose population grew. In 1974, the first drawing allocated permits to twenty-five goose hunters. Two years later, the first tundra swans and snow geese stopped at the refuge on their way north. The three traditional wintering areas to the south are

I could capture only one-third of the enormous flock (late February).

the tidal marshes in Delaware, Maryland, and North Carolina. Over the next nineteen years the number of migrating snow geese that visited grew to only 1,500, but between 1995 and 1997, stopovers exploded to 150,000.

Management. The refuge is managed for the benefit both of wildlife and humans, but wildlife takes priority. Most of the property is open grassland that is seasonally mowed, with some controlled burning and cultivated grain fields. Oak/hickory woodlands provide ideal habitat for cavity-nesting birds, deer, and turkey. From fall to late spring, dikes flood fields planted with millet. The 360-acre lake is shallow, with an island in the middle for nesting waterfowl. Human encroachment is controlled by the 756-acre propagation area that surrounds most of the lake. Middle Creek could not support its huge numbers of geese and swans without the local agricultural fields as an additional source of food. The Game Commission and conservation organizations formed the Middle Creek Initiative to protect this valuable farmland from housing and commercial development.

Wildlife. Middle Creek WMA was designated a globally significant important bird area because it provides ideal habitat for a large percentage of the continent's eastern population of snow geese and tundra swans. Few other places in Pennsylvania have the diversity of birds that are found here. Approximately 280 species of birds have been recorded, including nesting bald eagles; a blue heron rookery; twenty-three species of overwintering waterfowl; ospreys; numerous species of owls, hawks, and shorebirds; northern harriers; bobolinks; meadowlarks; and redheaded woodpeckers. The refuge woodland and adjacent 1,800-acre game land forest are home to turkey, ruffed grouse, and woodcock. Middle Creek was also designated an important mammal area for its expansive fields, which support prey such as northern short-tailed shrews, meadow voles, and field mice. Short-eared owls and northern harriers can be seen cruising over the fields in search of their next meal.

Snow Geese. During the 1970s, the eastern population of snow geese began to change their source of food from aquatic vegetation and marsh grasses to agricultural fields. The improved diet is believed to have caused their numbers to increase to the point where US wildlife managers fear that snow geese are degrading their tundra habitat by overgrazing. To see the snow geese as they leave the lake en masse, you should arrive at Willow Point before sunrise and then wait. They usually leave to feed during early morning, but I have been there when they left midday. The geese return from the fields at the end of the day. A noticeable increase in quacking is your ten- to thirty-second warning that they are about to take off.

Visitor Center. Before exploring the refuge, stop at the visitor center to pick up maps and view the large collection of mounted birds and mammals,

Tundra swans

Behind me were another twenty photographers.

Watching 30,000 snow geese take off together is an unforgettable experience.

including golden and bald eagles, owls, hawks, waterfowl, shorebirds, and meadow birds. The staff will gladly provide information about locations for viewing specific species and recent bird sightings. Their guide describes seven prime locations to view wildlife along the loop road. You can view waterfowl through the expansive glass wall overlooking the lake, using binoculars provided by the center. The staff and naturalists conduct environmental-education programs and lectures, post waterfowl count updates (visit their website), and conduct trap and transfer projects and annual bird banding. Special events include the Wildlife Art Show, Waterfowl Show, and Ned Smith Art Auction.

Feeding in the field along the Tour Road

The visitor center has excellent wildlife displays and a view of the lake.

Saw a whet owl sleeping in the warm sunlight.

Recreation. The WMA has hiking and interpretive trails, three picnic areas, and a small fishing pond. A 40-acre section of the lake is designated for kayaking and canoeing between May 16 and September 14. Fishing from shore and ice fishing are allowed in the public recreation area. An excellent way to view the property and wildlife is by driving the self-guided loop road (one-way traffic), which is open from March 1 until mid-September, weather permitting. The ADA-accessible Willow Point Trail provides access to the best observation area overlooking the lake. Special seasons and regulations for hunting have been established, and certain types of hunting require a permit. Goose hunting from pit blinds is available for those selected in the public drawing. Information and applications are posted on the Game Commission and Middle Creek WMA websites.

SE7 French Creek State Park and Hopewell Furnace National Historic Site, Berks County

French Creek SP is a beautiful, well-maintained, 7,730-acre recreational park with forests, meadows, lakes, and wetlands. The park is in the center of Pennsylvania's southeast region, the most developed and populated region in the state. It is the largest block of contiguous forest between Washington, DC, and New York City. Within the state park is the 848-acre Hopewell Furnace National Historic Site, one of the best examples of a preserved iron furnace complex in Pennsylvania.

History. When you visit the park, make sure you allocate some time to visit Hopewell Furnace. I was impressed with everything: the pastoral setting, the restoration work, the well-designed production layout, and the large home, barn, and buildings that house the furnace, waterwheel, and charcoal. In 1771, Mark Bird built the iron furnace complex in an area rich in iron ore. Not far from the park, forty-five million tons of ore were mined by Bethlehem Steel from 1958 to 1977. Hopewell's rural location meant that in addition to the furnace and associated buildings, a self-supporting community had to be built. The most productive years were 1816–1831. Changing technology and competition from large plants built in the cities forced the furnace to close in 1883. The descendants of the third ironmaster, Clement Brook, used the 15,000-acre property as a summer home until the Great Depression. In 1935, the family sold it to the federal government, which planned to develop it as the French Creek Recreational Demonstration Area. The young men of the CCC built most of the park's facilities that you see today, including the two dams. The men also began restoration work on the Hopewell Furnace property. The federal government turned over the recreational demonstration area to the commonwealth in 1946.

Recreation. The state park has two lakes: 22-acre Scotts Run Lake and 68-acre Hopewell Lake. Both lakes have a boat launch, seasonal moorings, and

Hopewell Lake

A scenic location for the pool

The fishing pier

electric-motor-only policy. Boat rentals and a long fishing pier are available at Hopewell Lake. The clear, cold water of Scotts Run Lake supports trout that are stocked three times during the year. Hopewell's warm-water fish include bass, walleye, pike, pickerel, muskellunge, and panfish. Hunting is permitted on 6,000 acres. A very nice swimming pool and food concession situated on a grassy slope along Hopewell Lake provide a picturesque view of the lake. The modern, 200-site campground has wide, deep sites in a shaded woodland. Other accommodations include three cottages, two yurts, ten modern cabins, two organized-group tent areas, and two large, organized-group cabin camps with dining halls, washhouses, and staff quarters.

The park's nine hiking trails with a total of more than 35 miles are maintained and marked. The 8-mile Horseshoe Trail—the only equestrian trail

The ironmaster's mansion

The furnace support buildings and waterwheel

in the park—is part of the 130-mile trail between Valley Forge and the Appalachian Trail near Harrisburg. Mountain bikes are permitted on 20 miles of trails that are rated as difficult. The park is well known for its permanent self-guided orienting course and competitions that attract people from multiple states. Orienting-course maps are provided by the park. The competitions are timed cross-county races where competitors use a map and compass to find a series of distant points. The park also has a disc golf course.

Nature. The evenly aged trees in the park and historic site's deciduous forest are predominately white, black, red, and chestnut oak. Other trees include yellow-poplar, hickory, beech, dogwood, black birch, cherry, walnut, and willow. More than 500 plants have been identified in the two parks. In wet areas of the forest are skunk cabbage, arrowhead, sweet flag, and numerous species of ferns. Other plants include showy and ragged fringed orchid, Canadas mayflower, and false Solomon's seal.

Pine Swamp Natural Area is a deciduous swamp forest with several wet meadows and no pine trees. The habitats support 200 plant species and thirty-three types of trees and shrubs. The dominant trees are mostly red maple, swamp, white, and pin oak. Shrubs include highbush blueberry, swamp rose, and arrowwood. A half-dozen plants of concern are found here, along with an incredible seventeen different types of ferns and a large variety of flowering plants that bloom from early April to September. The park is an island of excellent habitat, which is why 185 species of birds have been recorded in the two parks.

SE8 John Heinz National Wildlife Refuge, Delaware and Philadelphia Counties

John Heinz NWR is the most surprising place I have visited in Pennsylvania. The 1,000-acre refuge encompasses six types of habitats, 10 miles of easy-to-walk trails through wetlands, great viewing access, a 4.5-mile canoe and kayak trail, and a long list of birds and wildlife, making it one of the best birding places in Pennsylvania. The surprising part is that the refuge is surrounded by the Philadelphia metropolitan area. It is adjacent to the International Airport and borders I-95, the main corridor along the eastern US.

History. As far back as the mid-1600s, Dutch, Swedish, and English settlers diked and drained part of 5,700-acre Tinicum Marsh for grazing. By 1918, the marsh was reduced to 200 acres. Gulf Oil Corporation donated 145 acres at the eastern end in 1955, but filling and dredging in other areas continued to reduce the size of the marsh. It was declared a national natural landmark in 1965, and seven years later, Congress authorized the purchase of 1,200 acres to establish the Tinicum National Environment Center. In 1991, the center was given its current name, John Heinz NWR at Tinicum.

Visitor Center. Begin your visit at the Cusano Visitor Center for information, maps, brochures, and exhibits, to watch a short film, and to borrow binoculars. The trails are open every day of the year from sunrise to sunset, and the center is open 8:30 a.m.–4:00 p.m. except on federal holidays. The refuge, within a 10- mile radius of 1.7 million people and a two-hour drive of thirty-five million people, has a prominent role of exposing the public to the natural environment, wildlife, education, and the NWR system. Every weekday, the staff conducts programs and guided tours for about eighty students, with a maximum of 150. During spring migration the refuge attracts birders from distant states. I recommend arriving early in the morning on a weekday.

Refuge. The refuge is owned and managed by the US Fish and Wildlife Service as one of 560 properties in the National Wildlife Refuges System. John Heinz NWR is the first urban refuge in the US. The main trails in the wetland areas are wide, level, and well above the water. Brush is partly cleared to ensure good views. One boardwalk bridge crosses the impoundment and another boardwalk (not shown on the map) leads to an observation deck in the tidal marsh. Three observation areas, one of which is a two-level deck, project into the impoundment, and a covered deck is in the marsh. Kiosks and signs along the trails provide interesting information, and nest boxes are placed throughout the refuge. Warbler Woods is a small

Overlooking the impoundment area from the two-story deck

Great egrets chasing each other

The boardwalk over the tidal marsh to the observation decks

Goslings looking for mom

Painted turtles were everywhere.

forest with trails and markers that identify trees. Surprisingly, whenever I visit the refuge, I rarely hear jets because they take off at a 90- degree angle to the refuge, and the prevailing wind is toward the airport.

Habitat. Diverse ecosystems in the refuge include tidal and nontidal freshwater marsh, open impoundment water, freshwater tidal creek, mudflats, coastal plain and riparian forests, and early successional grasslands. The 258-acre freshwater tidal marsh, the largest in Pennsylvania, is one of nature's most biologically productive ecosystems, containing high plant diversity and more birds than any other type of wetland. The marsh experiences water-level fluctuations of up to 6 feet between high and low tide. The most-common plant species are arrowhead, pickerelweed, and spadderdock. The marsh also supports six plant species that are rare in Pennsylvania. The Fish and Wildlife Service drains most of the water in the impoundment in early fall to create large mudflats for the benefit of migrating shorebirds and wading birds. They raise the level a few weeks later for migrating waterfowl. The refuge has another 56 acres of nontidal open water that includes several ponds, such as 5-acre Hoy's Pond.

A 4.5-mile segment of Darby Creek flows through the refuge and is a good way to see a variety of plants and wildlife. The creek's waters are tidal, so you can travel in the creek only between two hours before and after high tide. Fishing in the creek or impoundment from the dike's trail is permitted. Species include catfish, carp, crappie, and small striped bass, panfish, and largemouth bass.

Wildlife. The combination of diversified habitat and its location on the Atlantic Flyway has driven the bird count to more than 300 species, of which eighty-five nest in the refuge, including the bald eagle. Their nest, built in 2009, can be seen by looking across the impoundment from the trail past the double-deck observation deck. I also saw three mature eagles flying back and forth from their perch in a lone tree across the marsh. A

A graceful landing at the tidal marsh

A recently scavenged turtle nest (early June)

mallard hen and her ducklings were hiding together under vegetation along the bank. Several swallows were sitting on nests they had built in the observation deck's ceiling beams. Numerous great egrets and blue herons feed in the impoundment's shallow water. Other possible sightings include black-crowned night herons, green-winged teal, northern shovelers, northern pintails, and black ducks. During migration, mergansers, ducks, grebes, and American coots are regularly observed. The refuge is a wintering ground for more than twenty species of waterfowl, with a daily average of 1,200 individuals. The mudflats during migration attract up to 10,000 semipalmated and least sandpipers, several hundred greater and lesser yellowlegs, and many other wading birds and shorebirds. Marsh wrens, swamp sparrows, least bittern, and other marsh birds are heard more often than seen. In the woods and fields, observers have recorded thirty-five warbler species, Baltimore and orchard orioles, indigo buntings, cedar waxwings, scarlet tanagers, flycatchers, and thrushes. On a recent trip to the refuge I saw a yellow warbler in the parking area before I stepped out of my car.

The forest habitat near water is home to three species of snakes. Turtles of various sizes can be seen lined up on nearly every log in the refuge. The ten turtle species include the endangered eastern mud turtle, the northern diamond-backed terrapin, and the eastern redbelly turtle, the latter on the state's threatened-species list. Walking along the dike, I saw where a critter had dug out part of a turtle nest, eaten about three eggs, and then left. Eight species of frogs and toads inhabit the refuge, including the state-endangered southern coastal plain leopard frog. The Pennsylvania Wildlife Federation designated the refuge as an important mammal area for its occasional use by river otters, mink, and beaver, and it is the state's potentially last location for the marsh rice rat. It also has populations of short-tailed shrew, least shrew, meadow vole, white-footed mouse, and several other species of rodents.

SE9 Harrisburg Islands, Conewago Potholes, and Chickies Rock, Dauphin and Lancaster Counties

Lower Susquehanna. The Susquehanna River is the longest river in the eastern US and is the largest nonnavigable river in the US. From its beginning in New York, the 400 miles of river has an average drop of 2.5 feet per mile. From Conewago Falls to the Chesapeake Bay, it drops 4.7 feet per mile. The 43-mile section from Columbia drops 5.39 feet per mile. The Susquehanna is the only river in the East with a steeper incline at its end than in its upper sections. When electricity became a commodity, this section of the river, with its mountainsides, high rate of flow, and rapid elevation drop, was an ideal location for hydroelectric generation.

The first hydroelectric dam was built in 1904 at Conewago Falls near Falmouth. At the time, the 8,000-foot-long stone dam and plant was the largest power plant in the world. It is still in operation today. Next was the 55-foot high Holtwood Dam, completed in 1910, which became the second-largest dam in the world and the largest electric producer in the US. In 1928, the 105-foot-high Conowingo Hydro Electric Station in Maryland, 5 miles south of the Pennsylvania border, became the world's largest electric generation facility. The fourth dam, Safe Harbor, was completed in 1931. Coal and nuclear power plants followed. Many of the rapids are now under reservoirs, but on a positive note, virtually all of the land on

Great white egrets on one of nearly 100 islands in the Susquehanna River in Harrisburg

Strange-looking holes sculpted into a boulder at Conewago Rocks, Falmouth

Another view of the endless boulders upstream when the water level was low.

both sides of the lower Susquehanna and most of its islands are undeveloped and protected because it was, and still is, owned by the utility companies. Recently, PPL donated nearly 5,000 acres to conservation organizations. The lower Susquehanna has countless islands, many with sheer rock faces and elevations of 60–300 feet above the river. Bald eagles, osprey, blue herons, great white egrets, and otters feed on the plentiful fish. Overall, it is one of the best places in Pennsylvania for scenic beauty, overlooks, boating, kayaking, fishing, birding, wildflowers, and sightseeing.

Wade Island. The Game Commission's 3-acre Wade Island in Harrisburg is home to the state's largest rookeries of black-crowned night herons and great egrets. Both birds are listed in Pennsylvania as endangered because the number of nesting pairs is low and vulnerable. Why they chose Wade Island is not known. What is known is that they prefer to nest in colonies on islands with tall trees, near a good source of food, and where they are undisturbed. Wade Island is protected and boaters are not allowed to get close. The Game Commission has monitored Wade Island's bird population every spring since 1985, and all of the Sheets Islands were designated an important bird area. Egrets and black-crowned night herons nesting on Wade Island are threatened by the increasing number of nesting double-crested cormorants. The first cormorant nest was confirmed in 1996, and numbers have increased rapidly. The Game Commission, along with the federal Fish and Wildlife Service, began a program in 2006 to protect the colonies of the two endangered species by culling cormorants, but in 2012 the number of nests still increased to 188. The future for all of the wading birds requires making tough management decisions, protecting more habitats, improving the health of the river, and maintaining a low level of disturbance.

View upstream toward the dam and countless
boulders in the river

The other Pennsylvania endangered heron is the yellow-crowned night heron. In the first decade of the twenty-first century, the state's only rookery was across the river from Harrisburg, but they dispersed and established a rookery of ten nests in Harrisburg's Bellevue Park. In 2012, they moved to midtown Harrisburg, one block from the river. A dozen nests are in tall sycamore trees along several city blocks. Experts believe that this location poses less of a predatory threat from animals such as raccoons. This unlikely location continues to be the state's only rookery for yellow-crowned night herons.

Since 2009, egrets have nested in only two Pennsylvania locations: Kiwanis Lake in York County has fewer than ten nesting pairs, and Wade Island averages fewer than 200 active nests. Other colonies were abandoned on the lower Susquehanna River in 1988, and on the lower Delaware River in 1991. Black-crowned night heron currently nest in Dauphin, Lancaster, York, and Berks Counties, but their numbers and range have declined in recent decades. On Wade Island, the colony peaked in 1990, with 345 nesting pairs. The five-year average in 2014 was only sixty pairs. Their nesting range outside Pennsylvania is from the Great Lakes to the coast of New England, but their numbers are also declining. The black-crowned night heron appears stocky and short necked and is less than half the size of the great blue heron. The yellow-crowned night heron is smaller and

The view from the top of Chickies Rock

more delicate looking. Both night herons forage on just about anything they find in the water, but their favorite food is crayfish. As their name implies, they are active between sunset and sunrise.

McCormick Island. North of Wade Island is 100-acre McCormick Island, which is owned by the Central Pennsylvania Conservancy. The island supports thousands of migrating waterfowl and the state's highest concentration of wading birds during breeding season. The island's habitat is primarily deciduous forest of birch, sycamore, silver maple, and poplar, plus forested wetlands, shallow foraging areas, and open water. You can expect to see blue heron, green heron, both night herons, egrets, and bald eagles.

Conewago Potholes. The fascinating carved potholes and sculptured rock are one of the country's best examples of the erosive power of water on igneous rock. The rock, called diabase, is between Three Mile Island dam and the PFBC Falmouth Boat Launch, and mostly on the eastern shoreline. The rocks are more exposed and accessible when the river's level is below 3.5 feet, as recorded on the USGS website, Harrisburg Gage 01570500. Nearly all of the thousands of boulders—up to 100 tons—are sculpted. The boulders also have every type of hole design imaginable: ten or more holes on one boulder, a hole within a larger hole, two holes that have a hole between them, or a hole with a hole to the outside of the boulder, and one 10-foot-high boulder had a 2.5-foot-wide hole perfectly straight down and 8 feet deep. The potholes were created when fast-flowing water carrying quartz sand and rocks formed a vortex and gradually ground a hole, which grew deeper over time. Geologists believe that the rocks were sculpted by massive amounts of water from the melting glacier and glacial ice dam breaks. There are two ways to reach the rocks. Take the trail from the corner of the Falmouth boat launch parking lot to the third power line, turn left, and head down to the boulders. Bushwhacking is almost impossible. You can also kayak from the launch upstream against the current to the third power line. Paddle or hike when the water level is very low, and you will be able to rock hop another half mile upstream. This rock-strewn area is an excellent place to fish for smallmouth bass.

Climbing Chickies Rock

Chickies Rock. The top of the rock is a popular overlook with a tremendous panoramic view of the Susquehanna River. The parking lot is on Route 441, 0.9 miles north of Route 30. A 0.7-mile dirt road heads straight back, then turns right. After another 200 yards, turn left onto the short trail to the rock. Unless you are bird watching, do not take the side trails. The rock, trees, and sheer cliff are impressive. Do not miss visiting the bottom of the rock face. Drive north on Route 441 down the mountain, and take the first road to the left, called Furnace Road. The park's paved trail is immediately on the left, and four public parking spaces are ahead on the right. If they are taken, drive a short distance to the county's parking lot. The 442-acre park encompasses the rock and the beautiful paved biking-and-hiking trail that crosses Chickie Creek. The massive rock is a short walk down the trail. In the wooded area, study the rock's layers and notice how they form a perfect arch. This fold is called an anticline, and it is the largest exposed anticline in the eastern US. On any nice weekend, rock climbers will be scaling the 220-foot rock face. It is fascinating to watch them climb straight up by hand, with ropes used only for safety. The trail continues for several miles.

SE10 Conejohela Flats, Shenks Ferry Wildflower Preserve, Tucquan Glen Nature Preserve, and Pinnacle Overlook, Lancaster County

Conejohela Flats. Conejohela's shrub and forest islands, surrounded by a vast area of mudflats, are one of the best and least-known birding places in Pennsylvania. More than 250 species of birds have been recorded, and it is designated an important bird area. Other than local residents and serious birders, few people are aware that this magnificent place exists, because access and viewing are limited and it is not marketed. The mudflats and alluvial islands are built-up deposits of sediment. The safe harbor dam, built 6 miles downstream in 1931, created a lake that flooded some areas and created new flats and islands at Conejohela. Major floods can alter the configuration of the channels and islands.

Beginning in late February or early March, thousands of migrating tundra swans stop at the flats. In March and early April, you will see large flocks of ducks and gulls. The next wave is the shorebirds that arrive from late April through May. During the summer months, great and snowy egrets and great blue and little blue herons leave their nesting areas and arrive to feed in the shallow water. Ibises and other wading birds are also occasionally seen. Between April and November, thirty-eight species of shorebirds have been recorded, and historically the average total is more than 15,000 shorebirds. During the fall migration, the greatest variety of species and most of the rarities are recorded on the flats. A short list of birds that are observed are pied-billed and horned grebe; American bittern; osprey; eagle; merlin; peregrine falcon; Caspian, common, and Foster's terns; sora; laughing gull; marsh wren; and red-throated loon.

Bird watching along the east shore by using a 30x scope can be done at two places. One is at the junction of Pennsylvania 441 and Pennsylvania 999; toward the river is an unpaved parking lot. The other location is 0.9 miles south at the Blue Rock Boat Launch. Birding is much better by boat, and Blue Rock is the only launch on the east shore close to the flats. After launching, park on the east side of the tracks. Birding by boat is still limited because the mudflats are so large and inaccessible. Kayaks and canoes are best in the shallow water, and they do not make noise. Avoid walking the tracks because Norfolk Southern is strict about trespassing. To view the flats near the west shore, take PA 462 across the river, then take two right turns onto Pennsylvania 624 and head south for 3.2 miles.

Shenks Ferry Wildflower Preserve. In spring, nature lovers visit this well-known preserve to see the profusion of wildflowers that grow and blossom before the forest trees leaf-out and block the sunlight. It was also nice to visit on a hot day in June, when I was the only person in the cool, shaded forest and the only sounds were the babbling stream, a melodious wood thrush, and the squawking of a pileated woodpecker, a red-bellied woodpecker, and a kingfisher. Seventy species of flowering plants have been identified, but most impressive is the quantity of flowers covering the forest floor. Most plants bloom between the second week in April and mid-May, with the peak occurring the last week in April. Two that bloom early are bloodroot and hepatica, followed by Virginia bluebells, white trillium, Dutchman's breeches, yellow and white trout lilies, blooming violets, wild blue phlox, yellow corydalis, and showy orchid. An interesting orchid is putty root, which shoots out a single leaf at the end of summer. The leaf is semi-evergreen, lies on the ground, and dies out in April. The stalk emerges and blooms in May, and by June it has gone to seed and disappeared until it starts the cycle again.

The wildflowers were not always here. At one time the area had a hotel, gristmill, ferry service, and dynamite factory. In 1906, the factory exploded, killing eleven young men and destroying the entire village. The ravine sat untouched for years, allowing the plants to establish themselves. The plants are prolific here because the ravine cuts through limestone, unlike the surrounding region's more acidic soil. The ravine's plants also live in a protected microclimate. The preserve is on Green Hill Road, which is a rough dirt road to the bottom of the mountain. It turns left, and 300 yards ahead is the preserve's trail. There is room for only five or six cars to park. You can also park at the left turn and walk. Return the way you came in; do not continue on Green Hill Road up the opposite side of the valley. The preserve's trail is up and back, is about a half mile long, and parallels Grubbs Run. Past the power line you enter another beautiful section of woods. The Lancaster County Conservancy wants everyone to stay on the main trail and allow the side trails to grow in naturally.

Tucquan Glen Nature Preserve. This preserve protects one of the most scenic, pristine, and wild ravines along the lower Susquehanna River. Tucquan Creek and its tributary, Clark Run, were designated a Pennsylvania wild and scenic river. From River Road you can follow a trail down to the bottom of the ravine and return on the opposite side, for a round trip of 2.4 miles. There are two small parking lots along River Road that fill early on weekends. The preserve is owned by Lancaster Conservancy, and on busy weekends they station two people who monitor parking and provide information about alternative scenic preserves nearby.

From the smaller lot take the yellow trail that parallels the right side of the creek. In April and early May, many of the thirty-five species of

Blue phlox line the path at Shenks Ferry Wildflower Preserve in late April.

A newborn fawn hiding behind a rock at Shenks Ferry Wildflower Preserve trailhead (mid-June)

wildflowers bloom along the trail's upper section. The preserve also protects more than twenty types of ferns and forty species of trees. Halfway down the mountain, turn right onto the orange trail, which heads uphill and veers away from the stream. The trail descends the mountain to the road at the bottom, where you turn left and cross Tucquan Creek. After a good rest and soaking in the scenery, hike up the south side of the stream on the blue trail. The creek is filled with boulders that create pools of water and mini-waterfalls. The trail is steep and maneuvers around the

The lower section of Tucquan Glen Nature
Preserve in late April

boulders, rhododendron, and hemlock trees, and it is one of the toughest sections of trail you will find in Pennsylvania. The landscape is well worth the effort. The trail becomes less steep and parallels the stream to the end, where you can take your boots off to cross the stream through the shallow, chilly water.

Pinnacle Overlook. The overlook is located 380 feet above the Susquehanna River and provides a great view upriver. Technically, you are looking at Lake Aldred above the Holtwood Dam. At the end of Pinnacle Road there are two parking lots with a gate between them. Be aware that the gate is closed and locked at sunset, so park accordingly. The rock outcrop is a few hundred yards from the gate. To capture dramatic photographs, arrive before sunrise or stay past sunset. Winter scenes with snow and the frozen reservoir are also dramatic. The Pinnacle was part of PPL Company's 5,000-acre Holtwood property, but since 2014, most of the property was transferred to the Lancaster Conservancy. The conservancy has since transferred ownership of 80 acres at the Pinnacle to Pennsylvania's DCNR. It is now managed with Susquehannock SP. Several trails from the overlook connect to the conservancy's Kelly's Run Nature Preserve, and the Conestoga Trail connects with Tucquan Glen Nature Preserve.

View from the Pinnacle Overlook

Conejohela Flats from the lookout. This
shallow section of river attracts shorebirds
and wading birds.

SE11 Holtwood Dam, Muddy Run Recreation Area, Susquehannock State Park, and Ferncliff Nature Preserve, Lancaster and York Counties

Holtwood Dam. The hydroelectric dam—operating since 1910—was owned by PPL until 2015 and is now owned by Brookfield Renewable Energy Partners. East of the full-length spillway are turbine-driven generators and a fish lift for migrating shad and other fish. On the west side is a new, world-class whitewater playboarding park. A concrete channel was sculpted to create large waves and a hydraulic hole where experienced kayakers spin, surf, and do freestyle tricks called loops, squirts, and cartwheels. Whitewater releases at the park are scheduled for February, March, October, and November, so effects on migrating fish and endangered plants are minimized.

River of Rocks. Before the dams were built, the section of the river between Columbia, Pennsylvania, and Perryville, Maryland, was known as Susquehanna Gorge. The exposed bedrock, boulders, tree-covered rock islands, and numerous vertical cliffs below Holtwood Dam provide visitors with a sense of what the entire section of river looked like. The Susquehanna River is the oldest and longest river on the East Coast. For more than 350 million years, rain, wind, and gravity have eroded the Appalachian Mountains, which were as tall as the Rockies. The most powerful force on the riverbed

View looking south from the Route 372 bridge. Notice the tiny two-person kayak.

Great blue herons waiting for an easy meal below Holtwood Dam

Holtwood Hydroelectric Dam

occurred during multiple ice ages. As the climate warmed, mile-high glaciers produced an inconceivable amount of meltwater that raced down the river valley. River rocks found in valleys 300 feet above today's river indicate that the river's floor was much higher than it is now, and on several occasions the river was 200 feet deep, flooding all the side valleys. During the maximum extent of each glacial period, the elevation of the Atlantic Ocean was more than 400 feet lower than today, and at one time there was no Chesapeake Bay. The river's huge volume of silt flowed into the ocean to form the Delmarva Peninsula and, by default, the bay.

The rock islands and channels below Route 372 are fantastic places to kayak, but it requires some strength and experience to paddle against the current. Keep in mind that the Holtwood Dam releases water through their turbines at random times, increasing the mild current and raising the water level by 12 to 18 inches within one hour. Boaters and kayakers use the PFBC's launch along River Road on the western shore, 2 miles below the bridge. The islands are straight ahead, and the 2-mile-long channel is to the left. Halfway up the channel, take the right fork to view the section of the channel that is the most scenic. The only other launch in this section is at Fisherman's Park on the eastern shoreline, but the launch is not as good.

Overlooks. The four impressive overlooks are Holtwood Overlook off Old Holtwood Road, Susquehannock SP's Hawk Point and Wissler's Point, and the drive over the Route 372 bridge. For a closer view, visit the "deeps," a cut through rock near the west shore. Park at York County's Lock 12 parking area on River Road, near Route 372. Hike south on the Mason Dixon Trail past Lock 13, below the bridge, then out onto the rock area. Also visit any of the parking areas along River Road between the bridge and dam. Another location is the Fishing Park at Exelon's Pump Station.

Muddy Run Recreation Area. Muddy Run is a combination of Exelon's recreational area and the pumped storage reservoir. The recreational area

The upper and lower Bear Islands create a 2-mile channel along the west bank.

Sailing at Muddy Run RA

is a beautiful, well-maintained, 500-acre park with a 100-acre lake, boat rentals, launch, modern 189-site campground, camp store, and food concession with a second-story screened porch to enjoy a meal or ice cream. The expansive grass lawns, fields, forest, and lake attract an impressive list of birds. Visit the Pennsylvania Society of Ornithology's excellent website (https://pabirds.org) for a list of species and the best places to find them. The Lake Shore Trail circles the lake and its two long, narrow coves. It crosses the spillway and a dam that separates the recreational lake from 1,000-acre Muddy Run Reservoir. A side trail leads to a high platform with an active osprey nest. Two other great trails are the Bluebird trail and the Trail of Changing Times.

Fisherman's Park. At the river below Muddy Run Reservoir is Exelon's pump station and hydroelectric generation facility, and their small Fisherman's Park. During off-peak hours, using low-cost electric, they pump water from the river's Conowingo Reservoir by using four 25-foot-diameter vertical shafts—343 feet long—up to Muddy Run Reservoir, where it is stored. During peak day-use demand the water flows back down through the shafts to eight turbines that generate electricity that sells for a higher rate. The park is a great place to bird watch or fish, and it has a boat launch, pavilion, toilet facilities, and a view of three rock

View looking south from Susquehannock
SP's Hawk Point Overlook

One of the many rock cliffs at the head of the islands

An island with its tight channel to the right

islands and the two bear islands. I have been there several times and always see eagles, cormorants, and osprey. To visit the park, take River Road across the top of the 250-foot-high, 4,800-foot-long dam and take the first right past the dam onto Fishing Park Road. The road winds down a steep ravine along Wissler Run to the park on the right.

Susquehannock SP. The day-use park has two nice lookouts. Hawk Point is the main lookout 380 feet above the river, with a view upriver and a better view downriver. Wissler's Run Overlook has a distant view of the natural rocky riverbed and the pump station below.

Ferncliff Nature Preserve. The 64-acre park is owned by Lancaster Conservancy and is designated as a national natural landmark for its old-growth trees. Park along Bald Eagle Road and walk around the gate and down the 0.8-mile dirt road that follows Barnes Run. The road crosses the small creek twice before reaching the railroad tracks and river. The hike down the ravine is not as steep or wild looking as other ravines along the river, but the number of noticeably large trees on both sides is impressive. The trees are the lucky survivors of the logging era. The conservancy plans to reestablish and mark a separate trail through the old-growth forest. The dominant old-growth tree is yellow-poplar. Other trees are hemlock, beech, chestnut, red and white oak, sycamore, and red and sugar maple. Rhododendron and mountain laurel are also present. Springtime wildflowers include round-leaved stemless violet, trillium, putty root, and crane-fly orchids. On most weekdays you will have the park to yourself, but on summer weekends the younger crowd will be hiking to or from the large rock that juts out into the river reservoir 200 yards south of the end of the trail. The top of the rock is large and about 25 feet high, with a sheer cliff and deep pool below that is perfect for jumping off. I do not recommend doing this, but I did enjoy spending time with about twenty "kids" one-third my age. Watching them jump and having fun was a pleasant way to end a memorable day along the river.

The rock islands are amazing and a pure pleasure to paddle around.

The rock is a favorite hangout and a great place to jump 20 feet above the river.

Bibliography

Adovasio, James M. *The First Americans: In Pursuit of Archeology's Greatest Mystery*. New York: Modern Library, 2002.

Bonta, Marcia. *Outbound Journeys in Pennsylvania: A Guide to Natural Places for Individuals and Group Outings*. University Park: Pennsylvania State University Press, 1990.

Bonta, Marcia. *More Outbound Journeys in Pennsylvania: A Guide to Natural Places for Individuals and Group Outings*. University Park: Pennsylvania State University Press, 1995.

Brown, Scott E. *Pennsylvania Waterfalls: A Guide for Hikers and Photographers*. Mechanicsburg, PA: Stackpole Books, 2004.

Czarnecki, Greg, and Karen Czarnecki. *Highroad Guide to the Pennsylvania Mountains*. Atlanta: Longstreet, 1999.

Fergus, Charels. *Wildlife of Pennsylvania and the Northeast*. Mechanicsburg, PA: Stackpole Books, 2000.

Fergus, Charels. *Natural Pennsylvania: Exploring the State Forest Natural Areas*. Mechanicsburg, PA: Stackpole Books, 2002.

Gadomski, Michael. *Reserves of Strength: Pennsylvania's Natural Landscape*. Atglen, PA: Schiffer, 2013.

Gadomski, Michael. *The Poconos: Pennsylvania's Mountain Treasure*. Atglen, PA: Schiffer, 2015.

Harding, John J., and Justin J. Harding. *Birding the Delaware Valley Region*. Philadelphia: Temple University Press, 1980.

Kosack, Joe. *The Pennsylvania Game Commission, 1895–1995: 100 Years of Wildlife Conservation*. Harrisburg: Pennsylvania Game Commission, 1995.

Maass, Eleanor. *Forestry Pioneer: The Life of Joseph Trimble Rothrock*. Harrisburg: Pennsylvania Forestry Association, 2003.

Michaels, Art. *Pennsylvania Overlooks: A Guide for Sightseers and Outdoor People*. University Park: Pennsylvania State University Press, 2003.

Mitchell, Jeff. *Paddling Pennsylvania: Kayaking and Canoeing the Keystone State's Rivers and Lakes*. Mechanicsburg, PA: Stackpole Books, 1974.

Mitchell, Jeff. *Backpacking Pennsylvania: 37 Great Hikes*. Mechanicsburg, PA: Stackpole Books, 2007a.

Mitchell, Jeff. *Hiking the Allegheny National Forest: Exploring the Wilderness of Northwestern Pennsylvania*. Mechanicsburg, PA: Stackpole Books, 2007b.

Newman, Boyd, and Linda Newman. *Great Hikes in the Poconos and Northeast Pennsylvania*. Mechanicsburg, PA: Stackpole Books, 2000.

Niering, William A., and Nancy C. Olmstead. *Field Guide to Wildflowers: Eastern Region*. New York: Alfred A. Knopf, 2001.

Ostrander, Stephen J. *Great Natural Areas in Eastern Pennsylvania*. Mechanicsburg, PA: Stackpole Books, 1996a.

Ostrander, Stephen J. *Great Natural Areas in Western Pennsylvania*. Mechanicsburg, PA: Stackpole Books, 1996b.

Peterson, Rodger Tory. *Eastern Birds*. Boston: Houghton Mifflin, 1980.

Saenger, Peter G., Barbara C. Malt, and Kevin F. Crilley. *Birds of the Lehigh Valley and Vicinity*. Emmaus, PA: Lehigh Valley Audubon Society, 2014.

Thwaites, Tom. *50 Hikes in Eastern Pennsylvania*. Woodstock, VT: Countryman, 2003.

Whiteford, Richard, and Michael Gadomski. *Wild Pennsylvania: A Celebration of Our State's Natural Beauty*. St. Paul, MN: Voyageur, 2006.

Willen, Matt. *The Best in Tent Camping. Pennsylvania*. Birmingham, AL: Menasha Ridge, 2006.

Young, John L. *Hiking Pennsylvania: 55 of the State's Greatest Hiking Adventures*. Guilford, CT: Globe Pequot, 2008.

Jeff is a landscape, architectural, and aerial photographer specializing in Pennsylvania's natural environment. He retired from a career in construction management and lives near Bethlehem, Pennsylvania, with his wife, Alice. Jeff's outdoor interests include fly fishing, skiing, kayaking, mountain biking, hiking, birding, nature study, and exploring remote areas. He has traveled extensively throughout the US and during a period of five years traveled more than 30,000 miles to photograph Pennsylvania's natural world. Jeff's photographs have been used by businesses, Pennsylvania's DCNR, Governor Corbett's Inaugural Ball, and federal and state agencies and have been published in magazines and calendars. Visit Jeff on Facebook.